Spirituality, Theology and Mental Health

Multidisciplinary Perspectives

Edited by

Christopher C. H. Cook

scm press

© The Editor and Contributors 2013

Published in 2013 by SCM Press
Editorial office
3rd Floor
Invicta House
108–114 Golden Lane,
London EC1Y 0TG

SCM Press is an imprint of Hymns Ancient & Modern Ltd
(a registered charity)
13A Hellesdon Park Road
Norwich NR6 5DR, UK

www.scmpress.co.uk

British Library Cataloguing in Publication data

A catalogue record for this book is available
from the British Library

978-0-334-04626-4

Typeset by Regent Typesetting, London
Printed and bound by
Lightning Source

Contents

Author Affiliations

Patricia Casey, Professor of Psychiatry, University College, Dublin.

Christopher C. H. Cook, Professor of Spirituality, Theology and Health, Department of Theology and Religion, Durham University.

John Cottingham, Professorial Research Fellow, Heythorp College, University of London.

Douglas J. Davies, Professor of the Study of Religion, Department of Theology and Religion, Durham University.

Colin Jay, Chaplaincy Co-ordinator with Tees, Esk and Wear Valleys NHS Foundation Trust.

Christopher MacKenna, Director, St Marylebone Healing and Counselling Centre.

Alexandra Pârvan, Lecturer in Philosophy and Psychology, University of Pitesti, Romania.

Simon D. Podmore, Lecturer in Systematic Theology, Liverpool Hope University.

Loren T. Stuckenbruck, Chair of New Testament and Ancient Judaism, Evangelisch-Theologische Facultät, Ludwig-Maximilians-Universität München.

Mark Wynn, Professor of Philosophy and Religion, School of Philosophy, Religion and History of Science, University of Leeds.

Preface

Spirituality is increasingly recognized as having an important place in the clinical and research literature associated with mental health. This recognition has emerged as a result of a growing evidence base, and an increasingly confident voice of opinion arising from the users of mental health services. However, it has not been without its critics, and arguments based on empirical findings, as well as on assertions of the spiritual nature of mental suffering, have been countered by expressions of concern about the ethical, professional and scientific implications of what is being proposed.

The aim of this book is to take contributions from leading scholars from theology, anthropology, philosophy, psychiatry and other relevant disciplines as an illustration of the main areas of academic and professional debate concerning spirituality and mental health at the present time. These contributions provide a basis for reflection on some of the professional, methodological and epistemological issues that arise for academics, practitioners and those who suffer from mental disorders.

The book draws on the proceedings of a conference of the same title held at St John's College, Durham, 13–16 September 2010.[1] The book is built around the central conference themes, and all of the contributing authors also contributed papers at the conference (although the chapters here are not necessarily or exactly the same as the conference presentations). It thus reflects debates and discussion had at the conference, but has not been unnecessarily constrained by the conference proceedings. The book stands on its own terms as a contribution to interdisciplinary discourse and interprofessional dialogue in this field. It has been informed by the conference, and has benefited from dialogue that took place at the conference, but it is not a set of conference proceedings.

It is hoped that the book will provide a valuable teaching resource at postgraduate level, whether on specialist taught programmes such as the Masters programme in spirituality, theology and health at Durham University, or for generic modules in pastoral and practical theology, or for doctoral students writing dissertations on cognate topics. We hope that it will also be used by clinical students studying for intercalated degrees or professional qualifications.

---

1 http://www.dur.ac.uk/spirituality.health/?p=141#more-141.

The intention has been to produce a book that crosses a number of boundaries. First, it is aimed both at academics and professionals. Professional practice informs academic research and scholarship, and academic scholarship at its best has relevance to practice. Each needs the other. Second, it is aimed both at theologians and clergy, as well as at medical academics and healthcare professionals. Notwithstanding the presence of chaplains in many (in the UK most) hospitals and notwithstanding a common concern for human well-being, this boundary has been far too impermeable for far too long, to the detriment of both pastoral and clinical care, as well as academic enquiry. Third, a variety of other interdisciplinary and interprofessional boundaries are crossed, in order that the relevance of other academic disciplines to the topic at hand, including especially anthropology and philosophy, may be made clear.

The title of the book, with 'theology' interposed between spirituality and mental health, is a reflection of the emphasis that has been adopted from the very earliest stages of planning our Durham conference through to the final stages of editing the book. Although not all of the contributing authors are theologians, the relevance of theology to the present debate is being particularly asserted as an important part of the interdisciplinary endeavour. Some reasons will be offered in justification of this emphasis in the introduction, but it is important to acknowledge here that this is a distinctive feature of the approach that has been taken. Spirituality may be theistic or atheistic, and mental health problems may or may not reflect explicit theological concerns. However, spirituality (in the healthcare context) and mental health are both primarily discussed within a scientific framework, and theology has especially been neglected as a conversation partner. This neglect does not do justice either to the longstanding concerns of theology with human suffering or to the theological challenges that mental suffering presents to people of faith. This book seeks to contribute a corrective to the imbalance.

Christopher C. H. Cook
Durham University

Acknowledgements

This book has only been made possible through the vision, efforts, enthusiasm, patience and good will of many people. I would like to thank them all, whether I have mentioned them here by name or not. However, some names should not go unmentioned.

The book has been informed and inspired by a conference that was planned and undertaken by a large number of colleagues in Durham, including especially Douglas Davies, Matthew Guest, Charlotte Hardman, James Jirtle, Bernhard Nausner, Matthew Rattcliffe and Anastasia Scrutton, all of whom served on the conference planning committee that conceived the idea of the book. Contributions made to debate at the conference by a large number of delegates were also significant. I cannot thank them by name, but their part in the making of this book has not gone unnoticed. Some of them contributed their own experiences – spiritual, theological and otherwise – of struggling with mental illness, and we are indebted to their honesty, courage and willingness to share with us.

Charlotte Hardman had originally hoped to co-edit this volume with me, but changed circumstances prevented us from working together on the project as we had both hoped. I have missed her wisdom, scholarship and support in the editing process but benefited greatly from her help in the planning stages, and I am glad to acknowledge here the benefits that I gained from this.

I did not feel that it was right that other chapters should be peer reviewed but that my own should not, and I am very grateful to Andrew Powell and Douglas Davies for their helpful and constructive comments on my own contributions, which have certainly been enriched and improved as a result.

I would like to thank Natalie Watson and all the staff at SCM for their support and for their appreciation of the importance of the theme of this book.

Writing takes time, and I would not have had time available for this project but for the support of the Guild of Health, from whom I received a generous grant that made my time available for both the conference and this book. They have understood that spirituality and theology have something important to contribute to mental healthcare, and that a mutual dialogue between different disciplines and professions, including both clergy and doctors, is much needed. I am very grateful for their vision and support.

Finally, as always, my thanks go to my wife and family for their love, patience and encouragement in so many ways.

Introduction

CHRISTOPHER C. H. COOK

Spirituality and religion are receiving increasing interest in research and clinical practice concerned with mental health and mental disorders. Theology, in contrast, continues to receive little or no attention. A number of recent exceptions might be noted, including some significant work in selected areas such as addiction (Cook 2006; Mercadante 1996), and dementia (Swinton 2012). There has also been interest, mainly in the domain of pastoral theology, in the not too distant past, including the work of Frank Lake and Clinical Theology (Lake 1966), and the reflections of Anton Boisen on his own acute mental illness, which led to the development of Clinical Pastoral Education (Boisen 1952). We might further note some other important exceptions. There has been reflection on the relationships between mental disorder and faith in the lives of various biblical figures, saints and ascetics, including even Jesus of Nazareth, but this has not always been theologically well informed (Cook 2012b; Schweitzer 1948). There has also been interest on the part of some Orthodox theologians (Larchet 2005; Muse 2004; Chirban 2001), perhaps because of the particular attention that Orthodoxy has given to mental well-being (Cook 2011; 2012a). Indeed, it might well be thought that I have now acknowledged a sufficient number of exceptions to add up to something much less than evidence of a complete neglect. However, these exceptions do also serve to map out a significant area of neglect. Critical contemporary theological attention to current constructions of mental health and mental disorders seems to be lacking, at least in western Christianity.

There may be many reasons for this. For example, science and theology may be perceived as alternative frames of reference, which address different questions, and which have little common ground within which to engage together. If this is the case, it is still interesting that relatively little theological attention has been devoted to mental health. Illness in general has not so obviously been neglected and theological interest in health and healing may be identified in the work of Dame Evelyn Frost, among others (Frost 1985; Porterfield 2005; Shuman and Meador 2003; Watts 2011). Neither has the dialogue between science and religion been a subject that has been neglected in recent years (Barbour 1998).

There has been an historical antipathy between religion and psychiatry, which may have made many psychiatrists unlikely to see the relevance of theology and many theologians suspicious of a discipline that has often seen religious experience as evidence of mental disorder (Cook 2012b; Blazer 1998). However, against this, theologians have not been slow to respond vigorously to other controversial debates with other relevant disciplines (Watts 2002; Gill 1996) and have even effectively assimilated many professional insights from counselling and psychotherapy within their own perspectives on pastoral and practical theology (Carr 1997; Clinebell 1984; Litchfield 2006).

Perhaps a further possible explanation is to be found in the way in which spirituality, rather than religion, has come to be seen as important in clinical practice and research. The distinction between spirituality and religion is explored by Patricia Casey in Chapter 2 of the present volume, addressing the commonly encountered view that 'I am spiritual but not religious'. This perspective, which does indeed seem to be popular today, has generated a focus on spirituality dissociated from religious tradition, and thus perhaps also from theology. The clinical and research context, including the plural and secular nature of contemporary western society, has required that spirituality be seen as something that transcends particular faith traditions, and thus is an accessible mode of discourse for people from all faith traditions and none. Healthcare related research on this kind of spirituality has primarily been conducted from an empirical, scientific, point of view, not a theological one. However, theology does have an interest in spirituality as well as religion. In Chapter 8 of the present volume, I suggest that the language of transcendence may provide a fruitful point of theological engagement.

The relative lack of recent critical theological engagement with mental health and mental disorder thus remains something of a mystery. However, if it has been an oversight of the past, this is no reason for continuing neglect in the present. Indeed, there are various reasons why theological engagement with these topics might be seen as important.

First, we are now more aware than ever before that people who face adversity (whether this be physical or mental illness, or something else) are likely to draw upon spirituality and religious faith as an important coping resource (Pargament 2011). Chaplains and other clergy (not to mention counsellors, psychotherapists and sometimes other healthcare professionals) are therefore not infrequently engaged with the pastoral task of assisting such people in their own theological reflections upon their struggles. This is partly, but not exclusively, concerned with the quest for meaning, and the need to interpret the significance of what has happened within the context of the stories that our lives comprise, including the story of faith. However, there is a further complication, for the mental faculties that are employed in the process of undertaking such reflection are often themselves the very faculties that are disordered as a part of the condition in question.

Thus, for example, the guilt experienced by the person who is clinically depressed is both a matter requiring serious theological reflection in its own right and is to be distinguished in various ways from the attention that theology may have given to 'ordinary' or 'normal' guilt in the past, but it is also a part of the mental apparatus that the person concerned will necessarily bring to bear upon their own theological self-reflection. Guilt may thus be a symptom of the clinical condition, it might also be a contributing cause of the clinical condition, but, most importantly, it also distorts the ability of the person concerned to reflect theologically in what might be considered an objective fashion on their own spiritual well-being. The need for a critical theological framework within which to understand and manage such issues is therefore a practically, clinically and pastorally very important one.

Of course, if we have a model of mental well-being within which most of us are well, and only a minority (albeit perhaps a significant minority) suffer from diagnosable mental illness, then the kind of problem that I have just described will not affect most of us most of the time. In particular, we would not imagine that it will affect most academic or practical theologians going about their normal everyday work. But this is a questionable assumption. First, it is questionable because we now know that diagnosable mental illness is common in the general population (Mcmanus et al. 2009). Second, it is questionable because diagnoses according to the International Classification of Diseases (World Health Organization 1992), or the Diagnostic and Statistical Manual of the American Psychiatric Association (American Psychiatric Association 1987), are not the only way of defining what mental well-being is not. If we adopt the broader perspectives of psychology, counselling and psychotherapy, there is a sense in which many of us, perhaps all of us, find ourselves in places that do not reflect complete mental well-being, at least sometimes and perhaps often. These are therefore issues that potentially affect the way in which all theologians undertake their task of doing theology. Considered in this light, one may well wonder why theology has hitherto given so little attention to this problem.

Mark Wynn provides a helpful analysis, with great relevance to this task, in Chapter 7. In particular, he suggests that 'mental health consists in part in the realization of an appropriate match between a person's fundamental values and beliefs and the appearance of the sensory world'. Mental health, values and beliefs, and our experiences of the world around us, are all interrelated. Theology, or at least the sense that we make of our own theologies and the theology of others, I would suggest, therefore cannot satisfactorily be separated from either our state of mental well-being or our experiences of the world around us.

Second, theology in the broadest sense (including all its sub-disciplines) has a contribution to make to our understanding of the human condition – including conditions of mental health and ill-health. At a time when the relevance of the humanities to medicine is being appreciated more than ever before (Barritt 2005), theology has its part to play as a partner in a full multidisciplinary engagement, alongside the (other) human and social sciences. It is this kind of engagement that has been sought, with the help of authors from a variety of academic disciplines, both in the conference that prepared the way for this book and, now, in the book itself. The benefits of this engagement make themselves apparent in a wide variety of ways. One significant example, however, will be found here in the attention to concepts of narrative, addressed by Douglas Davies in Chapter 9, and about which I shall say more in Conclusions and Reflections at the end of the book.

Third, contextual theology increasingly recognizes that theology is itself shaped by its context, and that this context includes the full social, cultural and scientific understanding of the human environment (Peers 2010). Theology may, therefore, be beneficially informed and influenced by engagement with other disciplines, including those various social and biological sciences that engage with issues of mental health and disorder. This will not be a theme that is explored at any length in this book, although we might see some potentially fruitful ground for pursuing it further in a number of chapters.

There are doubtless also other reasons for seeing value in theological engagement with issues of mental health, well-being and disorder. However, it will be difficult to pursue such questions too much further without clarity of understanding of what theology is. While this important question cannot be exhaustively explored here, at least some attention to it is required.

What is theology?

Augustine of Hippo suggested that theology is 'reasoning or discussion about the divinity'.[1] Like Anselm of Canterbury's famous definition of 'faith seeking understanding' (Davies and Evans 1998, p. xxi), this presumes a position of belief or faith which asserts that there is a divinity with respect to whom reason and discussion might be pursued. For anyone who does not share such a commitment, theology might be seen as irrelevant although, in a broader sense, it is taken as incorporating atheistic systems of religious thought such as Buddhism. In any case, it still addresses the situation of the great majority of people worldwide who report theistic belief. Even for those who do not believe, it is at least important as a discipline within which the reasonings and discussions of others may be delineated and understood. For those who do believe, this is the space within which what they believe is explored, challenged and defined. The nature of what emerges is of wide importance as a characterization of what gives many people meaning and purpose in life, of what they resort to as a basis for coping in times of adversity, and as something that has, for better or worse, enriched, influenced and formed much of human history and culture.

---

1 *City of God* VIII.1

However, I think that the relevance to all of us is more even than this. To believe that there is no God (or gods) is itself a theological statement. Indeed, it is a very important theological statement, about which there has been very much debate. But such belief, or at least such a line of reasoning and thought, is not solely the concern of the atheist. Understood as 'doubt' it has afflicted many people of faith, including such figures as Thérèse of Lisieux (Foley 2008) and Mother Teresa of Calcutta. It is also understandable as an experience of thought that goes beyond what may adequately be conveyed by the concept of 'doubt'. A 'perception' of the absence of God, or an interpretation of experience that raises the question of the absence of God, is not the domain only of the atheist. Thus, for example, in *The Dark Night*, St John of the Cross (Kavanaugh and Rodriguez 1991) explores what it might mean for Christian faith and spirituality to engage faithfully and lovingly with places in life within which God seems noticeably absent. In Chapter 11 of the present volume, Simon Podmore explores such a line of thought in relation to Christ's cry of dereliction from the cross. Theology, it might be argued, is as much about grappling with the seeming absence of God as with God's seeming presence. It is concerned with unbelief, and inability to believe, as much as it is with belief.

Theology may be subclassified in a variety of ways. No attempt will be made here to explore the history of such taxonomies, but a threefold division proposed recently by Rowan Williams (2000) will be taken as helpful in the process of further exploring the relevance of theology to the present volume. Williams suggests that theology may be divided into celebratory, communicative and critical 'styles'.

Theology begins as a celebratory phenomenon, an attempt to draw out and display connections of thought and image so as to exhibit the fullest possible range of significance in the language used. (p. xiii)

This beginning is perhaps most often thought of in positive affective terms, and Williams draws on examples of hymnody and worship. However, as already suggested, it may also incorporate descriptions of places of despair and loss, including loss of hope and loss of faith. Perhaps for our present purpose, of considering the relevance of theology to mental non-wellbeing, it is especially important that it does so.

But theology does not remain within this style, and it moves beyond any celebratory place of beginning. Williams suggests:

Theology seeks also to persuade or commend, to witness to the gospel's capacity for being at home in more than one cultural environment, and to display enough confidence to believe that this gospel can be rediscovered at the end of a long and exotic detour through strange idioms and structures of thought. This is what I mean by the 'communicative': a theology experimenting with the rhetoric of its uncommitted environment. (p. xiv)

Theology is thus informed by disciplines of thought other than its own. We might even see here an echo of John Henry Newman's proposal, in *The Idea of a University*, that all disciplines of academic thought are interrelated and belong together (Newman 1996). Theology needs the other disciplines, and they need theology. This has been a central ethos of the present project – both the conference that paved the way for the present book and the book itself. Thus contributions from philosophy (e.g. Chapter 10, by John Cottingham) and anthropology (Chapter 9, Douglas Davies) have been seen as just as important and theological as those from biblical studies (Chapter 6, Loren Stuckenbruck). Similarly, where drawing on practice-based experience and scholarship, the resources of both the chaplain (Chapter 3, Colin Jay) and the clinician (Chapter 2, Patricia Casey) have been seen as vital. Some of us cross disciplinary and professional boundaries both in our own practice and in our contributions to the present volume. Thus, Chris MacKenna (Chapter 5) writes both as a psychotherapist and a priest; Alexandra Pârvan (Chapter 4) writes both as a psychotherapist and a philosopher; and my own contributions are made from my perspectives both as theologian (Chapter 8) and psychiatrist (Chapter 1).

Williams sees a further style of theology, however, which denies the temptation towards a comfortably descriptive kind of approach, within which different disciplines are seen merely as complacently corroborating discourse about the divine.

> But there can come a point here where the passage through unfamiliar media of thought provokes a degree of crisis: is what is emerging actually identical or at least continuous with what has been believed and articulated? This is a question that prompts further probing of what the 'fundamental categories' really mean. Is there a stable conceptual area in the discourse of belief that will always remain unaffected by mediation in other idioms? And, if not, what, if any, kind of continuity and coherence belongs to this discourse? This nagging at fundamental meanings is what constitutes a critical theology, alert to its own inner tension or irresolutions. (Williams 2000, pp. xiv–xv)

Williams suggests that there are two possible outcomes to this style of theology, one which moves towards agnosticism, nihilism or atheism, and another which rediscovers the celebratory, and I think it is important for the integrity of the theological quest that we always acknowledge this reality. Theology sometimes leads us to uncomfortable places. It is in the nature of the present volume where mental disorder, a place of non-wellbeing, is to be considered that such critical thinking, and openness to where it may lead, is deeply necessary. I think that Simon Podmore's exploration (in Chapter 11) of the place of desolation typified by Christ's cry of dereliction from the cross, a place of the seeming absence of God, is an important exploration of this style of theology.

Finally, like Rowan Williams's *On Christian Theology*, from which this classification of scriptural styles has been drawn, we will confine ourselves in this book to Christian theology. This engagement will inevitably acknowledge in various places the secular context of pluralism of belief, and various forms of unbelief including atheism. However, it would not be possible in a single book of this length to engage in sufficient depth with other important theological traditions such as those of Islam or Judaism,[2] or any of the eastern religious traditions. It is much to be hoped that similar work will be undertaken in future from within these traditions and that this in turn will allow a comparative study of theologies of mental health across and between the world's major faith traditions.

Spirituality, theology and mental health

Spirituality, theology and mental health are all intimately related. The part that theology plays will be explored further throughout the present book, but it will not be possible adequately to engage with this task only in the explicit language of theology. The professional discourse of clinical practice, the pastoral experience of chaplains and clergy, the academic rigour and insights of other disciplines, all have their part to play in working towards a more critical theological engagement with mental health and mental disorder.

References

American Psychiatric Association (1987), *Diagnostic and Statistical Manual of Mental Disorders*, Washington DC: American Psychiatric Association.

Barbour, I. G. (1998), *Religion and Science*, London: SCM Press.

Barritt, P. (2005), *Humanity in Healthcare: The Heart and Soul of Medicine*, Oxford: Radcliffe.

Blazer, D. (1998), *Freud vs God*, Downers Grove IL: InterVarsity Press.

Boisen, A. T. (1952), *The Exploration of the Inner World: A Study of Mental Disorder and Religious Experience*, New York: Harper.

Carr, W. (1997), *Handbook of Pastoral Studies*, London: SPCK.

Chirban, J. T. (ed.) (2001), *Sickness or Sin? Spiritual Discernment and Differential Diagnosis*, Brookline: Holy Cross Orthodox Press.

Clinebell, H. (1984), *Basic Types of Pastoral Care and Counselling*, London: SCM Press.

Cook, C. C. H. (2006), *Alcohol, Addiction and Christian Ethics*, Cambridge: Cambridge University Press.

Cook, C. C. H. (2011), *The Philokalia and the Inner Life: On Passions and Prayer*, Cambridge: James Clarke.

Cook, C. C. H. (2012a), 'Healing, psychotherapy, and *The Philokalia*', in B. Bingaman and B. Nassif (eds), The Philokalia: *A Classic Text of Orthodox Spirituality*, Oxford: Oxford University Press, pp. 230–9.

---

2 In Chapter 6, Loren Stuckenbruck does however engage with some important Hebrew scriptural texts, as well as with Christian Scripture.

Cook, C. C. H. (2012b), 'Psychiatry in Scripture: sacred texts and psychopathology', *The Psychiatrist* 36:6, pp. 225–9.

Davies, B. and Evans, G. R. (1998), *Anselm of Canterbury: The Major Works*, Oxford: Oxford University Press.

Foley, M. (2008), *The Context of Holiness: Psychological and Spiritual Reflections on the Life of St Thérèse of Lisieux*, Washington DC: ICS Publications.

Frost, R. (1985), *Christ and Wholeness*, Cambridge: James Clarke.

Gill, R. (1996), *Theology and Sociology: A Reader*, London: Cassell.

Kavanaugh, K. and Rodriguez, O. (1991), *The Collected Works of St John of the Cross*, Washington DC: Institute of Carmelite Studies.

Lake, F. (1966), *Clinical Theology*, London: Darton, Longman & Todd.

Larchet, J. C. (2005), *Mental Disorders and Spiritual Healing: Teachings from the Early Christian East*, Hillsdale: Sophia Perennis.

Litchfield, K. (2006), *Tend My Flock: Sustaining Good Pastoral Care*, Norwich: Canterbury Press.

Mcmanus, S., Meltzer, H., Brugha, T., Bebbington, P. and Jenkins, R. (eds) (2009), *Adult Psychiatric Morbidity in England 2007: Results of a Household Survey*, London: The NHS Information Centre for Health and Social Care.

Mercadante, L. A. (1996), *Victims and Sinners*, Louisville KY: Westminster John Knox Press.

Muse, S. (ed.) (2004), *Raising Lazarus: Integral Healing in Orthodox Christianity*, Brookline: Holy Cross Orthodox Press.

Newman, J. H. (1996), *The Idea of a University*, New Haven: Yale University Press.

Pargament, K. I. (2011), *Spiritually Integrated Psychotherapy*, New York: Guilford.

Peers, A. (2010), *Doing Contextual Theology*, London: Routledge.

Porterfield, A. (2005), *Healing in the History of Christianity*, Oxford: Oxford University Press.

Schweitzer, A. (1948), *The Psychiatric Study of Jesus: Exposition and Criticism*, Boston: Beacon.

Shuman, J. J. and Meador, K. G. (2003), *Heal Thyself: Spirituality, Medicine, and the Distortion of Christianity*, Oxford: Oxford University Press.

Swinton, J. (2012), *Dementia: Living in the Memories of God*, Grand Rapids MI: Eerdmans.

Watts, F. (2002), *Theology and Psychology*, Farnham: Ashgate.

Watts, F. (ed.) (2011), *Spiritual Healing: Scientific and Religious Perspectives*, Cambridge: Cambridge University Press.

Williams, R. (2000), *On Christian Theology*, Oxford: Blackwell.

World Health Organization (1992), *The ICD-10 Classification of Mental and Behavioural Disorders*, Geneva: World Health Organization.

Controversies on the Place of Spirituality and Religion in Psychiatric Practice

CHRISTOPHER C. H. COOK

Summary

Recent controversies concerning the place of spirituality in psychiatry in the UK have reflected a variety of concerns among mental health professionals and service users. On the one hand, research and clinical interest in spirituality as a positive factor in mental healthcare has been on the ascendant. On the other hand, there have been concerns that the inclusion of spirituality within the practice of psychiatry crosses important professional boundaries. Boundaries are important for good professional practice, and three particular boundaries emerge in this debate as being of especial concern: the boundary of specialist expertise, the boundary between secular and religious spheres of interest, and the boundary between personal and professional values. Proper professional observance of these boundaries does not require that spirituality or religion be excluded from psychiatry (an impossible aim, in any case) but it does require that they be examined carefully and critically, both by individual clinicians in the course of their practice and by the professional community in the course of ethical, academic and clinical debate.

Spirituality and religion have attracted increasing interest in the field of mental healthcare in recent years, among academics, clinicians and service users. Research evidence suggests that better attention to spirituality might improve treatment outcomes, and service users have expressed a desire that spirituality and religion should be addressed during the course of treatment. However, there has been significant professional and academic debate as to the merits and dangers of this trend. This chapter will consider the nature of spirituality, the increasing interest given to it in academic and professional debate and the nature of the controversies that have arisen. In particular, attention will be given to examining the nature of the professional boundaries that have been identified as a concern where spirituality and religion are to be addressed in clinical practice and their proper management.

The nature of spirituality

Spirituality is not easily defined and represents a disputed concept about which there has been much debate (Cook 2004; Sims and Cook 2009). Some would argue that it is distinct from religion and others that it amounts to much the same kind of thing. But, religion is also not easily defined, and the oft promoted view that spirituality is individual, subjective and experiential, as contrasted to the institutional, traditional and doctrinal nature of religion, does justice neither to the social and traditional aspects of spirituality nor to the individual experience of religion. For many, spirituality and religion are about meaning and purpose in life, but it is doubtless the case that meaning and purpose are often found by others without spirituality or religion ever being mentioned. Similarly, even though many people understand spirituality in terms of relationships (for example with self, others and a higher power or wider order), it is difficult to define those relational aspects of spirituality that cannot otherwise be framed in purely psychological terms, unless perhaps they are concerned with transcendence (and even here, psychological accounts abound).

Despite these observations, spirituality is preserved here as a term that is seen to be useful, partly because it is so widely used (and hardly likely to be abandoned in the foreseeable future) but also because it is thought to retain some validity. Further, it is useful to have a term that can be employed to refer to a universal aspect of human well-being (even if it is not universally accepted), without introducing the specificity and particularity that religion usually implies.

Spirituality and mental health

A search of Medline citations reveals that increasing numbers of papers on spirituality have been published in the healthcare literature since the early 1980s (Cook 2004). The proportion of papers on spirituality and mental health has similarly been rising year on year, and this increase does not simply reflect the increasing numbers of papers published year on year but actually represents a growing proportion of papers in the database (see Figure 1).

When the first edition of the widely cited and influential *Handbook of Religion and Health* was published in 2001 (Koenig, McCullough et al. 2001), it reported that almost 80 per cent of 100 studies on religion and measures of well-being such as happiness, life satisfaction and morale found a positive correlation. Religious involvement was found to be associated with (among other things) low hostility, higher levels of hope, optimism and self-esteem, less delinquency among young people and greater social support and marital stability.

The *Handbook* reviews of research on specific psychiatric disorders generally demonstrated positive effects of religiosity. For depression, for

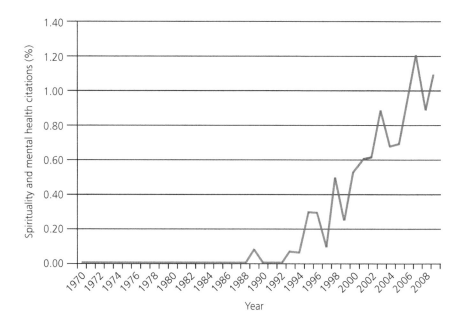

Figure 1: Spirituality and mental health – Medline citations

example, it was concluded that religious affiliation and social involvement (where associated with intrinsic religiosity) were generally associated with less depression, that religious people recover more quickly and that religious involvement helps people to cope with stress. Of 68 studies, 84 per cent showed an inverse relationship between religious involvement and suicide. Intrinsic religiosity was, on the whole, found to buffer against anxiety. Nearly 100 studies were found to support a deterrent effect of religion against substance misuse. While religion was not thought to influence the occurrence of the psychoses, it was thought to provide an important coping resource to people suffering from such conditions. In general, however, it was also acknowledged that the methodology of many studies left much to be desired, and particularly that more longitudinal studies were needed.

When the second edition of the *Handbook* was published, just over ten years later (Koenig, King et al. 2012), the conclusions of the first edition generally seemed to be reaffirmed and supported by more recent research. Thus, for example, 78 per cent of 224 studies on well-being undertaken since the year 2000 found positive associations with greater religiousness. But as in the first edition, not all findings were positive. For example, out of a total of 443 quantitative studies on depression included in the first and second editions, 61 per cent found that greater religious/spiritual involvement was associated with less depression or faster recovery, but 22 per cent found no association and 6 per cent found an association with greater depression. Furthermore, some of the studies finding no association or finding an association with greater depression were rated as being of good quality methodology. The authors note a variety of possible reasons for this. For example, in contrast to the United States, in less religious but affluent countries it is suggested that people suffering from depression might turn to religion as a coping mechanism and thus that an apparent association between religion and depression might emerge.

The rising numbers of published research papers internationally and the associated scientific debate have been paralleled by an increasing level of public and professional debate. Much of this has taken place in the United States, but the debate in the United Kingdom will be taken here as an example of the way that spirituality has become a topic of increasing interest in the field of mental health. In particular, interest in this topic within the Royal College of Psychiatrists is taken as an example and indicator of professional and academic interest generally, but it is of note that during the same period the debate has also reflected the interests of service users, policy makers and other professional groups (Mental Health Foundation 1997; Mental Health Foundation 2002; Mental Health Foundation 2007). Indeed, service user concerns and policy initiatives are almost certainly among the key factors that have fuelled interest and driven change in services (Eagger, Richmond et al. 2009).

In 1991, HRH The Prince of Wales, addressing the Royal College of Psychiatrists as its patron, drew attention to the spiritual task that is at the heart of mental healthcare:

> We are not just machines, whatever modern science may claim is the case on the evidence of what is purely visible and tangible in this world. Mental and physical health also have a spiritual base. Caring for people who are ill, restoring them to health when that is possible, and comforting them always, even when it is not, are spiritual tasks. (HRH The Prince of Wales 1991)

In 1993, successive presidents of the Royal College of Psychiatrists addressed the subject of spiritual care in their lectures at College meetings. Professor Andrew Sims, in his valedictory lecture, warned members that they ignore the topic at their patients' peril:

> For too long psychiatry has avoided the spiritual realm, perhaps out of ignorance, for fear of trampling on patients' sensibilities. This is understandable, but psychiatrists have neglected it at their patients' peril. We need to evaluate the religious and spiritual experience of our patients in aetiology, diagnosis, prognosis and treatment. (Sims 1994)

Reflecting on why psychiatrists neglect the spiritual, he suggested that there might be several reasons:

(a) It is considered unimportant.
(b) It is considered important but irrelevant to psychiatry – like assuming the hospital has a safe water supply.
(c) We feel we know too little about it ourselves to comment, or even to ask questions.
(d) The very terminology is confusing and hence embarrassing; it is not *respectable*.
(e) There may also be an element of denial in which it is easier to ignore this area than explore it as it is too personally challenging. (Sims 1994)

Professor John Cox, as the incoming president in the same year, emphasized the importance of religious perspectives as an aspect of culturally aware psychiatry in a plural society:

> [I]f mental health services in a multi-cultural society are to become more responsive to 'user' needs then eliciting the 'religious history' with any linked spiritual meanings should be a routine component of a psychiatric assessment, and of preparing a more culturally sensitive 'care plan'. (Cox 1994)

In 1997, the Archbishop of Canterbury was invited to address an annual meeting of the College (Carey 1997). In the course of asking how the barriers between religion and psychiatry might be transcended, he noted the common inheritance that they share. Both recognize health as something 'beyond the physical'. Both value faith, hope and love (although psychiatry might not so often use this language). Because they share so much and yet retain their own distinctiveness, he argued that religion and psychiatry actually need each other. On the one hand, religion needs the psychological and professional insights of psychiatry. On the other hand, psychiatry needs to understand the experiences associated with the religious quest, at least if its practitioners are to find any empathy with the many users of mental health services who are themselves associated with or engaged in this quest. Moreover, the Archbishop asserted, society needs religion and psychiatry to work together for the good of people who suffer from mental disorders if it is to respond effectively to the needs of people with mental disorders in primary care and in local communities.

In 1999, a Special Interest Group for Spirituality and Psychiatry (SPSIG) was formed within the College, under the founding chairmanship of Dr Andrew Powell, with a view to promoting professional debate on spirituality and psychiatry (Shooter 1999; Powell and Cook 2006; Powell 2009). Among other things, the group was established as a forum within which to discuss:

- 'the significance of the major religions which influence the values and beliefs of the society in which we live, also taking into account the

spiritual aspirations of individuals who do not identify with any one particular faith and those who hold that spirituality is independent of religion';
- 'specific experiences invested with spiritual meaning, including the meaning of birth, death and near-death, mystical and trance states to distinguish between transformative and pathological states of mind';
- 'protective factors which sustain individuals in crisis and otherwise contribute to mental health'. (Shooter 1999)

At the time of writing, the membership of the SPSIG stands at nearly three thousand.

Within a decade, the topic of spirituality had thus moved from something rarely or never mentioned within public and professional discourse at College meetings to being a topic that attracted sufficient interest to warrant the forming of a new Special Interest Group. In 2009, just a decade after this, a book conceived and written largely by members of the SPSIG and published by Royal College of Psychiatrists Press outlined the current state of the field of spirituality and psychiatry in clinical practice (Cook, Powell et al. 2009). Two years later, the College adopted as policy a position statement making recommendations for psychiatrists concerning spirituality and religion (Cook 2011), a statement that had also been drafted and proposed by the SPSIG.

The contemporary debate

The contemporary debate about spirituality and mental health arises in the context of a much longer history of tension between religion and psychiatry. From the very birth of psychiatry there seems to have been a desire to establish a distance from religion, perhaps as a part of the need to affirm scientific credentials for this new medical speciality (Koenig, King et al. 2012, pp. 30–1). This distance became coupled with more active antagonism on the basis of various allegations that religion is associated with emotional immaturity, guilt, neurosis or even major mental illness (Neeleman and Persaud 1995). However, the relationship has always been complex and any deepening or lessening of the tensions at different points in history might be seen as reflecting varying attempts at establishing a balance or rapprochement between two different worlds of thought – the religious and the scientific – in an area of shared concern about the nature of mental suffering and the proper means of finding healing from it.

Internationally, one of the strongest critics of the place of spirituality in healthcare in recent times has been Richard Sloan (Sloan, Bagiella et al. 1999; Sloan and Bagiella 2002; Sloan 2006). Sloan's objections are across a range of scientific, ethical and practical domains, summarized in his book *Blind Faith: The Unholy Alliance of Religion and Medicine*, and are by no means focused only on mental health issues. However, among the many examples that he gives as basis for his concerns, he draws attention to the way in which prayer is often used as a coping mechanism by patients with psychiatric conditions who are not receiving support from mental health professionals. He takes this to mean that these people must have thought that prayer was sufficient in the absence of medical care, and thus that it makes them think that they do not need professional help (2006, p. 189). As another example drawn from the world of psychiatry, he refers to literature linking brain serotonin levels to religiosity and spirituality and to neuro-imaging studies of meditating subjects (pp. 243–54) and expresses concern that such reductionistic approaches to research are at least unsatisfying to religion and at worst might even be understood as blasphemous. Sloan is clearly concerned not only with good science and professional practice but also with the dangers of misapplying religion to the detriment of health and science to the detriment of religion.

Much of the literature around this debate, including Koenig's *Handbook* and Sloan's *Blind Faith*, has been published in the USA. The debate concerning spirituality and psychiatry in the UK seems to have taken off following publication of an editorial by Harold Koenig in *Psychiatric Bulletin* in 2008 (Koenig 2008). Under the title 'Religion and mental health: what should psychiatrists do?', this editorial succinctly presented arguments that had previously been made elsewhere – either by Koenig himself, by various contributors to the debate at Royal College of Psychiatrists' meetings (briefly summarized above), or by others, in print and at conferences. It evoked a vigorous correspondence. The main items of contention, some of which echo Sloan's concerns, are therefore worthy of some further attention here.

Noting the history in psychiatry of an understanding of religious beliefs and practices as pathological, Koenig went on to say: 'Recent research, however, has uncovered findings which suggest that to some patients religion may also be a resource that helps them to cope with the stress of their illness or with dismal life circumstances.'

Drawing on the work of Neeleman and Persaud (Neeleman and Persaud 1995) and noting that psychiatrists are likely to be less religious than their patients, Koenig suggested that psychiatrists may not appreciate the value of religion as a resource to help in coping with illness. Further, the experience of psychiatrists is in dealing with pathological (e.g. delusional) manifestations of religion and they therefore may be more aware of the potential of religion to cause dependence and guilt, all of which may bias them against recognition of the therapeutic values of healthy religion. He noted also that, in contrast to biological psychiatry, religion is perceived as non-empirical and subjective.

Koenig proposed a number of interventions that psychiatrists 'should consider'. These included taking a spiritual history, supporting healthy religious beliefs, challenging unhealthy beliefs, praying with patients (but only in 'highly selected cases') and consultation with, referral to, or joint working with trained clergy. In conclusion, Koenig stated, 'Ignoring the religious beliefs will cause the psychiatrist to miss an important psychological and social factor that may be either a powerful resource for healing or major cause of pathology.'

The prolonged and vigorous correspondence that followed in *Psychiatric Bulletin* (later renamed *The Psychiatrist*) was revealing of the concerns of British psychiatrists (Lepping 2008a; Lepping 2008b; Poole, Higgo et al. 2008; Poole, Higgo et al. 2010), and the debate has continued since in other journals (Dein, Cook et al. 2010; Poole and Cook 2011; Poole and Higgo 2011). Spiritual history-taking was thought to be intrusive and showed lack of respect, it was said, for non-believers. Like Sloan, correspondents thought that judgements about which beliefs should be supported and which challenged were value laden. Attention was drawn to the potential risks of the proposed interventions, notably in the case of the patient with religious delusions or of the clinician with an agenda for proselytizing. The possibility of praying with patients (cautious though Koenig had been about this) was found to be especially controversial. Spirituality was considered to be a 'culture-bound' concept and was contrasted with the 'neutral' space of secularity. It is hard to sum up all of these concerns under one heading but perhaps if one were to try to do so it would be under the heading of concern about boundary violations. The proposals that Koenig summarized in his editorial were seen, at least by some psychiatrists, as prejudicing accepted professional boundaries.

Boundaries

It is interesting to consider exactly what the boundaries may be that Koenig and others who wish to promote the place of spirituality in psychiatry are actually considered to be in danger of breaching. It seems to me that at least three have featured prominently in the debate: the boundary of specialist expertise, the boundary between secular and religious spheres of interest and the boundary between personal and professional values.

Spirituality, it is argued, is essentially not the business of psychiatrists. It is not a part of their special professional expertise. It belongs, rather, to chaplains, clergy and other spiritual advisers whose training has focused on such things and who are the properly recognized experts to whom the person with spiritual concerns should resort. Not only do psychiatrists not have the specialist training that might equip them to deal with spiritual things, but when they do transgress this boundary, it is argued, the patient may not be aware that it is spiritual rather than psychiatric advice that they are receiving. In other words, there may be (intentional or inadvertent) misrepresentation of the grounds for commending a particular course of action and the possibility of abuse of the privileged position that the psychiatrist occupies as a recognized expert. This boundary thus both defines and protects the arena within which psychiatric expertise may be said to exist, but also protects against confusion of this specialist knowledge with other kinds of specialist knowledge. In practice, the boundary tends to be fairly permeable when it is other kinds of scientific knowledge that are under consideration. It is therefore not a boundary within the sciences within which psychiatry is seen as distinct. It is really, I think, a boundary to keep out non-scientific (including not only explicitly spiritual and religious but also other non-empirically based) modes of thought. Thus, for example: 'Psychiatrists are essentially applied biopsychosocial scientists, who work within a clear set of humanitarian values and ethical principles in order to get alongside service users and facilitate their recovery from a mental illness' (Poole, Higgo et al. 2008).

The boundary between secular and religious spheres is a somewhat different boundary, although it does serve a very similar and overlapping function. Thus, it similarly selects between kinds of knowledge that are appropriate to psychiatry (i.e. science) and those that are not (e.g. religion), but it also serves to define space within which the clinical encounter may take place. This space, importantly, must be neutral. It must be shared space within which a patient can safely seek help (without fear of, for example, proselytizing) and within which a professional can safely offer help (without fear of, for example, accusations of unprofessional conduct). It is this function of defining neutral space that makes this boundary important to professional practice and different (at least in principle) from the boundary defining specialist expertise.

The neutrality that is sought within this safe space, at least in the present context, is concerned with neutrality towards matters of religion. Thus, the Christian psychiatrist should not attempt to convert his Muslim patient, nor the Muslim psychiatrist her Christian patient. Neither should judgements be formed as to the benefits of one religion over another. This is not solely a religious issue, of course, for the same neutrality is sought in respect of political and moral beliefs, among others. The boundary is one that safeguards generally against judgemental attitudes that might cause harm to a vulnerable patient. Secularity, it is argued, provides this neutral, safe, space.

Finally, there is the boundary between personal and professional values. The concern here, I think, is that the psychiatrist should be professional (which is surely not unreasonable) and that this requires an approach to the clinical encounter that keeps the personal and private values of the clinician at bay, or at least identifies them as in need of separating out. Thus, any religious concerns that the professional may have personally concerning morality, truth or values must be kept out of the consultation in order to allow a non-judgemental stance to be adopted, within which the patient can safely know that it is scientific, professional and impartial advice that they are receiving. As with the previously described boundaries, this protects against proselytizing. It ensures that advice given is known to be based on objective, scientific concerns, not on hidden religious principles.

These three boundaries, then, the boundary of specialist expertise, the boundary between secular and religious spheres of interest and the boundary between personal and professional values, have similar and overlapping functions, but they operate in differing epistemological and social domains. The first is more concerned with the differences between scientific and non-empirical forms of knowledge. The second is more concerned with the location of the clinical encounter within secular space and its isolation from religious discourse. The third is more concerned with the nature of professional roles and their separation from the personal or private aspects of the professional's life.

The continuing professional and academic debate about the place of spirituality in psychiatry must surely be a good thing, and it is to be hoped that it will result in time in greater consensus as to how the research evidence should be interpreted and greater clarity about where the proper boundaries lie and what good practice in this domain looks like. A recently published contribution to the debate would suggest that this is already beginning to happen (Cook, Poole et al. 2012). There seems to be agreement that it is not possible to exclude matters of spirituality and religion from all aspects of clinical practice, that it is important to understand the role of spirituality and religion in a patient's life, that it is sometimes appropriate to involve chaplains and other religious advisers in the process of helping people with mental health problems and that psychiatry is in any case not the complete solution to people's problems: 'psychiatry cannot offer total solutions to mental illness and human unhappiness ... in practice psychiatry is the application of a flawed science in the context of shared (but sometimes contended) professional values' (Cook, Poole et al. 2012).

However, while there might be cause for encouragement in the clarifying of this common ground, significant differences still remain concerning the extent to which it is possible or appropriate for psychiatrists to incorporate spirituality into clinical practice. My own view has been that recognition of a spiritual dimension to treatment adds meaning to a patient's experience and that, at least in some cases, there seems to be evidence that it might also improve outcomes. It does also raise complex and important questions concerning the appropriate observance of professional boundaries. However, the highlighting of these issues and the debate that ensues upon this provides the space within which good practice is clarified. An opposing view has been that spirituality takes psychiatrists outside the boundaries of their special expertise and might be seen to imply that psychiatry has all the answers. According to this view spirituality creates confusion, rather than clarifies boundaries (Cook, Poole et al. 2012).

Boundary disputes

All of the professional boundaries towards which attention has been directed in the debate surrounding the place of spirituality in psychiatry have their place (at least in some form or another), and it is not the intention here to demolish or dismantle them. Indeed, preservation of professional boundaries is essential to good clinical practice, and the clarity that they bring protects both psychiatrist and patient alike. However, it is clearly also not necessary to imagine that these boundaries are so fragile, or that the complexities of the topic of spirituality are so great, as necessarily to exclude all professional and ethical possibility of addressing spiritual concerns within clinical practice. Nor do I imagine that this is what most of the opponents of spirituality want. Rather, a boundary is being drawn (it seems to me) between the minimal attention that spirituality and religion are necessarily seen as unavoidably requiring in clinical practice and the excessive or inappropriate attention that some psychiatrists are seen as actually or potentially giving to them. The question is thus really about the appropriate location of this boundary and, indeed, whether or not it is either possible or desirable to define its location precisely. In effect, this is the first of the boundaries referred to above, the boundary of specialist expertise. What legitimately falls within the boundaries of the specialist expertise of the psychiatrist, and what falls outside?

It is clear that the special expertise of the psychiatrist is already highly multidisciplinary. Psychiatry is not a discrete science set apart by unique methods and areas of concern, but draws widely on the natural and social sciences. Similarly, the professional clinical practice of psychiatry draws extensively on general medicine and psychotherapy, as well as having its own distinctive approach to psychological medicine. Psychiatry also, increasingly, draws on philosophy and the humanities as providing broader contexts of understanding good practice. Why, then, not spirituality, theology or religious studies? Spirituality and religion are, after all, domains of human experience within which many people find self-understanding. If the clinician is to understand the religious or spiritual patient well, do they not need to understand and have empathy for their religious and spiritual beliefs and experiences? If professional training has not historically attended well to this, then perhaps that needs to change? Even if it does not, and even if psychiatrists are not experts on spirituality per se, they are experts (we might hope) on the art of enquiry into their patients' concerns. This surely should include the clarification and elucidation of what their most deeply held spiritual beliefs and values are? This specialist expertise, at least, is inherent to the core of psychiatry and it is antithetical to proselytizing.

What is clear, and what this boundary should legitimately protect, is that the sharing of expert knowledge that takes place within a psychiatric consultation should be according to clear and transparent principles. An opinion offered by a psychiatrist that mindfulness might be helpful as relapse prevention for depression, based on the research evidence and on a knowledge of accepted national guidelines (National Institute for Health and Clinical Excellence 2009), might reasonably be considered within the sphere of her specialist expertise. Encouragement by a psychiatrist of someone in similar circumstances to pursue Buddhist meditation practices more generally might not be considered so reasonable or justifiable, although a full analysis of this would require an understanding of the spiritual and religious history of the patient and the faith tradition of the clinician. A Christian psychiatrist recommending such a course of action to a patient with a known history of affiliation to Buddhism and basing this advice on a general understanding of the research demonstrating the benefits of spirituality for mental health might reasonably be said to be operating within her specialist expertise. A Buddhist psychiatrist recommending the same course of action to a Christian patient who is already actively engaged in a quest to renew their spiritual commitment within the Christian tradition might well be thought to have transgressed an important boundary. Yet another psychiatrist, being generally aware that their patient might benefit from further exploring spiritual practices, but not feeling equipped to address this and perhaps not being familiar with the tradition to which the patient belongs, may simply need to acknowledge the limitations of their knowledge and seek the help of an appropriate chaplain or spiritual adviser.

The second important boundary referred to above is that between secular and religious 'space'. It is in fact highly debatable as to whether or not secularity is 'neutral' space at all (Cook, Powell et al. 2011). Indeed, it is difficult to imagine what truly neutral space would look like (Poole and Cook 2011). However, it is also difficult to see why the religious person should be any less capable of adopting a neutral attitude than the atheist or agnostic. Doubtless much partiality has been justified on religious grounds, but it is also the case that mental health service users have often found that they cannot discuss religion with their psychiatrist for fear that it will be labelled as pathology (Mental Health Foundation 1997 and 2002). The intrusion of secular atheism (or political and other belief systems) into the clinical encounter is no less a violation of the proper neutrality of clinical space than is the intrusion of religion. The boundary that needs to be maintained is therefore, properly, not that between secularity and religion but that between patient-centred, clinical impartiality (or 'neutral space') and an adverse partiality based on values or beliefs, both explicit and implicit, that are threatening to the neutrality of the space in which the clinical encounter takes place. These values or beliefs will usually be those held by the clinician (even if unconsciously) but may be imposed from outside (e.g. by fear of censure for mentioning the topic of religion). I have called the space in which such clinical encounters occur 'aligned space', because it is aligned with such adverse values and beliefs, rather than with those of the patient and of good practice.

Aligned space is not characterized by being either religious or secular, although it can be encountered in either of these forms among others. Its presence and dangers are not always obvious. The religious form must include, as Sloan and others have pointed out, the intrusion into the consulting room of overt forms of proselytizing, as well as more subtle and covert intrusion of religious values into the advice and recommendations made by psychiatrists to their patients on ostensibly scientific grounds. However, the secular form must equally include the prejudicial labelling of religious experience as pathological, as well as the more subtle messages that patients receive which make them feel that it is not safe to discuss their spiritual or religious experiences with their psychiatrist. Secular space can be firmly aligned, not safe and far from neutral for the spiritual or religious (or indeed the non-religious) person.

Neutral space is made possible by a clinical encounter within which secular and religious domains are allowed to overlap, even if only by a small margin. (If they did not, presumably all mention of religion or spirituality would be completely excluded from the clinical encounter.) The safety of this space is defined by the ability of the clinician to make a sensitive and affirming enquiry of the patient about spiritual and religious (and other) matters. It is characterized by encouragement, empathy and compassion on the part of the clinician. Neutral space is a precious and vulnerable clinical asset. It is easily desecrated by carelessness, various forms of alignment to external social influences or the misaligned priorities of a clinician with a personal agenda. It needs to be actively fostered and jealously guarded.

Clinical practice is also essentially a personal encounter, and this brings us back to the third of the important boundaries that I referred to above – the boundary between personal and professional values. Many patients wish to meet with professionals who are also human beings and who do not hide behind their professionalism. Human beings have personal views and values of all kinds, including spiritual values, which are better recognized and acknowledged than ignored or denied. Now this does not mean that the clinician should foist all (or even any) of their personal views upon their patient (thus claiming the consulting room as aligned space), but it does mean that the clinician also has to be a 'person' and not a coldly empirical, unfeeling or inhuman creature who seeks to eliminate from their professional practice all value judgements and all personal mores. Rather, it is in self-awareness that the clinician can best find the grounds for empathy and protection against partiality. Sometimes, exceptionally, this may involve disclosing a personal commitment to a particular spiritual or faith tradition, or other philosophy, but proper disclosure will only ever be in the patient's interests with due regard to the neutrality of the space in which it is made and with the purpose of empathy. More often, the proper self-awareness of the clinician will take a more silent form in the consulting room, only to be vocalized in supervision or recorded in the notes. In psychotherapy, manifesting as counter-transference, it may assume particular therapeutic significance. But, always, the clinician will be on guard against their tendency to impose personal values and views, covertly or otherwise, upon their patient.

The boundary between personal and professional values, then, if too strictly imposed, might leave the patient feeling that they have only encountered a professional and not a person. I suspect that this does more to subvert the spiritual aspects of good psychiatric practice than anything, and it does not, in my view, foster empathy or support a genuine positive regard towards one's patients. However, if it is ignored, it opens the floodgates to all kinds of confusion and malpractice. This boundary – like all boundaries – must be constantly monitored. Here, perhaps more than elsewhere, recognition that the boundary is not absolute is important. In order to ensure that the balance in managing ingress and egress across this boundary has been maintained at an appropriate level, self-awareness, good supervision and unfailing honesty will be important.

Observance of these and other professional boundaries will generally be fostered by a familiarity with, and respect for, the principles outlined in *Good Medical Practice* (General Medical Council 2006) and *Good Psychiatric Practice* (Royal College of Psychiatrists 2010). Among the principles enshrined in this guidance are recognition of personal limitations, sharing of knowledge, self-awareness and respect for patient autonomy. I have reflected elsewhere on the common ground that these principles share with the fundamental nature of prayer (Poole and Cook 2011), and I think that they share much in common with spirituality in general. That is, an authentic spirituality will show awareness of personal limitations, will seek to share knowledge appropriately, will be in search of personal awareness and will respect the autonomy of others.

Recommendations for psychiatrists on spirituality and religion

The Position Statement adopted as policy by the Royal College of Psychiatrists in 2011 makes a series of seven recommendations for good practice (Table 1).

While the development of such policy statements requires consensus and compromise and thus will not be without shortcomings in the eyes of some psychiatrists (Poole 2011), it will be seen that these recommendations do go a significant way towards addressing the concerns that the debate on spirituality and psychiatry has raised over recent years. They address at least four of Koenig's proposed interventions (taking a spiritual history, supporting healthy religious beliefs, challenging unhealthy beliefs, and consultation with, referral to, or joint working with trained clergy), although expressing appropriate caution in how some of these tasks should be undertaken. They do not refer to the matter of praying with patients although, as already indicated, this has been the subject of special attention in a debate published in the *British Journal of Psychiatry* (Poole and Cook 2011). They also reflect and address at least some of the concerns raised in the published correspondence that followed Koenig's editorial, and they refer both to the

Table 1: Royal College of Psychiatrists' Recommendations for Psychiatrists on
Spirituality and Religion (Cook 2011)

1 A tactful and sensitive exploration of patients' religious beliefs and
spirituality should routinely be considered and will sometimes be an
essential component of clinical assessment.

2 Psychiatrists should be expected always to respect and be sensitive
to the spiritual/religious beliefs and practices of their patients or to
the lack of them and of the families and carers of their patients. This
should normally include allowing and enabling patients to engage
in the practice of their chosen spiritual or religious tradition. Where
the psychiatrist has reason to believe that this may be harmful, any
advice or intervention offered concerning this should be sensitive to:
the patient's right to practice their religion; the influence upon their
spiritual/religious choices of any illness from which they may be suffering; the views of the family and/or faith community; and advice
offered by chaplains or spiritual care advisors.

3 Psychiatrists should not use their professional position for proselytizing or undermining faith and should maintain appropriate
professional boundaries in relation to self-disclosure of their own
spirituality/religion.

4 Psychiatrists should work to develop appropriate organizational
policies which promote equality, understanding, respect and good
practice in relation to spirituality and religion.

5 Psychiatrists, whatever their personal beliefs, should be willing to
work with leaders/members of faith communities, chaplains and
pastoral workers in support of the well-being of their patients and
should encourage all colleagues in mental health work to do likewise.

6 Psychiatrists should always respect and be sensitive to spiritual and
religious beliefs, or lack of them, among their colleagues.

7 Religion and spirituality and their relationship to the diagnosis, aetiology and treatment of psychiatric disorders should be considered
as essential components of both psychiatric training and continuing
professional development.

published evidence base and existing guidance concerning good practice, as
provided by the General Medical Council and the Royal College of Psychiatrists. They also share common ground with the rather shorter policy
published 20 years earlier by the American Psychiatric Association (Committee on Religion and Psychiatry 1990), although that document appears
to have been primarily concerned with the problem of proselytizing and the

influence that a psychiatrist's religious beliefs might have upon their professional practice.

To the extent that these guidelines still leave some scope for interpretation and do not cover all eventualities, a number of observations might be made here. First, it is arguably good that professional practice is not too tightly confined within guidelines and that further debate is not restricted in an area where there is considerable diversity of legitimate professional opinion. Second, however, there are probably limits to what can be achieved on the basis of general principle. It is to be hoped that the future debate will be further informed by attention to real-life clinical dilemmas and the complex and sometimes conflicting concerns that they raise (Cook, Poole et al. 2012). Remarkably little empirical information is currently available as to the views of psychiatrists on such matters and further research is clearly needed.

Conclusion

The increasing interest in, and the present debate about, the relevance of spirituality and religion to clinical practice and research in psychiatry over recent decades raises a series of important questions. These are of a scientific, ethical and professional nature, but appear especially to be concerned with maintaining good boundaries, among which I have proposed that three appear to be especially important. First, the boundary of specialist expertise concerns itself with whether or not spirituality lies within the proper domain of psychiatry. Paradoxically, this boundary is being questioned at a time when increasing amounts of psychiatric research expertise are being devoted to the study of spirituality and religion in relation to a wide variety of mental disorders. Yet, clinically, the expertise that is required here is a very traditional ability to conduct a sensitive, affirming and compassionate enquiry into a patient's beliefs, values and concerns, whether they be explicitly spiritual or religious or not. While we might argue that psychiatrists need to be better informed about spirituality and religion, it would seem that they have long understood the core skills necessary as being central to their clinical expertise.

I have suggested that the second important boundary of concern is that between secular and religious spheres of interest, but that this can really better be understood as one defining the neutral space within which a proper clinical enquiry concerning spirituality and religion can safely be conducted. Threats to this boundary come from various forms of personal or social alignment and are not the sole prerogative of either secularity or religion. However, it is clear that proselytizing within clinical practice (whether in its religious or atheistic form) is one of them and that this is completely antithetical to the kind of sensitive, affirming and compassionate enquiry into matters of spirituality and faith that is being advocated here.

Third, and finally, the boundary between personal and professional values requires that the clinician be self-aware and skilful in managing clinical relationships. The patient-centred focus on encouragement, compassion and sensitivity to spiritual matters that I am advocating here is undermined both by an overly familiar or self-serving intrusion of personal values into the clinical agenda (even if unconsciously undertaken) and also by a cold, aloof form of professionalism that has no place for compassion. This is a difficult tension to manage, but I do not think it is unique to this aspect of psychiatry. It is a skill that good clinicians have long applied in all areas and specialties of medicine.

Recommendations for practice, such as those developed by the Royal College of Psychiatrists, are helpful in managing boundaries but cannot deal with every eventuality. More attention is needed to the individual complexities of real cases, while maintaining a degree of latitude for good clinical judgement. Qualities such as empathy, encouragement and compassion are not easily taught or prescribed. Sometimes found lacking in clinicians who might otherwise describe themselves as spiritual or religious and sometimes wonderfully present in those who regard themselves as neither spiritual or religious, they are, without fail, the cornerstone of all good clinical practice.

References

Carey, G. (1997), 'Towards wholeness: transcending the barriers between religion and psychiatry', *British Journal of Psychiatry* 170:5, pp. 396–7.

Committee on Religion and Psychiatry (1990), 'Guidelines regarding possible conflict between psychiatrists' religious commitments and psychiatric practice', *American Journal of Psychiatry* 147:4, p. 542.

Cook, C. C. H. (2004), 'Addiction and spirituality', *Addiction* 99:5, pp. 539–51.

Cook, C. C. H. (2011), *Recommendations for Psychiatrists on Spirituality and Religion*, London: Royal College of Psychiatrists Press.

Cook, C. C. H., Poole, R. et al. (2012), 'Holistic psychiatry', *The Psychiatrist* 36:6, pp. 235–6.

Cook, C. C. H., Powell, A. and Sims, A. (eds) (2009), *Spirituality and Psychiatry*, London: Royal College of Psychiatrists Press.

Cook, C. C. H., Powell, A. et al. (2011), 'Spirituality and secularity: professional boundaries in psychiatry', *Mental Health, Religion and Culture* 14:1, pp. 35–42.

Cox, J. L. (1994), 'Psychiatry and religion: a general psychiatrist's perspective', *Psychiatric Bulletin* 18:11, pp. 673–6.

Dein, S., Cook, C. C. H. et al. (2010), 'Religion, spirituality and mental health', *The Psychiatrist* 34, pp. 63–4.

Dobbelaere, K. (2011), 'The meaning and scope of secularization', in P. B. Clarke (ed.), *The Oxford Handbook of the Sociology of Religion*, Oxford: Oxford University Press, pp. 599–615.

Eagger, S., Richmond, P. et al. (2009), 'Spiritual care in the NHS', in Cook, Powell and Sims (eds), *Spirituality and Psychiatry*, pp. 190–211.

General Medical Council (2006), *Good Medical Practice*, London: General Medical Council.

HRH The Prince of Wales (1991), 'Lecture by HRH The Prince of Wales, as Patron, to the Royal College of Psychiatrists, Brighton, Friday 5 July 1991', *British Journal of Psychiatry* 159, pp. 763–8.

Koenig, H., King, D. et al. (2012), *Handbook of Religion and Health*, New York: Oxford University Press.

Koenig, H. G. (2008), 'Religion and mental health: what should psychiatrists do?', *Psychiatric Bulletin* 32:6, pp. 201–3.

Koenig, H. G., McCullough, M. E. et al. (2001), *Handbook of Religion and Health*, New York: Oxford University Press.

Lepping, P. (2008a), 'Is psychiatry torn in different ethical directions?', *Psychiatric Bulletin* 32:9, pp. 325–6.

Lepping, P. (2008b), 'Religion, psychiatry and professional boundaries', *Psychiatric Bulletin* 32:9, p. 357.

Martin, D. (2005), *On Secularization: Towards a Revised General Theory*, Aldershot: Ashgate.

McFadyen, A. (2000), *Bound to Sin: Abuse, Holocaust and the Christian Doctrine of Sin*, Cambridge: Cambridge University Press.

Mental Health Foundation (1997), *Knowing Our Own Minds: A Survey of How People in Emotional Distress Take Control of their Lives*, London: Mental Health Foundation.

Mental Health Foundation (2002), *Taken Seriously: The Somerset Spirituality Project*, London: Mental Health Foundation.

Mental Health Foundation (2007), *Making Space for Spirituality: How to Support Service Users*, London: Mental Health Foundation.

National Institute for Health and Clinical Excellence (2009), *Depression: The Treatment and Management of Depression in Adults*, London: National Institute for Health and Clinical Excellence.

Neeleman, J. and Persaud, R. (1995), 'Why do psychiatrists neglect religion?', *British Journal of Medical Psychology* 68:2, pp. 169–78.

Poole, R. (2011), 'Praying with patients: Belief, faith and boundary conditions', *British Journal of Psychiatry* 199, p. 518.

Poole, R. and Cook, C. C. H. (2011), 'Praying with a patient constitutes a breach of professional boundaries in psychiatric practice', *British Journal of Psychiatry* 199:2, pp. 94–8.

Poole, R. and Higgo, R. (2011), 'Spirituality and the threat to therapeutic boundaries in psychiatric practice', *Mental Health, Religion and Culture* 14:1–2, pp. 19–29.

Poole, R., Higgo, R. et al. (2008), 'Religion, psychiatry and professional boundaries', *Psychiatric Bulletin* 32:9, pp. 356–7.

Poole, R., Higgo, R. et al. (2010), 'Concerns over professional boundaries remain unresolved', *The Psychiatrist* 35:5, pp. 211–12.

Powell, A. (2009), 'The Spirituality and Psychiatry Special Interest Group of the Royal College of Psychiatrists', in Cook, Powell and Sims (eds), *Spirituality and Psychiatry*, pp. xv–xviii.

Powell, A. and Cook, C. C. H. (2006), 'Spirituality and Psychiatry Special Interest Group of the Royal College of Psychiatrists', *Reaching the Spirit: Social Perspectives Network Study Day, Paper 9*, London: Social Perspectives Network, pp. 33.

Royal College of Psychiatrists (2010), *Good Psychiatric Practice: Continuing Professional Development*, London: Royal College of Psychiatrists Press.

Salem, M. O. and Foskett, J. (2009), 'Religion and religious experiences', in Cook, Powell and Sims (eds), *Spirituality and Psychiatry*, pp. 233–53.

Shooter, M. (1999), 'Proposal for a Special Interest Group in Spirituality and Psychiatry', *Psychiatric Bulletin* 23:5, p. 310.

Sims, A. (1994), '"Psyche" – Spirit as well as mind?', *British Journal of Psychiatry* 165:4, pp. 441–6.

Sims, A. and Cook, C. C. H. (2009), 'Spirituality in Psychiatry', in Cook, Powell and Sims (eds), *Spirituality and Psychiatry*, pp. 1–15.

Sloan, R. P. (2006), *Blind Faith: The Unholy Alliance of Religion and Medicine*, New York: St Martin's Press.

Sloan, R. P. and Bagiella, E. (2002), 'Claims about religious involvement and health outcomes', *Annals of Behavioral Medicine* 24:1, pp. 14–20.

Sloan, R. P., Bagiella, E. et al. (1999), 'Religion, spirituality and medicine', *Lancet* 353:9153, pp. 664–7.

Swinton, J. (2007), *Raging with Compassion: Pastoral Responses to the Problem of Evil*, Grand Rapids MI: Eerdmans.

Watts, F. (2002), *Theology and Psychology*, Farnham: Ashgate.

2

'I'm spiritual but not religious'

Implications for Research and Practice

PATRICIA CASEY

Summary

There is an assumption, among some mental health service users, clinicians, researchers and others, that religiousness and spirituality are the same construct. A consideration of the history of these concepts shows that, over time, each has become separated from the other. Both require careful definition. The definitions of spirituality are heterogeneous and, with important implications for research and practice, some encompass mood states. The failure to separate spirituality and religiousness, and the confounding of spirituality with mood states in some research in psychiatry, makes interpretation of the findings difficult. Greater clarity and precision will be required in future research, including, if possible, attempts to provide distinctive operational definitions of spirituality and religiousness.

Since the turn of the millennium there has been a visible increase in interest among psychiatrists and psychologists in the role of religion and spirituality in illness and health, including mental health. From ambivalence and even downright hostility, the pendulum has swung dramatically and in the 30 years prior to 2000 (Koenig 2008) there were 724 quantitative studies on religion/spirituality and mental health in peer-reviewed journals, while in the 8 years post 2000 there were 6,774 such articles published and the majority of these pointed to a positive association between religion/spirituality and mental health benefits. The first *Handbook of Religion and Health* was published in 2001 (Koenig et al. 2001) and a second edition followed in 2012.

The growth of interest in the link between religion/spirituality and mental health was recognized by the development of best practice guidelines by the American Psychiatric Association (1990) and more recently by the General Medical Council of Britain (2008). The American College of Graduate Medical Education now mandates that all students receive training in the religious and spiritual factors that can influence mental health. The Royal College of Psychiatrists in Britain (2011) published a twelve-page position statement stating:

> [T]here is now a sufficient body of evidence to suggest that spirituality and religion are at least factors about which psychiatrists should be knowledgeable insofar as they have an impact on the aetiology, diagnosis and treatment of mental disorders. Further, an ability to handle spiritual and religious issues sensitively and empathically has a significant potential impact upon the relationship between psychiatrist and patient.

There are now also a number of peer-reviewed journals dedicated to publishing on the topic. Some are specific to the study of health and religion while others are broader but also publish papers on health and religion/ spirituality. These include.

- *International Journal for the Psychology of Religion*
- *Journal of Religion and Health*
- *Journal of Religion, Spirituality and Ageing*
- *Journal for the Scientific Study of Religion*
- *Journal of Spirituality in Mental Health*
- *Journal for the Study of Spirituality*
- *Mental Health, Religion and Culture*
- *Research in the Social Scientific Study of Religion.*

In addition, all the major mental health journals are also publishing on this topic (see References at the end of this chapter).

Historically the relationship between psychiatry and religion fluctuated. The writings and actions of some early psychiatrists were favourable to the role of religion and spirituality in the care of the mentally ill. The founder of the first mental hospital in Britain, William Tuke, was a Quaker, and he was impelled to charitable works by his faith. 'Moral Therapy' was offered to patients. The first psychiatric hospital in Ireland was founded by Dean Jonathan Swift, the Anglican Dean of St Patrick's Cathedral in Dublin, in 1747. Throughout Europe the earliest mental hospitals were founded by religious individuals acutely aware of the mistreatment and pariah status of those with mental illness. The Hotel-Dieu was founded by St Landry in Paris in 651, while monasteries offered sanctuary to the homeless mentally ill.

However Jean-Martin Charcot (1825–93), a physician, and his pupil Sigmund Freud (1856–1939), had a more jaundiced view of religion, and they linked psychiatric conditions such as hysteria and other neuroses to it. An exception to this at the time was Carl Jung (1875–1961). The negative view of religion and its relationship to mental illness dominated into the late twentieth century. In 1980, Albert Ellis, the founder of rational emotive therapy wrote, 'devout theists often deny, ignore or hallucinate about reality; the more devout they are – as the long history of religion shows – the more delusionary and hallucinatory they seem to be' (Ellis 1980). While a Canadian psychiatrist, Wendall Watters, wrote, 'Christian doctrine and liturgy have been shown to discourage the development of adult coping behaviour and the human to human relationship skills that enable people to cope in an adaptive way with anxiety caused by stress' (Watters 1992).

It is difficult to identify the reason for the change in attitude, but the increased interest among psychiatrists in the role of religion and spirituality in mental health was averred to in the *American Journal of Psychiatry*, which editorialized on the topic (Curlin et al. 2007) and commented that the long-standing lack of interest among psychiatrists concerning the religious beliefs of patients may be passing.

Causation or association?

The upshot of the increase in interest in religion/spirituality and mental health is that now there are numerous studies identifying positive associations between them in diverse conditions and behaviours including depression, anxiety, suicidal behaviour, coping styles and adolescent behaviour as well as recovery from physical illnesses.

But association does not imply causation. There are two ways to approach this question in science. To show that A causes (or helps) B requires that subjects are randomized to either receiving or not receiving A and then examining the numbers who develop B in each group. Studies of this type are termed controlled experiments. In the case of religion/spirituality, it is not possible to conduct such studies since random allocation to regular religious activities based on faith is generally not feasible or ethical (except for studies of remote prayer), so instead observational studies are conducted.

Observational studies are carried out when A is outside the control of the investigator. In this instance the population under study, say adults in the general population, will be selected and those who possess or do not possess attribute A (religiousness/spirituality) identified, so that the effect this has on the likelihood of developing B, for example depression, will be measured.

But answering the question as to whether it is religiousness per se that influences the chance of developing depression is not so simple. For example, the positive association between religious practice and reduced risk of depression might simply be that those who are not depressed are more motivated to engage in religious practices such as church attendance. Alternatively, it may be that the presumed benefits on mental and physical health are simply due to lifestyle habits that are likely to be more sober in those who are religious/spiritual. Another possible explanation is that the friendship and support people find by regular church attendance is responsible – if so then being a member of a football club would generate equal benefits. In order to answer the question as to whether it is religious practice per se that is cause, these third variables mentioned above such as lifestyle habits and social supports (also called confounders) must be controlled for statistically in the analysis of the collected data.

In addition, questionnaires to measure religiousness and depression must be developed and statistically evaluated to ensure that they are valid (measuring what it is they claim to measure) and reliable (the same results will be obtained when administered by two separate investigators to the same group or when measured on two separate occasions). These methodological requirements are clearly laid out in many statistics textbooks.

The studies must take place in a variety of settings, such as the general population, mentally and physically ill in-patients and out-patients and so on, and there must be a period of follow-up.

It is only when these requirements have been met that a causal rather than an associated link is demonstrated. These criteria have been enunciated by Bradford Hill (1965).

'I'm spiritual but not religious' – fact or fiction?

In the area of religious research, religion and spirituality have traditionally been interlinked. The word *spiritualitas* was used first in the fifth century in reference to the influence of God in human lives, while by the twelfth century it referred more specifically to the psychological or interior aspects of the human experience. All the faith traditions developed spiritual dimensions. The Jewish faith saw the growth of the Kabbalah movement, Islam the Sufi movement and Christianity the Gnostics. Individuals also developed their own forms of spirituality, and one such was the seventeenth-century mystic Madam Guyon, whose focus was on prayer and 'Quietism', a state of intellectual and interior stillness so as to attain perfection and union with God. St Teresa of Avila was another. While most of these were condemned to varying degrees (Teresa of Avila is now one of the few female Doctors of the Church), their focus was still trained on God and the Divine. The Enlightenment, culminating in the French Revolution, mounted a challenge to orthodox religion and consequently to the temporal power of the Church.

By the time the twentieth century arrived, the Church's influence had waned significantly and avowedly atheistic states were on the horizon. The social revolution of the 1960s saw the search for direction and ethical guidance renewed, but not from the Church, which was by now in serious decline. The New Age movement began in England in the 1960s and quickly became international. Devotees did not have group rituals, and nor did they adhere to any single dogma. There was no one learned text to offer guidance. Rather, adherents were encouraged to adopt whichever set of beliefs and practices they felt most comfortable with, including meditating, divination (foretelling the future), channelling and so on. Their search was located in the individual and they defined their own gods. Many Christians have incorporated elements of New Age beliefs into their lives, while others, with no affiliation to a traditional theology, have become avid followers of New Age thinking. Elements have been incorporated into political thinking also, such as environmentalism.

The book by Wade Clark Roof (2001), *Spiritual Marketplace: Baby Boomers and the Remaking of American Religion*, was a watershed in understanding the new spirituality. For the first time, everybody could appropriate claims to being spiritual, even those who were non-believers.

While previously spirituality and religiously related activities such a prayer, fasting and meditating were inextricably linked, the new understanding viewed spirituality as something that everybody possessed, yet was uncoupled from a religious core. This is illustrated very comprehensively by Koenig (2008) in Figures 1 and 2 below.

In Figure 1a spirituality is seen as a core element of religiousness. The outer perimeter of the circle represents those who are superficially religious. Both of these are distinct from those who are secular, that is, neither religious nor spiritual. All contribute to meaning, purpose and so on, and have an effect on emotional states and behaviour. In this model, spiritual persons can be compared with less spiritual people, and each can be compared to those who are secular. This model also allows examination of the effect of these constructs on anxiety, depression and so on, since they are distinct.

Figure 1b shows a shift that represents a more recent understanding in that spirituality is now broader than religion and includes those from diverse religious groups and from none. Here we can see the emergence of a spiritual but not religious group, while the secular group is still distinct. How the new 'spiritual but not religious' group is defined is unclear as the grounding in religiousness (see Figure 1a) has been erased. Despite the absence of a clear definition, this model, in theory, still allows for comparisons between the three groups, religious, 'spiritual but not religious', and secular, and also points to the possibility of examining the impact of these on mental health.

Figure 2 points to a new way of conceptualizing religiousness and spirituality and their relationship to each other and to other attributes such as purpose, meaning and so on.

Ask the question to most people in the western world today, 'Are you religious?', and they will usually say that they are spiritual but not religious. Occasionally, when questioned specifically, they will tell you that they also attend church and engage in personal religious activity such as prayer, fasting and so on, but for most there is no connection to formal religious practices (Figure 2a).

Figure 2b represents the conceptualization of spirituality, religiousness and secularism. Here spirituality is increasingly equated with personal well-being. So feelings of happiness and contentment are viewed as equated with spirituality. This creates significant methodological problems in research examining the contribution of spirituality to mental health (see below).

Figures 1a and 1b: Older relationship between religion and spirituality

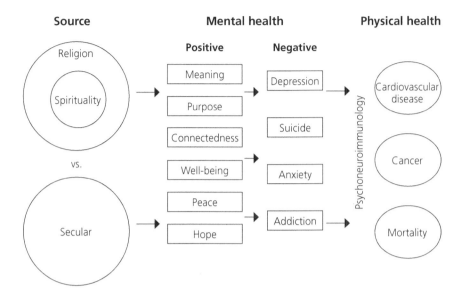

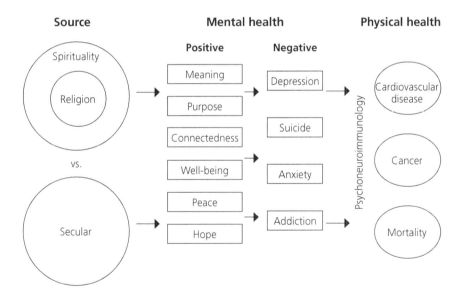

Reproduced by kind permission of Wolters Kluwer Health.

Figures 2a and 2b: Modern relationship between religion and spirituality

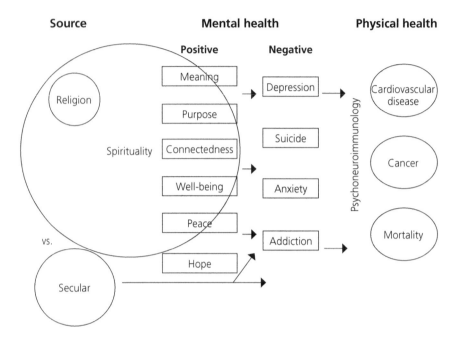

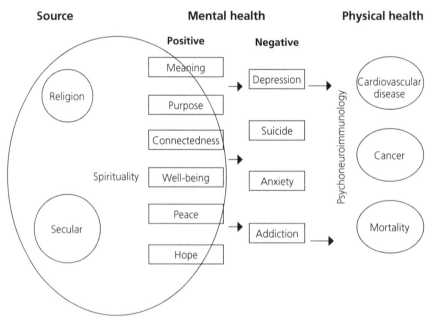

Reproduced by kind permission of Wolters Kluwer Health.

The models above point to four possible groupings between religiousness and spirituality, shown in Table 1.

Table 1: Classification of spiritual, religious and secular persons

1 Spiritual and religious – this classification represents the traditional view of the relationship of one to the other.
2 Spiritual but not religious – this is the newest group.
3 Neither religious nor spiritual – this is the secular group.
4 Religious but not spiritual – this group has received little scientific attention.

The group that is spiritual and religious conform to the traditional view of the relationship between these attributes. The person engages in religious practices and adheres to beliefs and rituals associated with the specific tradition as well as engaging in spiritual activities such as meditating, fasting and reading illuminating texts, sacred and secular. Spiritual and religiousness in this group are hand in glove and each enriches the other.

The group described as spiritual but not religious tend to view religiousness in a negative light, to be more independent of others, to hold 'New Age' beliefs and to have mystical experiences (Zinnbauer et al. 1997). They view spirituality and religion as non-overlapping constructs and these differences are shown in Table 2.

Table 2: Religion vs spirituality

Authoritarian	From within
Denominational	Personal
Linked to community	Autonomous
Ritualistic	Not hidebound
Stipulates behaviours and rituals	Morality individualized
Personal God or supernatural	Supernatural not necessary
Beliefs	Experiential

The third group in Table 1 above, those who are secular, are not much studied and, if the model shown in Figure 2b is applied, they are likely to become extinct since feelings and mood states will be equated with spirituality also and thus experienced by everybody as part of day-to-day existence. The merging of the secular into the spiritual group is one which secularists may wish to eschew.

The fourth group, religious but not spiritual, have not received any attention nor are they mentioned in the scientific literature specifically although they might conform to the group described by Allport and Ross (1967) as showing an extrinsic religious orientation, that is, engaging in the practice of religion but not in its spirit and not internalizing its message. They may be motivated by appearances and gain rather than by the inherent value of faith. Allport and Ross (1967) distinguished this group from those of intrinsic orientation who tried to assimilate the codes of their faith and to incorporate them into their personal conduct. Unfortunately, this group is often viewed by the general public as engaging in practices that are dry and arid, based on convention and habit rather than on any deeper perspective. This unhelpfully pits religiousness (bad) against spirituality (good), as has been demonstrated by Zinnbauer et al. (1997) above.

That these groups are more than the imaginings of anthropologists is exemplified by a study (King et al. 2006) that found that 17.7 per cent identified themselves as neither religious nor spiritual, 13.1 per cent described themselves as spiritual but not religious, while 69.2 per cent described themselves as religious and spiritual. Interestingly, nobody described themselves as religious but not spiritual.

That the construct known as spirituality is heterogeneous and means different things to different people is apparent from a study by Bibby (1995) in which Canadian adults were interviewed and 52 per cent expressed their spiritual needs in conventional religious terms such as belief in God, attending church and so on, while 48 per cent expressed these in more abstract terms, such as wholeness, reflection and so on.

In religious and theological circles there is an understandable tendency to equate spirituality with religiousness or, at least, with the sacred. This must now be seen as an oversimplification.

What is spirituality, what is religiousness?

Concerns about these constructs, particularly spirituality, have been articulated by Koenig (2008), who demonstrates the disparity and, at times, vagueness in the various definitions of spirituality in the scientific literature.

Religiousness is relatively easily defined but mainly encompasses

1 adherence to a set of beliefs, practices and rituals
2 that are related to the sacred and
3 to a particular tradition
4 they encompass belief in a personal God for most, although it is accepted that the Buddhist tradition does not necessarily imply belief in God.

The sacred is defined as 'that which relates to the numinous (mystical, supernatural) or God, and in Eastern religious traditions, to Ultimate Truth or Reality. Religion may also involve beliefs about spirits, angels, or demons' (Koenig 2009).

By contrast, spirituality is more difficult to define and several definitions exist. One that is widely accepted is that of Ellison (1983):

> Spirituality is universal, yet unique to every person ... (spirituality) enables and motivates us to search for meaning and purpose in life. It is the spirit which synthesises the total personality and provides some sense of energizing direction and order. The spiritual dimension does not exist in isolation from the psyche and the soma. It affects and is affected by our physical state, feelings, thoughts and relationships.

This definition is difficult to understand and it is cumbersome without adding clarity. It presents a very broad and rhetorical description. A more easily understood one is that of Hill et al. (2000) which defines spirituality as:

> The feelings, thoughts, experiences and behaviours that arise from a search for the sacred. The term 'search' refers to attempts to identify, articulate, maintain or transform. The term 'sacred' refers to a divine being, divine object, Ultimate reality or Ultimate Truth as perceived by the individual.

This clearly places spirituality in the supernatural or sacred arena and is akin to that of the traditional view of spirituality.

Another definition by Cook (2004) says:

> Spirituality is a distinctive, potentially creative and universal dimension of human experience arising both within the inner subjective awareness of individuals and within communities, social groups and traditions. It may be experienced as relationship with that which is intimately 'inner', immanent and personal, within the self and others, and/or as relationship with that which is wholly 'other', transcendent and beyond the self. It is experienced as being of fundamental or ultimate importance and is thus concerned with matters of meaning and purpose in life, truth and values.

This definition suggests the universality of spirituality in that it is present in everybody as part of the experience of being human. There is also a transcendent element that is concerned with values and meaning.

The World Health Organization Quality of Life Assessment – spiritual, religious and personal beliefs (WHOQOL–SRPB) questionnaire (1998) does not directly define spirituality but in the instructions to the questionnaire it has defined spirituality very broadly indeed, as in the example below.

> The following questions ask about your spiritual, personal or religious beliefs. These questions are designed to be applicable to people coming from many different cultures and holding a variety of spiritual, religious or personal beliefs ... Alternatively you may have no belief in a higher,

spiritual entity but you may have strong personal beliefs or followings such as beliefs in a scientific theory, a personal way of life ... While some of these questions will use words such as spirituality, please answer them in terms of your own personal belief system, whether it be religious, spiritual or personal.

This definition is clearly an attempt to make spirituality 'whatever you want', a catch-all ranging from the recognizably religious to a personal theory such as, for example, life on Mars or a belief in the value of skin-diving. It also encompasses within its domain feelings of well-being and harmony. By broadening the boundaries, it includes not simply religious or broadly sacred experiences but also aspects of mood and well-being (see Figure 2 above).

A more focused but complex definition of spirituality has been developed by King and Koenig (2009), which encapsulates four domains as follows:

1 Belief
   An assent to or conviction about a domain or existence that goes beyond the material world. This includes all manner of religious or other beliefs that are not based on materialism.

2 Practice
   Spiritual or religious practice at this level occurs without conscious awareness of, or relationship to, the spiritual realm addressed. Although it involves exercises of imagination and desire such as contemplation, prayer, reading or reflection, the self is not moved by any direct experience of relationship with or connection to the other.

3 Awareness
   There is an awareness of being moved intellectually and/or emotionally. It includes contemplation, prayer, meditation or reflection when there is conscious awareness of, or response to, this dimension.

4 Experience
   A discrete experience that may include diffusion of the mind, loss of ego boundaries and a change in orientation from self towards or beyond the material world. The experience usually comes unbidden but may follow a period of reflection, meditation, stress or isolation. Ecstatic experiences are of this type, but experience may be much less intense and more prolonged.

A further definition by La Pierre (1994) described the characteristics of spirituality as follows:

• a search for meaning in life
• an encounter with transcendence

- a sense of community
- a search for the ultimate truth or highest value
- respect and appreciation for the mystery of creation
- personal transformation.

This, like the definition by Hill et al. (2000), is much more traditionally religious and trained on the transcendent.

Is separating religiousness and spirituality important?

Some may believe that questioning the overlap or separation between religion and spirituality is an exercise in hair splitting that is irrelevant in clinical and pastoral settings. This is only partially true. In arenas such as pastoral counselling, the difference is not relevant, since all counsellors, pastors and therapists should work within the framework of the person's world-view, whether it be a largely religious one, a spiritual one without any religious connotations, neither or a combination of both. All should be offered hope and meaning whatever their perspective.

However, if we wish to examine scientifically questions concerning the relationship between spirituality/religion and health then it becomes highly relevant.

The scientific study of religion and spirituality and their impact on peoples' lives is relatively new and began in 1972, when George Comstock, an epidemiologist at Johns Hopkins Medical School, published a paper examining the link between mortality and church attendance in the general population. Spirituality and religion have traditionally been viewed as overlapping aspects of the one construct but, as argued above, this is no longer the case and both, increasingly, are seen as distinct constructs that inform peoples' lives, although each probably in a different manner.

Notwithstanding this overlap between religiousness and spirituality in some definitions, equating spirituality with religiousness is likely to lead to a misunderstanding of their respective roles in building mental health resilience. Furthermore, failure to recognize this distinction will not enable scientists to answer questions that are waiting to be asked and answered. These include:

- Is religion beneficial or harmful to mental health?
- Is spirituality beneficial or harmful to mental health?
- Are both equally important?
- Does each influence the same or different domains of mental health and its outcome?
- How do they exert their benefits, for example social support, prayer, meaning, hope, lifestyle, moral injunctions, church attendance, and which emanate from religiousness, which from spirituality?

Other more specific questions relating to specific mental disorders could also be asked, including, 'Do religious practices and spirituality contribute equally to recovery from depressive illness?', 'Are suicidal thoughts more or less common in those with spiritual beliefs as compared to those who engage in religious practices?', 'Do moral objections protect against suicide in mental illness?' (Dervic et al. 2011).

If there are no differences in the answers to these questions then the distinction is irrelevant. If, however, it were shown that, for example, religiousness benefited mental health through solidarity with like-minded individuals and that spirituality assisted in problem-solving, then clearly this would be relevant information that could help in identifying interventions tailored to individual attributes and strengths. If it were established that those who are religious are less likely to engage in suicidal behaviour than those who are spiritual, then this has important public health ramifications. Just as mental health professionals are interested in the role of social supports in assisting in recovery from illness, so other attributes such as religiousness and spirituality are also important components of the individual to be examined.

It is also important to answer the question 'How?' What is the mechanism by which religiousness assists people – is it through meaning and values, is it because of the lifestyle they live? Is it because of the friends and social supports that religion brings? What is the mechanism by which spirituality effects peoples' emotional state – is it through enhancing self-esteem, is it by encouraging self-empowerment?

Questionnaires that measure religiousness and/or spirituality

A number of questionnaires have been developed to measure spirituality and/or religiousness. Some of these measure both religiousness and spirituality in a single scale while others focus on one or the other. The researcher deciding on which scale to use will be challenged for three reasons:

1   The scale should clearly distinguish religiousness from spirituality. Some questionnaires achieve this by means of separate subscales within the overall scale (Kendler 2003; King et al. 2001), while others (Koenig et al. 1997) have developed schedules that specifically measure one or other attribute.
2   Spirituality should be clearly defined within the scale.
3   Spirituality should not overlap with or be open to contamination from mood or general well-being. So questions that relate to having a purpose in life or to optimism would inevitably be influenced by low mood and falsely result in the conclusion that the absence of spiritual beliefs was associated with low mood.

A number of scales will be outlined and critiqued in order to assist a researcher faced with a maze of schedules from which to choose. For further information on questionnaires measuring religiousness and spirituality the reader is directed to Koenig (2011), Koenig et al. (2012) and the Fetzer Institute Report (2003).

One of the most widely used measures of spirituality/religiousness is the Functional Assessment of Chronic Illness – Spiritual Well-Being (FACIT-Sp) (Brady and Cella 1999). This has been used in many studies in cancer patients, and it is endorsed by the National Cancer Institute in the USA as a measure of spirituality. There are many versions available: the original had 12 questions while the newest (FACIT-Sp-Ex) (Peterman et al. 2002) has 23, which measure the role of faith/spirituality (e.g. I find strength in my faith or spiritual beliefs; I feel connected to a higher power or God) and the role of meaning/peace (My life lacks meaning and purpose; I feel loved) in those with chronic illnesses. This schedule does not distinguish spirituality from religiousness and many of the questions are related to emotional well-being, although some are spiritual in content (I feel compassion for others in the difficulties they are in). However, studies purporting to use this as a spiritual/religious measure will clearly find a strong positive association with the emotional responses to physical illness.

The Spiritual Well-Being scale (Paloutzian and Ellison 1982) is one of the most widely used scales, having been used in several hundred studies. It consists of 20 items, ten measuring religious well-being and ten existential well-being. Questions include, 'I feel life is a positive experience', 'I feel very fulfilled and satisfied with my life'. These questions are clearly identifying features of mental health and unless both domains are analysed separately there will be a strong association between the score on this scale and psychopathology. It is also questionable if the existential well-being questions are measuring anything uniquely spiritual rather than tapping into general measures of happiness.

The World Health Organization has developed the World Health Organization Quality of Life measure (WHOQOL) (WHOQOL Group 1998) with a subscale that measures spirituality, religion and personal beliefs (WHOQOL-SRPB). While describing eight dimensions (connectedness to a spiritual being/force, awe, meaning of life, wholeness/integration, spiritual strength, inner peace/serenity/harmony, hope/optimism and faith) that might capture religiousness and spirituality, the instructions for completing the questionnaire remove any meaning linked to religiousness and instead broaden the definition of spirituality beyond recognition to include personal beliefs and theories. This makes for the possibility that belief in aliens constitutes a spiritual dimension.

One of the results of this broad definition was shown in a study of relationship between quality of life and spiritual, religious and personal beliefs (Saxena and WHO QOL Group 2006). Using the WHO questionnaire and interviewing 5,089 people from 18 countries, it found that in the analysis the measure of spirituality/religiousness explained 65 per cent of the variance in the quality of life score. A contribution of this size is implausible and is almost certainly due to the broadness of the definition and the fact that feelings of well-being (such as hope and optimism) were included as measures of spirituality and also as measures of quality of life.

Another measure is the Multidimensional Measure of Religiousness/Spirituality (MMRS) (Fetzer Institute 1999/2003). This was the outcome of a report that presented 12 questionnaires measuring domains of religion/spirituality. The composite of these became the MMRS, and a briefer version, with 38 selected items from the total, formed the Brief Multidimensional Measure of Religiousness/Spirituality (BMMRS). This is widely used and it is gaining popularity due to the establishment of norms for the BMMRS in the general population. This makes it easy to compare results from research populations against national baseline scores. There are subscales measuring meaning, forgiveness and values. Questions include, 'The meaning of my life comes from feeling connected to other living things', 'It is easy for me to admit that I am wrong', 'I am able to make up pretty easily with friends who have hurt me in some way'.

The Daily Spiritual Experiences Scale (DSES) (Underwood and Teresi 2002) is extensively used as a measure of spirituality in mental and physical health research. It is a subscale of the Multidimensional Measure of Religiousness/Spirituality mentioned above (Fetzer Institute 1999). It consists of 16 items rated on 6 anchor points from 'never or almost never' to 'many times a day'. Eight of the questions relate specifically to God although the instruction advises that God can be replaced by another that calls to mind the holy or the divine. The remaining 8 questions are more general, for example, 'I feel a selfless caring for others', 'I feel inner peace and harmony', 'I am spiritually touched by the beauty of creation'. This scale adopts a very broad definition of spirituality/religiousness, judging by the question content, and many of the items are likely to score negatively in those with low mood.

A schedule that has separate measures of spirituality and religiousness was developed by King et al. (2001). The Royal Free Interview for Spiritual and Religious Beliefs consists of 18 questions rated on a 10-point scale. The questionnaire begins by asking the person to indicate whether they are religious, spiritual, neither or both. Four of the subsequent questions relate to religiousness (public or private), 10 to spirituality and 3 to both. The questions relating to spirituality are independent of mood.

Kendler et al. (2003) developed a scale that reflects the multidimensional nature of religiousness and spirituality. It consists of 78 items selected from various other questionnaires, which measure 7 domains. These are general religiosity, social religiosity, involved God, forgiveness, God as judge, unvengefulness and thankfulness.

A specific measure of religiousness, which is the most simple to use, has been validated and meets the criteria delineated above is that by Koenig et al. (1997). This is a 5-item measure for use in health outcome studies, known as the Duke University Religion Index (DUREL). The first relates to church attendance or other religious meetings, the second to private religious activity such as prayer, meditation and Bible study, and the final 3 to the impact of these on one's life and approach to life. Each question is rated on a 5-point scale.

Is there evidence that religiousness and spirituality have different influences?

This question has not received much attention due to the inclusion of religion and spirituality into a single measure in most studies. A few have separated them and the results, while tentative, suggest that there may be value in exploring the different contributions of spirituality and religiousness in greater depth than has hitherto been the case.

A Canadian study (Baetz et al. 2004), arguably the largest of its kind, examined over 70,000 adults as part of a multi-wave longitudinal study. Its aim was to identify the relationship between spiritual or religious self-perception and religious worship to depressive symptoms. Background confounders that might cloud the picture were controlled and these included socio-economic, demographic (e.g. age) and health variables. Those who attended church more frequently had significantly fewer depressive symptoms, while those who stated that spiritual or religious values were important to them, or perceived themselves to be spiritual or religious, but who were not involved in religious institutions, had higher levels of depressive symptoms. Clearly the relationship between spirituality and religiousness is complex, but the findings suggest that formal involvement in worship carries benefits that are not obviously evident among those with more diffuse attitudes (such as merely perceiving or stating themselves to be spiritual or religious).

King et al. (2006) examined six ethnic groups in Britain. Comparing the combined religious/spiritual group with those who are neither, no difference in the prevalence of common mental disorders (CMDs) was found. However, when the spiritual groups who did not practice religion were compared with those who did engage in religious practice, CMDs where twice as common in the former.

A more recent study on suicidal behaviour (Rasic et al. 2009) found that self-harm behaviour such as overdosing and cutting was lower in a group who self-identified as religious in comparison to those who identified as spiritual after controlling for social supports.

A study that highlights the complexity of the relationship between spirituality, religiousness and depression examined the contribution of these to a lifetime history of depression (Maselko et al. 2009). Over 900 subjects were interviewed using standardized measures of depression. Religiousness was established by inquiry about the frequency of attendance at religious services, while spirituality was divided into existential and religious well-being using the Spiritual Well-Being scale summarized in the previous section

(Paloutzian and Ellison 1982). It found that regular religious attendance reduced the odds of having a depressive illness by 30 per cent. The two dimensions of spirituality had a more complex relationship with existential well-being, reducing the odds of depression by 70 per cent, while religious well-being increased the odds. A problem with the study is that the existential well-being scale contains questions that may be tapping into general well-being, so the association may be spurious. A number of other explanations may also account for the increased odds of depression in those with high religious well-being.

More recently a study by King et al. (2013) examined the responses of over 7,403 subjects from the third National Psychiatric Morbidity Study conducted between October 2006 and December 2007 across England. Information on whether the respondents had a religious outlook on life, one that was spiritual but not religious or one that was neither was gathered using an adapted version of the Royal Free Interview for Spiritual and Religious Beliefs (King et al. 2001). A battery of structured interviews to evaluate psychiatric disorders and substance misuse was also administered. The study found that people who had a spiritual understanding of life had worse mental health than those with an understanding that was neither religious nor spiritual. Those who were religious were broadly similar, in terms of prevalence of mental disorder and use of mental health treatments, to those who were neither religious nor spiritual after adjustment for potential confounders. However, they were significantly less likely to use, or be dependent on, drugs or alcohol. The study concluded that people who profess spiritual beliefs in the absence of a religious framework are more vulnerable to mental disorder. The authors suggested that one possible explanation is that they are engaged in an existential search that is driven by their emotional distress, but recommended that further qualitative and quantitative studies would assist in clarifying the nature of the association.

There is evidence that positive religious coping is prominent in those with long-term mental illness, with large numbers spending a significant amount of time in prayer (Tepper et al. 2001). For example, meditation and religious activity were identified as particularly helpful in a group with bipolar disorder (Russinova et al. 2002). Of 406 with long-term mental illness, 80 per cent used religious coping, 61 per cent spent more than 50 per cent of time in religious coping (e.g. prayer), and large numbers reported religious activities as the most beneficial alternative healthcare intervention.

Conclusion

There are numerous questions with respect to the relationship between religiousness or spirituality and mental health variables that beg to be answered. This endeavour requires research of the highest quality. One of the fundamentals of this approach is that construing spirituality and religiousness as similar dimensions is an over-simplification. Instead, greater attention needs to be paid to conducting studies that investigate religiousness and spirituality as separate and complex entities, each clearly defined with respect to their role in emotions, behaviour and functioning. Provided this is the strategy, whether people self-define as religious, spiritual, neither or both becomes irrelevant since each construct can be evaluated independently. In addition, the measure of spirituality must truly be tapping into a domain that is independent of mental well-being. The basic principles of epidemiological research can and should be applied to spirituality and religiousness so that the profound questions about meaning, purpose, God, the sacred, prayer, the supernatural and myriad related matters can be studied with confidence.

References

Allport, G. W. and Ross, J. M. (1967), 'Personal Religious Orientation and Prejudice' *Journal of Personality and Social Psychology* 5:4, pp. 432–43.

American Psychiatric Association (1990), 'Guidelines regarding possible conflict between psychiatrists' religious commitment and psychiatric practice', *American Journal of Psychiatry* 147:4, p. 542.

Baetz, M., Griffin, R., Bowen, R. et al. (2004), 'The association between spiritual and religious involvement and depressive symptoms in a Canadian population', *Journal of Nervous and Mental Disease* 192:12, pp. 818–82.

Bibby, R. W. (1995), 'Beyond headlines, hype and hope: shedding some light on spirituality', paper presented at the meeting of the Society for the Scientific Study of Religion, St Louis MS.

Bradford Hill, A. (1965), 'The environment and disease: association or causation', *Proceedings of the Royal Society of Medicine* 58:5, pp. 95–300.

Brady, M. J. and Cella, D. (1999), 'Assessing quality of life in palliative care', *Cancer Treatment and Research* 100, pp. 203–16.

Cook, C. C. H. (2004), 'Addiction and spirituality', *Addiction* 99:5, pp. 539–51.

Curlin, F. A., Lawrence, R. E., Odell, S. et al. (2007), 'Religion, spirituality and medicine: psychiatrists' and other physicians' differing observations, interpretations and clinical approaches', *American Journal of Psychiatry* 164:12, pp. 1825–31.

Dervic, K., Carballo, J. J., Baca-Garcia, E. et al. (2011), 'Moral or religious objections may protect against suicidal behaviour in bipolar disorder', *Journal Clinical Psychiatry*, 72:10, pp. 1390–6.

Ellis, A. (1980), *The Case against Religion: A Psychotherapists View and the Case against Religiosity*, Austin TX: American Atheist Press.

Ellison, C. W. (1983), 'Spiritual well-being: conceptualisation and measurement', *Journal of Psychology and Theology* 11, pp. 330–40.

Fetzer Institute (1999), *National Institute on Aging Working Group. Multidimensional Measurement of Religiousness/Spirituality for Use in Health Research: A Report of the Fetzer Institute*, 1st edn, Kalamazoo MI: Fetzer Institute.

Fetzer Institute (2003), *National Institute on Aging Working Group. Multidimensional Measurement of Religiousness/Spirituality for Use in Health Research: A Report of the Fetzer Institute*, 2nd edn, Kalamazoo MI: Fetzer Institute.

General Medical Council (2008), *Personal Beliefs and Medical Practice*, London: General Medical Council.

Hill, P. C., Pargament, K. I., Wood, R. W. et al. (2000), 'Conceptualising religion and spirituality: points of commonality, points of departure', *Journal of the Theory of Social Behaviour* 30:1, pp. 51–77.

Kendler, K. S., Liu, Q. X., Gardner, C. O. et al. (2003), 'Dimensions of religiosity and their relationship to lifetime psychiatric and substance use disorders', *American Journal of Psychiatry* 160:3, pp. 496–503.

King, M. B., Peck, P., Thomas, A. (2001), 'The Royal Free Interview for Spiritual and Religious Beliefs: development of validation of a self-report version', *Psychological Medicine* 31:6, pp. 1015–23.

King, M. B. and Koenig, H. G. (2009), 'Conceptualising spirituality for medical research and health service provision', *BMC Health Services Research* 9, p. 116.

King, M. B, Marston, L., McManus, S. et al. (2013), 'Religion, spirituality and mental health: results from a national study of English households', *British Journal of Psychiatry* 202:1, pp. 68–73.

King, M., Weich, S., Nazroo, J. et al. (2006), 'Religion, mental health and ethnicity. EMPIRIC – a national survey of England', *Journal of Mental Health* 51:2, pp. 153–62.

Koenig, H. G. (2008), 'Concerns about measuring "Spirituality" in research', *Journal of Nervous and Mental Disease* 196:5, pp. 349–55.

Koenig, H. G. (2009), 'Research on religion, spirituality and mental health: a review', *Canadian Journal of Psychiatry* 54:5, pp. 283–91.

Koenig, H. G. (2011), *Spirituality and Health Research: Methods, Measurements, Statistics, and Resources*, West Conshohocken PA: Templeton Press.

Koenig, H. G., King, D. and Carson, V. B. (2012), *Handbook of Religion and Health*, second edition, New York: Oxford University Press.

Koenig, H. G., McCullough, M. and Larsen, D. (2001), *Handbook of Religion and Health*, 1st edn, New York: Oxford University Press.

Koenig, H. G., Meador, K. and Parkerson, G. (1997), 'Religion Index for Psychiatric Research: A 5-item Measure for Use in Health Outcome Studies', *American Journal of Psychiatry* 154:6, pp. 885–6.

La Pierre, L. L. (1994), 'A model for describing spirituality', *Journal of Religion and Health* 33:2, pp. 153–61.

Maselko, J., Gilman, S. E. and Buka, S. (2009), 'Religious service attendance and spiritual well-being are differently associated with a risk of major depression', *Psychological Medicine* 39:6, pp. 1009–17.

Paloutzian, R. F. and Ellison, C. W. (1982), 'Loneliness, spiritual well-being and the quality of life', in L. A. Poplain and D. Perham (eds), *Loneliness: A Sourcebook of Current Theory, Research and Therapy*, New York: John Wiley and Sons.

Peterman, A. H., Fitchett, G., Brady, M. J., Hernandez, L., Cella, D. (2002), 'Measuring spiritual well-being in people with cancer: the Functional Assessment of Chronic Illness Therapy–Spiritual Well-Being Scale (FACIT-Sp)', *Annals of Behavioural Medicine* 24:1, pp. 49–58.

Rasic, D. T., Belik, S. L., Elias, B. et al. (2009), 'Spirituality, religion and suicidal behaviour in a nationally representative sample', *Journal of Affective Disorders* 114:1–3, pp. 32–40.

Roof, W. C. (2001), *Spiritual Marketplace: Baby Boomers and the Remaking of American Religion*, New Haven: Princeton University Press.

Royal College of Psychiatrists (2011), 'Recommendations for psychiatrists on spirituality and religion. Position Statement PS03/2011', London: Royal College of Psychiatrists.

Russinova, J., Wewiorski, H. J. and Cash, D. (2002), 'Use of alternative healthcare practices by persons with serious mental illness: perceived benefits', *American Journal of Public Health* 92:10, pp. 1600–3.

Saxena, S. and WHOQOL Group (2006), 'A cross-cultural study of spirituality, religion and personal beliefs as components of quality of life', *Social Science and Medicine* 62:6, pp. 1486–97.

Tepper, L., Rogers, S. A., Coleman, E. M. et al. (2001), 'The prevalence of religious coping among persons with persistent mental illness', *Psychiatric Services* 52:5, pp. 660–5.

Underwood, L. G. and Teresi, J. A. (2002), 'The Daily Spiritual Experiences Scale: development, theoretical description, reliability, exploratory factor analysis and preliminary construct validity using health-related data', *Annals of Behavioural Medicine* 24:1, pp. 22–33.

Watters, W. W. (1992), *Deadly Doctrine: Health, Illness and Christian God-Talk*, New York: Prometheus Books.

WHO QOL Group (1998), 'The World Health Organization Quality of Life Assessment (WHOQOL): Development and general psychometric properties', *Social Science and Medicine* 46:12, pp. 1585–96.

Zinnbauer, B. J., Pargament, K. L., Cole, B. C. et al. (1997), 'Religion and spirituality: unfuzzying the fuzzy', *Journal for the Scientific Study of Religion* 36:4, pp. 549–64.

3

What is Spiritual Care?

COLIN JAY

Summary

Within mental health services there is a growing recognition of the importance of a spiritual dimension to care. Care plans contain space for spiritual needs, acknowledging them as distinct from people's religious affiliation. What is often lacking is guidance about what those needs are and how they should be addressed. Even a brief look at the variety of 'spiritual needs assessment tools' now available makes evident that spiritual care is not just about what is done, but also about how it is done. A spiritual needs assessment will not necessarily ensure that spiritual care is offered. This chapter draws on the relational 'Ubuntu' theology of Desmond Tutu, the writings of John Swinton and the humanistic counselling theory of Carl Rogers to argue that 'spiritual care' should be defined not as a particular intervention or activity but as a quality of relationship offered to a person, marked by a number of distinct characteristics. Through this quality of relationship, both as offered by specialist practitioners, and as embodied, where possible, in relationships with other healthcare staff, recovery will be enhanced as people find affirmation of their human value and space to make sense of their situation.

Introduction: what is spiritual care?

This may seem a strange question for a healthcare chaplain to ask at a time when there is a growing interest in and appreciation of the importance of such care for promoting recovery and well-being. All kinds of professional bodies within mental health services now recognize the significance of spirituality for good mental health in many people, and both the Royal College of Nursing and the Royal College of Psychiatrists have recently issued guidance to their members for good practice in spiritual care (Royal College of Nursing 2011b; Cook 2011). Within my own trust, we have worked together with service users and carers and a multidisciplinary group of staff to develop a care pathway for spirituality. Discussions have taken place too about identifying 'spiritual care competencies' for nursing and other staff.

The question persists, however.

As they seek to clarify their purpose within their organization, many healthcare chaplaincy teams have chosen to rename their department as something like the 'Department of Religious, Pastoral and Spiritual Care'. (Personally, I value being a 'chaplaincy' and find that there is something positive and creative about people not quite being sure what it is that we do. It is not unusual for a referral to begin with the words, 'I'm not sure how I think you might be able to help, but ...', and that seems to sit comfortably with notions of spirituality and spiritual care.) It is questionable, though, whether such a change to a departmental name will really be any clearer or less confusing. Religious care, enabling people to practise and gain benefit from their religion, most people will understand. Pastoral care too is a concept of which most organizations will have some grasp. But what of spiritual care?

As individuals occupying different places within the healthcare system, a range of professional disciplines, a variety of experiences as patients and carers and various degrees of spiritual or religious commitment or involvement, we may each know what we think we mean by 'spiritual care', but that interpretation of the term remains largely a very individual one.

In the literature on spirituality and mental health there is a wide variety of definition and implicit assumption of what spiritual care entails. John Swinton's focus is on spiritual care as empathic understanding:

> It is an approach, or perhaps better an attitude, that seeks to enter into the experience of people with mental health problems, and in so doing, focus on ways in which that experience can be understood rather than simply explained. (Swinton 2001, p. 140)

This finds echoes in Margaret Goodall's discussion of spiritual care for people with dementia and her emphasis on the carer as one who is 'with me' and who 'knows me' (Goodall 2011). Eagger, Richmond and Gilbert (2009) see spiritual care more as a brand of therapeutic activity, with a particular aim of enabling people to find meaning in their particular situation, while others view spiritual care more in terms of assessing needs. Milner and Raffay (2011), for example, talk of assessing people's spiritual strengths and needs, while Moss, Clarke and Moody (2011) describe a process of looking for and attending to distinctively 'spiritual' dimensions within any clinical practice or situation. For the Catholic Bishops' Reference Group, on the other hand, this is a matter of 'pastoral mission' with a clear denominational emphasis and a resistance to 'professional' or 'practitioner' models of spiritual care (Healthcare Reference Group 2008, p. 2).

All these various understandings of the nature of spiritual care do, however, presuppose a particular quality of relationship that can enable such activities to take place. This paper seeks to explore ways in which it may be that relational dimension of the encounter that provides the distinctively 'spiritual' element of 'spiritual care' and stands as a common denominator across this rich variety of insights. As such it may then also offer a language with which to demonstrate the benefit of such care to people with mental health problems and to justify the time and resources devoted to it in hard-pressed mental health services.

Understanding spirituality

Implicit in any understanding of spiritual care is, of course, the interpretation of spirituality that lies behind it. It is not the intention here to revisit this debate, except to observe that the current context is one in which spirituality is generally understood by health professions and services to include, but also to go beyond, religious practice and conviction (see Swinton 2001; Cook et al. 2009; Gilbert 2011). 'Spiritual' issues of meaning, purpose, belonging, hope, peace of mind and so on are deemed to be of potential relevance to the well-being of all people, irrespective of religious affiliation (or the lack of it). Indeed, biologist David Hay goes one step further in his agreement with the conclusions of Alister Hardy, a zoologist rooted according to Hay in a 'stubborn empiricism', namely that spiritual awareness is part of the mainstream of human experience, a capacity rooted substantially in our physical nature and developed as those who 'chose' to attend to the spiritual dimension of their awareness gained an evolutionary advantage in the strength that this gave to cope with the dangers and difficulties of their physical and emotional environment (Hay 2006).

Such an understanding of spirituality is not without its detractors, however. John Paley is one of these (Paley 2008). He suggests that much of what is said about spirituality in nursing literature is vague and unsupported and that spirituality in a generic sense is an invention dating from the 1950s, which has been used by Christians to present religious practices in a more contemporary and politically acceptable way. He argues that once spirituality escaped the confines of a particular religion, it widened its terms of reference at an astonishing rate, becoming 'a sort of giant conceptual sponge' absorbing everything. Writing of the 'stretch dynamic' that applies to such an understanding of spirituality, Paley suggests:

[I]n order to justify the claim that it is 'present in all individuals', it is necessary to stretch the concept's denotation beyond anything directly associated with religion. If spirituality is to be universal, applicable not only to those who possess, but also to those who lack, a religious sensibility, it must saturate the terrain of human experience so thoroughly that there is no prospect of any atheist, agnostic, humanist or hedonist being able to wriggle out of it. Hence, the profusion, the sheer prodigality, of 'definitions' that pepper the nursing literature, with anything which could conceivably be of special interest to *somebody* being added to the list. (Paley 2008, pp. 5–6)

This idea of spirituality, according to Paley, is not merely artificial and unnecessary, it is also obscurantist, concealing other more effective approaches to supporting people in distress, and causing confusion among patients and clinicians.

Paley finds unlikely allies for some of his arguments in the Catholic Bishops' Conference of England and Wales who state in a parliamentary briefing:

> In recent years 'religious' care has been transformed in some policy dialogues into 'spiritual' care. This is intended to support diversity. Ironically, it can actually undermine diversity by not always appreciating that, to people of faith, spirituality only makes sense in a religious context ... This homogenisation of spirituality results in a recasting of traditional community and religious-based care which is more the product of a secular understanding of faith. (Healthcare Reference Group 2008, p. 1)

Chris Swift, in his history of healthcare chaplaincy, then wonders:

> Perhaps in order to influence the Department of Health, and harness NHS resources for the continuation and development of chaplaincy we are witnessing the rise of 'the myth of spiritual care'. (Swift 2009, p. 143)

There are, therefore, some awkward questions to answer. The work within my own trust to develop a spiritual care pathway is an attempt to ensure that there is a system in place for spiritual issues to be raised and addressed available to anyone who wishes this to happen. The intention is that spiritual care should become mainstream, routine, freed from the element of chance involved in whether someone happens to encounter a chaplain in person. It has been developed in the conviction, and upon the evidence, that this will help to improve well-being and promote recovery among our service users. At the same time, systems also have their disadvantages and limitations. At times, I am haunted by a rather grisly picture of a disinterested member of staff with a clipboard, grilling a patient and demanding, 'So what brings meaning and purpose into your life?'

What is clear is that having a spiritual needs assessment and care plan will not in itself guarantee that spiritual care is offered. Something extra is needed and the suggestion here is that this 'something extra' is not so much an additional intervention or activity as a quality of relationship.

Spiritual care as relationship: Rogers, Tutu and Swinton

The idea that the quality of a relationship offered is in itself therapeutically significant is of course nothing new but lies at the heart of person-centred counselling as described by Carl Rogers. Rogers' counselling theory revolves around a single central belief:

It is that the individual has within himself or herself vast resources for self-understanding, for altering his or her self-concept, attitudes and self-directed behaviour – and that these resources can be tapped if only a definable climate of facilitative psychological attitudes can be provided. (Kirschenbaum and Henderson 1990, p. 135)

Therapy, for Rogers, therefore is seen not as a technique or activity but as a special relationship characterized by the 'core conditions' of:

Congruence

The more the therapist is himself or herself in the relationship, putting up no professional front or personal façade, the greater is the likelihood that the client will change and grow in a constructive manner. (Kirschenbaum and Henderson 1990, p. 135)

Unconditional positive regard

When the therapist is experiencing a positive, non-judgmental, accepting attitude towards whatever the client is at that moment, therapeutic movement or change is more likely. (Kirschenbaum and Henderson 1990, p. 136)

Empathic understanding

This means that the therapist senses accurately the feelings and personal meanings that the client is experiencing and communicates this acceptant understanding to the client ... Listening of this very special, active kind is one of the most potent forces for change that I know. (Kirschenbaum and Henderson 1990, p. 136)

For Rogers, not only is the creation of a particular quality of relationship an effective means for change and growth in the person being supported, it is interesting that he also acknowledges a spiritual dimension to those times when this therapeutic relationship is most complete and healing for the client.

At those moments it seems that my inner spirit has reached out and touched the inner spirit of the other. Our relationship transcends itself and becomes part of something larger. Profound growth and healing and energy are present. (Kirschenbaum and Henderson 1990, p. 137)

This sense of the therapeutic or transformative importance of the quality of a relationship is seen also in Desmond Tutu's writing on Ubuntu. Ubuntu is defined by Michael Battle in his commentary on Tutu's thought as '[a]n

African concept of personhood in which the identity of the self is understood to be formed interdependently in community' (Battle 2009, p. 1). In contrast to a western understanding of personhood or identity, as formed and defined in perpetual competition with others, Ubuntu says that 'a person is a person through other people'. In Tutu's words:

> We don't come fully formed into the world. We learn how to think, how to walk, how to speak, how to behave, indeed how to be human from other human beings. We need other human beings in order to be human. (Battle 2009, p. 54)

I do not, therefore, discover that I am beautiful or clever or talented because I am more beautiful or clever or talented than another, because in such an economy there are always only losers. Rather, I find that I am those things because I find my beauty or intelligence or talent revealed or reflected in the other. To have Ubuntu is to have come to understand my identity positively in relationship to and interdependence with other people. If I dehumanize others I dehumanize myself. If I offer Ubuntu to others I make possible to them through my love a new realization of what it means to be human – as Tutu charges a group of medical students in one of his addresses:

> This is how you have Ubuntu – you care, you are hospitable, you're gentle, you're compassionate and concerned. Go forth as new doctors, conscious that everybody is to be revered, reverenced as created in God's image ... go forth to demonstrate your Ubuntu, to care for them, to heal them, especially those who are despised, marginalized. (Battle 2009, p. 54)

Tutu is not alone in formulating a relational model of personhood, but this emphasis on the despised and the marginalized gives what he has to say a particular resonance within the mental health field.

And all of this, for Tutu, is founded and modelled in the love of God, both as expressed within the Trinity and as directed out towards the world: 'God does not love us because we are lovable, but we are lovable precisely because God loves' (Battle 2009, p. 36).

Such a brief summary of Ubuntu fails to do justice to Tutu's thought. However, even this overview serves to enrich an understanding of spiritual care as a quality of relationship. If, in offering spiritual care, I am offering Ubuntu to another, that is, I am offering a quality of relationship within which they can discover something positive about what it means to be the unique human being that they are, then that potentially has huge power to be a force for healing and integration.

A third variation on this same theme comes from John Swinton's model of 'radical friendship' (Swinton 2000). Swinton argues that for many people with mental health problems, this is an experience of being de-personalized. It is very easy for a person with mental illness to be seen as the illness rather than the person. We tend to talk not of someone having schizophrenia, or suffering from schizophrenia, but of being a schizophrenic – all at once, they have become the illness. Swinton looks to Jesus' own friendships with people as a model for how to offer a different and life-changing quality of relationship:

> Jesus' relationships were always personal, as opposed to instrumental, primarily aimed at regaining the dignity and personhood of those whom society had rejected and de-personalised. Jesus' friendships reacted beyond the socially constructed identity of individuals and, in entering into deep personal relationships of friendship with them, he was able to reveal something of the nature of God and enable the development of a positive sense of personhood based on intrinsic value rather than on personal achievement or outward behaviour. (Swinton 2000, p. 143)

Swinton goes on to argue that where people can offer this kind of friendship, there is real possibility of 'resurrecting the person' and offering hope and new possibilities to people with mental health problems. In his book entitled *Resurrecting the Person* (2000), Swinton is writing primarily for church members and argues that being a Christ-like friend in this way is not so much about doing things for people as being something for them, being someone who is with them and for them in the same way that God is with and for us. In another title, *Spirituality and Mental Health Care* (2001), Swinton's writing is aimed more at mental health professionals. His language therefore is different, but the message is essentially the same:

> It is clear that spiritual care is much more than simply an added task to be done or an extra skill that has to be learned. Rather it has to do with seeing the world differently and, in seeing it differently, acting differently within it. Spiritual care has to do with asking different questions of those to whom we offer care and equally as importantly, being equipped and prepared to respond appropriately and openly to the answers one receives. Spiritual care is as much a way of being as a way of acting. (2001, p. 175)

These words are echoed by Susan Mitchell and Glenn Roberts in their writing on spirituality and psychosis. Spiritual care, they say,

> is not something extra that we do, but the application of insight and understanding to all that we do. It is as much a way of being as a way of doing ... Spirituality is not a special form of treatment; there are no technical routines that are inherently spiritual. It is the way in which the work is carried out that imparts the spiritual quality. (2009, p. 50)

The 2010 RCN Spirituality Survey (Royal College of Nursing 2011a) likewise suggests that '[s]piritual care is ... very much dependent upon the personal attributes and qualities displayed by the nurse in their interactions and dealings with patients'. Consequently the College's guidelines on spiritual care emphasize attitudes, behaviours and personal qualities: 'It is not just about "doing to" but "being with" them' (Royal College of Nursing 2011b).

In my own trust, some work was carried out with a service-user reference group looking at spirituality. Asked about how they would like spirituality to be addressed in their care, it was clear from the group's responses that this did not consist in wanting to be asked particular questions or offered particular activities, rather it was much more about the way in which all care was offered and all assessments carried out. The group's clear wish was that spiritual beliefs, practices and insights should be respected in all encounters with healthcare professionals. Their plea to those professionals might be summed up in a song title: 'It ain't what you do, it's the way that you do it.'

Tightening the definition

To argue, therefore, that spiritual care is best viewed as a quality of relationship or a way of being rather than a particular, distinct activity or intervention receives support from within a variety of disciplines and traditions, but further definition is still needed. In research published by Harriet Mowat and John Swinton (2005), they found that many chaplains spend a substantial amount of their time 'being around'. Most clergy will know precisely what is meant by this kind of 'loitering with intent' or 'paddling around', and for the chaplains involved in the research it was clearly a purposeful and carefully planned activity designed make clear their availability and encourage referrals. Healthcare providers and commissioners may, however, find it harder to understand why they are being asked to pay for people simply to 'be around'. If we are going to argue that spiritual care is a particular way of being available, we need to define further what this way of being, this quality of relationship is and how we think it is both distinctive and of benefit to people.

What follows is not an attempt to provide exhaustive definition of spiritual care, but from reflection on my own working experience in mental health services, these seem to be the key elements of the relationship that I as a chaplain try to offer.

A professional relationship

It is important to be clear, first of all, that what is being offered is a *professional* relationship. Some people may find that it does violence to the whole idea of spirituality to place it immediately within a professional context in that way, but this is the context of 'spiritual care' in a health service setting.

The moment we begin to think in terms of 'offering spiritual care' or 'meeting spiritual needs' we are into the realm of a professional relationship or activity. Indeed, where 'care' becomes a noun rather than a verb, where people are 'receiving care' rather than just being 'cared for' or 'looked after', it tends to be the case that we have moved into the professional sphere. There are clear problems with this: how do you professionalize things of the spirit? But there are important strengths to a professional relationship too. In particular there are the safeguards it provides for the person receiving care. An example from the code of conduct for healthcare chaplains issued by the United Kingdom Board for Healthcare Chaplaincy makes the point well:

> The only appropriate relationship between you and those in your care is a professional relationship committed to promote the spiritual good and best interests of particular individuals. Moving the focus away from meeting the particular needs of those in your care towards meeting your own needs is unprofessional and an abuse of your role. (2010, p. 8)

Another important benefit of a professional relationship is the boundaries inherent within it. If spiritual care is about offering a particular quality of relationship, being available to another person in a particular way, this is arguably only possible if there are very clear boundaries to that relationship. As the code of conduct puts it:

> Boundaries enable the effective functioning of caring and supportive relationships in which healthcare chaplains can respond to the spiritual and religious needs of those in their care. Boundaries frame behaviour and practice so that pastoral relationships are consistent and their limitations clear to all parties involved. (2010, p. 8)

Of course, professional relationships can never be the whole answer to the needs of a person's spirit, and one of the great gifts brought to mental health units by chaplaincy volunteers is the offer of someone to speak to who is not being paid for it. Swinton, too, identifies the fact that, while professional relationships are important, nonetheless, 'The need for genuine community is perhaps the most pressing need in the process of caring for those individuals' with mental health problems (2000, p. 60).

There are therefore limits to the significance and scope of a 'professional' relationship; that said, it is a professional relationship of spiritual care, within the safeguards and boundaries it offers, that is under consideration here.

A person-centred relationship

It is, however, a professional relationship focused on the 'person' rather than the 'patient'; on the human being, rather than the illness. Different professions clearly have to interpret this in different ways. Chaplains can in many ways 'demote' the illness in their list of concerns in a way that is not possible for doctors or nurses to do, but it should not be beyond the ability of any health professional – indeed, health services now expect it not to be beyond the ability of any health professional – to recognize the human being who inhabits the list of symptoms.

Swinton's analysis of the way in which we create non-persons of people who are mentally ill has already been mentioned. He writes:

> It is through the myriad of unnoticed social gestures and negative assumptions that people with mental health problems find their sense of self-worth and personhood constantly being eroded. It is through that same process that they come to be perceived, consciously or subconsciously, as 'non-persons' and consequently excluded from meaningful participation in society. (2000, p. 81)

This process seems to describe the very opposite of offering someone Ubuntu, and spiritual care might be defined as an attempt to reverse this process.

Roger Grainger, writing about ministry to people with mental health problems, offers a pertinent warning:

> The most important thing about mentally ill ... people is, in fact, that they are people ... These people are ourselves, bone of our bone, flesh of our flesh, blood of our blood ... A book about ministry to the mentally ill ... may easily do as much harm as good to its subjects, because it encourages us to adopt a kind of pseudo-scientific attitude towards them which deprives them of their humanity. (1993, p. 96)

I recently attended a day conference at a venue where the receptionist was wearing joyfully bright, exuberant and eccentric make-up. A number of participants noticed this and commented on it with enjoyment of the fact. The next day I found myself in a case conference where the fact that a service user was wearing, in the view of a staff nurse, excessive make-up was a clear sign that her condition was deteriorating. Clearly mental health professionals have to make assessments and that staff nurse will have had good reasons for her observations, but the needs of spiritual care would demand that this is done also with humility and humanity. Nowhere is this more necessary than when we move into the area of people's spiritual and religious beliefs and experiences. However ill the person, nothing is more undermining of their humanity than to have these immediately pathologized.

It is not that, in order to be 'spiritual', spiritual care has to ignore illness as a factor, or be excessively naive about the effect of illness on people, but simply that it takes care to recognize and affirm that they are people still and to have as its focus that human being, made, according to my own Christian tradition, in the image of God.

A mutual relationship

My third consideration of this quality of relationship explores how this then demands a degree of reciprocity or mutuality. By 'professional' we often understand a one-way relationship. A service user came to me one day not knowing whether to laugh or cry. She had approached a student nurse on the ward and, in a bid to strike up a conversation, had asked if she had seen *Coronation Street* the night before. She received the reply, 'We're told on our course not to divulge any personal information to patients.' It is good to know that the art of conversation is not dead!

My instinct as a chaplain is that, while working clearly within professional guidelines and boundaries, there is a sense that something significant is happening when I can let another person see that their life has in some way touched mine, that I have been affected by them, that I am learning from them, that I can also receive from them, perhaps as a first step towards their re-learning that they still have something to offer others.

I find, for example, that I have never been prayed for as much as I have since working as a mental health chaplain. People often ask me to pray for them, but when I have finished, they often then say, 'And now I'm going to say one for you', in a way that never or rarely happened when I was a parish priest. I am pleased to receive their prayers for me and believe that allowing myself to be prayed for is part of my spiritual care for them.

A key aspect of this mutuality of relationship is the extent to which the 'carer' can, within appropriate controls and guidelines, allow him- or herself to be known by the 'client'. This is perhaps less to do with divulging personal information than with consciously allowing another access to elements of our core being. Such a 'knowing' is well illustrated from Christine Bryden's moving account of her experiences as a person with dementia:

> The way I know people is in a spiritual and emotional way. There's a knowing of who a person really is right at their core. But I have no idea of who they are, in terms of who they are meant to be in your world of cognition and action, and labels and achievements. (Bryden 2003, p. 110)

It would follow that effective spiritual care for someone in her position would mean allowing entry beyond a purely professional front to deeper elements of the carer's identity and personhood. To put a block on these would inhibit any meaningful connection that might allow spiritual care to take place, and my suspicion would be that this applies more generally to people experiencing mental health problems and not just to those with dementia.

Such a position could potentially lead on to some quite dangerous ground ethically. It is therefore reassuring to read in a leaflet on spirituality and mental health released by the Royal College of Psychiatrists the following words:

> Spirituality emphasises our connections to other people and the world, which creates the idea of 'reciprocity'. This means that the giver and receiver both get something from what happens, that if you help another person, you help yourself. (2010)

This of course has to be held in creative balance with the professional demand to be focused on the needs of the service user and not to cross certain boundaries. It recalls us also to Rogers and to the need for congruence in a helping relationship, and poses a question for which it would be very difficult to legislate: how do you make a professional relationship also, within appropriate boundaries, a real relationship?

The psychotherapist Peter Lomas writes of the importance of keeping in sight that the therapeutic encounter is simply an extension or exaggeration of an ordinary human conversation. The ordinariness of therapy is essential to it. Unless the therapist can accept equality with the patient, the undertaking is jeopardized from the start.

> In so far as the psychotherapist sets himself apart from his patient, giving the impression – even if only implicitly by reticence – that he is a different order of being, his capacity to heal is reduced. (1994, p. 17)

> The skill required to help a troubled person is one that is primarily learned in the school of ordinary living. (p. 19)

Jean Vanier, too, writes of the working relationship with people with learning disabilities in the L'Arche communities:

> Before 'doing for them' we want to 'be with them.' The particular suffering of the person who is mentally handicapped, or of all marginal people, is a feeling of being excluded and unloved. It is through everyday life in community and the love that must be incarnate in this, that they can begin to discover that they have a value, that they are loved and so are lovable. (2006, p. 98)

And again:

> Communities which start by serving the poor must gradually discover the gifts brought by those they serve. (p. 142)

A discerning relationship

A fourth characteristic of spiritual care is that it might be described as a relationship concerned with 'discernment' rather than 'diagnosis'. For the purposes of this discussion, 'diagnosis' might be defined as putting people, actions and/or symptoms into categories or 'boxes' in order to identify them, while 'discernment' would be understood rather as beginning with the person, meeting the person where they are and moving together collaboratively from that point.

It is not my intention to argue that discernment is good and diagnosis bad. Effective medical care clearly requires accurate diagnosis. If I have a serious medical condition, I want someone to diagnose that and start treating it, not to begin with how I am feeling about my symptoms and see where we go from there. Similarly, if I have a depression or a psychosis or the first signs of dementia, I want someone to realize that and identify it, and to have some ideas about what they can do to improve the situation. It is evident from many conversations with mental health service users that a diagnosis is very often a source of considerable relief and reassurance as people learn that their disconcerting experiences are not unique to them, that they have a name and can be treated.

However, that process does also inevitably involve a degree of reduction of complex and beautiful human beings to cases and symptoms and body parts. There needs to be recognition that there also exists a person in the midst of this process; that some of the suggested solutions may deprive their life of things that they consider to be essential; that they may wish to take decisions that seem to fly in the face of sense or reason, because they are informed by a different instinct; and that their illness and suffering may have meanings that they do not wish to have trampled over in the rush for a cure or an answer.

Spiritual care, I believe, begins here with a process of discernment, a process that can work hand in hand with diagnosis but that is also an essential counterfoil to that reductionist tendency.

Powell and MacKenna describe with great elegance how spiritual care and diagnosis can come together, for example in the practice of a psychiatrist:

> The Doctor–patient relationship is crucial in the success of any treatment being offered. From the outset the patient needs to feel he or she is being valued and treated as a human being – to be sympathetically received, listened to without judgement being passed and helped to make some sense of what has gone wrong. The effect is to strengthen the 'therapeutic alliance' which in turn assists with relevant information-gathering, accurate diagnosis and ensuring the patient's full co-operation with the agreed treatment choices. All such therapeutic interventions, whether physical or psychological, will have the best possible effect when they are offered

with sensitivity, care and concern coming not from the self-interest of the ego, but from the magnanimity of the soul. (2009, p. 105)

It is to be hoped that all healthcare will have this spiritual element to it, but that activity which calls itself specifically 'spiritual care' will start distinctively from this place.

A non-fixing relationship

A relationship of spiritual care is one that will be unwilling to impose solutions.
Chris Swift writes:

In a world of productive knowledge and solution-focussed healthcare it can be hard to argue for the necessity of space and silence. In this respect the physical places associated with the chaplain are akin to the interventions that take place at the bedside. Rather than utility we find signs, space, prayer, reflection and (potentially) meaning. (2009, p. 167)

He also quotes Helen Orchard on the 'empty-handed' approach to healthcare chaplaincy:

Here delivering spiritual care is not about delivering anything, but about being present while the other person works it out for him- or herself ... And while a person can be an expert in matters of religion, the empty-handed approach requires no expertise; indeed it is not possible to be the expert on matters spiritual as no-one has the full facts, answers or truth. (2000, p. 139)

This approach is arguably, if not a specialist skill, at least a specialist capacity that is brought to healthcare by those who are professional spiritual carers, exercising ministerial skills and drawing on their own spiritual traditions and practices. It is a capacity that we cannot take for granted in clinical colleagues and that may sit uncomfortably with other professional expectations of them, but for which, with appropriate support, they might find space in their clinical practice.

Sheila Cassidy observes in her book *Sharing the Darkness* (1988) that for all of us there is some respite from pain when we can *do* something. For nurses, there is always something that they can do. Doctors too are happiest when they can adjust medication and so on. The hardest thing is to keep on visiting when all physical manoeuvres are exhausted. She is writing specifically about palliative care, but so much of her insight is directly applicable to mental health.

She illustrates her point with a number of pictures of a patient sitting, first of all with a doctor armed with his competence and instruments and

protected by an aide (a nurse); then sitting with a priest performing a sacra-
mental ministry, in stole and dog-collar, protected by having a role to play
and a ritual to perform; then with a doctor or priest when exhausted of the
physical aspects of their work, with hands empty but still with the resources
of their counselling skills available; and finally the patient and professional,
stripped of all resources, present to each other, naked and empty-handed as
two human beings. She writes of the importance of this moment of powerlessness and the need not to run away from it.

This resonates with my own experience of chaplaincy work among people
in mental distress. In the sheer exhaustion of sitting with someone who can
find no reason to live, and the knowledge that you cannot find a reason for
them either, the temptation is to offer a prayer, a sacrament, a word from
the Scriptures; but at that moment this would be to run away from spiritual
care.

However much today's world forces us to talk and think in terms of care
pathways and outcome measures, this element of being able to stay when
I have run out of things to offer remains at the heart of what we mean by
spiritual care.

Swift, again, concludes:

Standing in the place where there are no answers, no quick exits to open,
does not require the gifts of those whose hands are full. It is a situation
that calls for great patience, compassion and faithfulness to the value of
the human being in front of you. While some might argue that this kind
of availability is simple, I would contend that it is in fact the product of
considerable preparation, maturity and deep, personal self-knowledge.
(2009, p. 175)

A relationship open to mystery

In addition to all those qualities listed by Chris Swift, this kind of availability to people requires of us also that we are deeply rooted in our own
spiritual traditions and practices. It is surely a legitimate requirement still
that spiritual care practitioners are firmly located within an established
spiritual tradition, for without that, they would certainly be overwhelmed
by such a demand. This final feature of spiritual care is therefore its openness to what is non-material, non-rational; its openness to mystery. Indeed,
there is an inevitability that we end up there because (and I might have listed
this as yet another quality of spiritual care) we insist on the meaning and
value of each human life that we encounter – an insistence that sometimes
seems to fly in the face of the evidence before us.

While I am fully committed to the recognition of the spirituality and spiritual needs of people whether they are religious or not, I suspect also that God
will remain stubbornly within our talk of spirituality, simply because talk-

ing about spirituality, thinking about spirituality, working with spirituality will always push us to the edges of what we can understand or prove or measure; and God, whatever we may or may not understand by the term, is at very least a helpful shorthand for that mystery that lies just beyond our record of outcomes for a spiritual intervention.

Conclusion

I have sought to define spiritual care not as a particular activity or intervention, but as a quality of relationship that is a professional relationship, but one focused on the person rather than the illness, and that allows for a degree of reciprocity in order to be a real rather than a wholly one-sided relationship. It is concerned with discernment rather than diagnosis, it refrains from imposing solutions – indeed it has at its heart the ability to stay with a person when there are no solutions, no answers, and because of this is not afraid, indeed is obliged sometimes to stand without apology on the edge of mystery.

For some, this may seem too vague an answer to the question, 'What is spiritual care?' It may not translate easily into outcome measures or spiritual care competencies. But it does make sense of the attempt to promote a spiritual dimension to the care offered by other healthcare colleagues: notwithstanding the constraints imposed by their particular roles and disciplines; it is surely not too much to ask that any healthcare professional should be able to incorporate elements of what I have described into the relationships they form with the users of their services. And in times of financial constraint it highlights the continuing importance of a specialist spiritual care service that can concentrate on these aspects of relationship without some of the role conflicts and constraints experienced by those colleagues in other disciplines.

I do believe that that is a dimension of care that we can justify and evidence; that in these days of person-centred care, providers of mental health services want to be able to offer and for which receivers of that care are crying out.

References

Battle, M. (2009), *Ubuntu: I in You and You in Me*, New York: Seabury Books.

Bryden, C. (2003), *Dancing with Dementia: My Story of Living Positively with Dementia*, London: Jessica Kingsley.

Cassidy, S. (1988), *Sharing the Darkness: The Spirituality of Caring*, London: Darton, Longman & Todd.

Cook, C. C. H. (2011), 'Recommendations for psychiatrists on spirituality and religion', London: Royal College of Psychiatrists.

Cook, C. C. H., Powell, A. and Sims, A. (eds) (2009), *Spirituality and Psychiatry*, London: Royal College of Psychiatrists Press.

Eagger, S., Richmond, P. and Gilbert, P. (2009), 'Spiritual care in the NHS', in Cook, Powell and Sims (eds) (2009), *Spirituality and Psychiatry*.

Gilbert, P. (2011), *Spirituality and Mental Health*, Brighton: Pavilion Publishing.

Goodall, M. (2011), 'Loving attention: chaplaincy as a model of spiritual care for those with dementia', in A. Jewell (ed.) (2011), *Spirituality and Personhood in Dementia*, London: Jessica Kingsley.

Grainger, R. (1993), *Strangers in the Pews*, Peterborough: Epworth Press.

Hay, D. (2006), *Something There: The Biology of the Human Spirit*, London: Darton, Longman & Todd.

Healthcare Reference Group of the Catholic Bishops' Conference of England and Wales (2008), 'Spirituality and RC Chaplaincy. Parliamentary Briefing no. 3', London: Catholic Bishops' Conference of England and Wales.

Kirschenbaum, H., Henderson, V. L. (1990), *The Carl Rogers Reader*, London: Constable.

Lomas, P. (1994), *True and False Experience: The Human Element in Psychotherapy*, Piscataway NY: Transaction Publishers.

Milner, K. and Raffay, J. (2011), 'Valuing staff and training for spiritual care', in Gilbert (ed.) (2011), *Spirituality and Mental Health*.

Mitchell, S. and Roberts, G. (2009), 'Psychosis', in Cook, Powell and Sims (eds) (2009), *Spirituality and Psychiatry*.

Moss, B., Clarke, J. and Moody, I. (2011), 'Educating for spiritual care', in Gilbert (ed.) (2011), *Spirituality and Mental Health*.

Mowat, H. and Swinton, J. (2005), *What Do Chaplains Do? The Role of the Chaplains in Meeting the Spiritual Needs of Patients*, Aberdeen: Mowat Research.

Orchard, H. (2000), *Hospital Chaplaincy: Modern, Dependable?*, Sheffield: Lincoln Theological Institute for the Study of Religion and Society.

Paley, J. (2008), 'Spirituality and nursing: a reductionist approach', *Nursing Philosophy* 9:1, pp. 3–18.

Powell, A. and MacKenna, C. (2009), 'Psychotherapy', in Cook, Powell and Sims (eds) (2009), *Spirituality and Psychiatry*.

Royal College of Nursing (2011a), *RCN Spirituality Survey 2010*, London: Royal College of Nursing.

Royal College of Nursing (2011b), *Spirituality in Nursing Care: A Pocket Guide*, London: Royal College of Nursing.

Royal College of Psychiatrists (2010), 'Spirituality and mental health' (leaflet), www.rcpsych.ac.uk/mentalhealthinfo/treatments/spirituality.aspx.

Swift, C. (2009), *Hospital Chaplaincy in the Twenty-First Century*, Farnham: Ashgate Publishing.

Swinton, J. (2000), *Resurrecting the Person*, Nashville TN: Abingdon Press.

Swinton, J. (2001), *Spirituality and Mental Health Care: Rediscovering a Forgotten Dimension*, London: Jessica Kingsley.

UK Board for Healthcare Chaplaincy (2010), *Code of Conduct for Healthcare Chaplains*, London: UKBHC.

Vanier, J. (2006), *Community and Growth*, London: Darton, Longman & Todd.

4

Augustine's Concept of Evil and Its Practical Relevance for Psychotherapy[1]

ALEXANDRA PÂRVAN

Summary

This chapter investigates how Augustine of Hippo's metaphysical concept of evil can inform psychotherapists' ways of conceptualizing and approaching clients' experiences of harm suffered or harm done, and thereby facilitate appropriate therapeutic and healing interventions in clinical areas such as abuse, trauma, depression, anxiety, loss or violent behaviour. The discourse on evil currently entertained by various psychotherapeutic approaches is ambivalent and paradoxical: at the same time excluded from the technical language of psychotherapy, it is still used with reference to psychic structures. This is problematic for therapists' attitudes towards clients and clients' attitudes towards themselves. Augustine's ontological understanding of evil as deprivation or lack, as non-substantial and relational, as secondary to and dependent on good, as well as the difference he draws between 'being' and 'doing', may offer theoretical and practical solutions to such contradictory takes on evil, thus helping both therapists and clients (whether offenders or victims) in their struggle to understand and work with the reality of evil towards healing.

Evil in psychotherapeutic discourse

By tradition the term 'evil' is intentionally excluded from the language, thought and work of psychotherapists (Ivey 2005, p. 199; Phillips 1994,

1 This article is the outcome of research pursued on an Andrew W. Mellon Research Fellowship, at the Institute for Advanced Studies in the Humanities (IASH), University of Edinburgh. I am grateful both to the Mellon Foundation and IASH for their generous financial and institutional support, which made this research possible. The final version of the article was prepared during a research stay at the Eberhard Karls Universität Tübingen, funded by the Deutscher Akademischer Austausch Dienst (DAAD), for which I am equally thankful.

p. 59; Khan 1989, p. 144) and psychiatrists (Adshead 2006, p. 262; Powell 2002, pp. 1–11),[2] but also spiritual carers (Swinton 2002, pp. 1, 2), pastoral counsellors and pastoral ministers (Hall Davis 2008, p. 666). By generally discarding 'evil' from their vocabulary, mental health professionals aim at avoiding the theological connotations and religious references of this term (Diamond 2005, p. 188; Levine 2006, pp. 300–9; de Zulueta 1997, pp. 199–200; Gilligan 1996, esp. pp. 92–4, 258, 261; Greig 1996, p. 173), as well as the connection with contemporary political war discourse (Levine 2006, p. 296), in order to engage in scientific causal explanations of human behaviour and neutral therapeutic attitudes and language. However, 'evil' is also employed in psychotherapeutic literature, and still for the purposes of *scientific* explanations of psychic organizations (Mollon 2000, pp. 68, 71; Ivey 2002, p. 58; 2005, p. 205; Hering 1997, p. 212).[3]

Moreover, there is a further ambivalence within these two discourses as well. On the one hand, some have questioned the very possibility, necessity or benefit of exercising a neutral or impersonal therapeutic attitude, and proposed instead that therapists should practise moral challenge and moral condemnation towards clients responsible for reprehensible acts (Růžička 2010, pp. 196–7; Burns et al. 2012, pp. 7–9; Grand 2002, pp. 147–70; Martin 2006, p. 127). On the other hand, it was pointed out that explanations of *evil* psychic structures often reduce the explained persons to a subhuman level, which resembles the attitude towards their victims of the very persons termed as evil by therapists, and thus affects the treatment of such clients (Spinelli 2000, pp. 564–5; see Swinton 2002, pp. 3, 5, 7; Mason et al. 2002). Therefore, there are practitioners who use the term 'evil' while advocating the exercise of empathy, virtues and love in order to resurrect the personhood of their clients, even when moral judgement on their acts is not suspended (Prins 1994, p. 300; Goldberg 1996, p. 209 and elsewhere; Swinton 2002, pp. 5–9; Adshead 2002, p. 7). Such an approach may, however, be ambiguous and problematic, as it may work rather to affirm therapists' moral superiority than clients' potential goodness, a goodness that actually needs to be affirmed, in a credible and non-contradictory way, as a means of catalyzing change.

In my view, what causes this conflict as well as therapists' professional ambivalence towards evil is the fact that, as a discipline, psychotherapy aimed at a scientific discourse that would part from ethics, while at the same time assimilated in its scientific accounts a strictly moral understanding of

---

2 The word 'evil' is avoided in the literature on criminology as well (Mason et al. 2002, p. 83; Greig 1996, p. 163).

3 At the beginning of the twentieth century, evil was medicalized in the clinical category of the psychopath (Mason 2006, pp. 89–108). Recently, some have proposed that 'evil' should be considered as a diagnostic category separate from antisocial personality disorder (APD) and psychopathy (Wilson 2003, pp. 3–4), or as a subcategory of narcissistic personality disorder (Peck 1983, p. 128).

evil.[4] It is my contention that this impasse can be broken by introducing a metaphysical understanding of evil in therapeutic theory and practice, which would also help clarify what would constitute a moral involvement appropriate to this profession, where the morality both of therapists and of clients needs to be dealt with and not left aside.[5] The psychotherapists who demand the expelling of 'evil' from their discipline understand it exclusively as a moral judgement, unable to shed light on the *origins* of evil, of what made it possible and how it can be prevented. My claim is that these issues can be better addressed by first answering the question 'What is evil?' within a metaphysical framework. This would allow for a morally neutral conceptualization of both harm done and harm suffered as 'evil', and would correspondingly supply new frames for explanation and intervention in clinical areas dealing with *evil done* (conditions associated with violent behaviour) and *evil suffered* (trauma, abuse, loss, anxiety, depression, bereavement, etc.).

In line with Freud's commitment to separate the scientific from what is purely speculative, no psychotherapist of whatever approach has so far explored, employed or worked with 'evil' as a metaphysical category. As a result, both those who accept and those who reject evil from psychotherapeutic vocabulary confuse between the ontological and moral standing of a person and perpetuate the contradictions and disputes surrounding 'evil'. In this chapter, I want to suggest that Augustine's view on evil joining ontological and moral aspects without confusing them can help therapists to assume appropriate therapeutic attitudes towards their clients, and guide their clients – whether they be perpetrators or victims of evil acts – to adopt healing attitudes towards themselves.

The substantialization of evil in popular culture and psychotherapeutic literature

Throughout our early childhood and onwards, we are socialized to distinguish between good and evil and to situate them on the same level of reality. When threatened or harmed and in order to be able to fight back or protect ourselves, we identify evil as an agent and in so doing we substantialize it: evil becomes a person, a thing or an act (with autonomous existence),

---

4 Freud's repressed 'evil wishes', the 'bad objects' in psychodynamic theories, or the evil structures, evil states of mind, bad selves, and malevolent personalities in the vocabulary of contemporary psychiatry and psychotherapy are all *morally* evil in so far as threatening and harming to the individual's and others' life and identity. The pathology most associated with evil, APD, is defined in the Diagnostic and Statistical Manual of Mental Disorders (DSM) by moral-transgression attributes, as Martin (2006, p. 127) points out.

5 If the client is encouraged and expected to be a moral agent, then this represents in itself a moral stance of the therapist.

who is against us. Once substantialized, evil can only 'disappear' if we win the battle, but this outcome is crucially obstructed by the substantialization itself. In fact, winning involves a process of de-substantialization by virtue of which the identified evil ceases to be perceived as an active threat per se, our relation to it changes, and there is no longer need for a dichotomized interpretation and opposing positions. When the de-substantialization is not effected, our perpetuated relation with evil as a substantialized entity endows it with strength, persistence and hold on us, making it function as a self-governed, destructive reality that clings to us. This is what I call *solidi-fied* evil. When evil is substantialized in external or internal objects whose action upon us is solidified in our mind in a fixed, stereotyped, self-instan-tiating form, it becomes for us a permanent companion. This brings us to a second level of substantializing evil: an act (or person) substantialized as evil leads to the substantialization of the experience of that act (or person) as evil. Therapists work to counter the effects of this second substantializa-tion of evil while at the same time they are paradoxically endorsing the first substantialization of evil.

Psychoanalysts, psychiatrists and clinical psychologists speak of evil per-sons (Mollon 2000, pp. 68, 71–2; Ivey 2002, p. 58; 2005, p. 205; Hering 1997, p. 212; Tangney and Stuewig 2004, pp. 337–8; Peck 1983, p. 81) and *evilness* (Kinzie 2006, p. 249; Wilson 2003, p. 9), and describe evil as an independent, agentive principle 'bent on destruction of goodness' (Ivey 2005, p. 201; Hering 1997, pp. 209, 216; Royston 2006, p. 24). By empha-sizing the incomprehensibility, unspeakability and mystery of evil (Kinzie 2006, pp. 249, 255, 257; Grand 2002, pp. 9, 12, 14; Greig 1996, pp. 167, 173) they are adding to the substantialization of evil an idealization of evil, and in some contexts this feeds the belief that those deemed 'evil' are beyond help and treatment (Mason et al. 2002). At the same time, most psycho-therapists would agree on the fact that evil is constitutive of our nature as humans: we are selves composed of both good *and* bad parts, which means our badness is normal and needs to be acknowledged as such. Evil is a part of us, expressing itself in mild or extreme forms. This stands for a double substantialization of evil, this time on the part of therapists and not evil-suf-ferers: we are doing/suffering evil, because we are all partly evil beings. By supporting such a view against Augustine's metaphysical treatment of evil, which he radically misconstrued (see Pârvan 2013), C. G. Jung argued that the badness of human nature is such that it makes us capable of an 'infinite amount of evil' (Jung 1959, pp. 46, 49–54ff.). Augustine is mentioned by other psychotherapists in their examination of evil, but his ideas, besides being often misunderstood, are not explored or put to any practical use (de Zulueta 2006, pp. 19–33, 342; Swinton 2007, pp. 22–6; Mason 2006, pp. 93–4; Adshead 2002, p. 5; Kinzie 2006, p. 254; Alford 1997, p. 118; Goldberg 1996, p. 10; Powell 2002, p. 8).

In the following, I will both examine Augustine's views on evil and pro-pose ways for them to be practically worked with and support healing interventions, in clinical and non-clinical *secular* contexts.[6] His metaphysics indicates how it is possible to recognize the reality and pervasiveness of evil without substantializing it in action or being, and also without confusing action and being.

Augustine's account of evil and its therapeutic potential

Ontological deprivation and wrongful habituation in evildoers

For Augustine, everything that is possesses metaphysical goodness (*conf.* 7,12,18)[7] by the intrinsic and valuable attributes of mode (or measure), form and order that define every being or substance (*nat. b.* 23; 14; 3; 6; *lib. arb.* 2,20,54; *civ.* 11,15; 12,5; *vera rel.* 18,35). A substance is that which makes a thing be what it is (*en. Ps.* 68 I,5), and every substance is a good unto itself,[8] although it may relate with others in ways that lack agreement or accordance (*conf.* 7,13,19; *mor.* 2,11–12). Nothing destructs itself by its very act of being, of existing, which means that evil exists without a being of its own,[9] and therefore it is not some-thing, but *nothing*, not any particular thing or object.

Having no being, in order to exist evil must occur in a being: it is *nothing* existing on something, which it corrupts by the very fact that it deprives that something of a degree of goodness that properly belongs to it. Thus, Augustine calls evil *privatio boni*, the deprivation of good.[10] This means evil is being less, *minus esse* (*doctr. chr.* 1,32,35; *lib. arb.* 2,20,54; 3,7,21; *mor.* 2,2; 2,8; 2,9; *imm. an.* 7,12; *ench.* 11; *c. Iul.* 1,9,42; *civ.* 12,7; *vera rel.* 17,34; *en. Ps.* 38,7 and 22; 143,11; *nat. b.* 17; *s.* 7,7). It represents a lack of something that ought to be there in the deprived substance, whether it be a quality previously possessed or one whose due acquisition failed (see Patout Burns 1988, p. 12).

---

6 For the limited scope and length of this chapter I will single out and comment only on the main elements of his metaphysical conception of evil, which I think can be employed regardless of the religious or non-religious views of therapists, clients or others. To keep a focused and balanced interdisciplinary discourse, dialogue with Augustine's interpreters on particular aspects of his theory of evil will be restricted to a minimum.

7 All references and citations from Augustine are taken from *Patrologia Latina* (PL), texts available at www.augustinus.it (= PL 32–45). The translations are mine. The abbreviations of Augustine's works follow those used by the *Augustinus-Lexikon*, available on the website www.augustinus.de, with the exception of replacing 'u' with 'v' where appropriate.

8 'Every nature is good' (*omnis natura bonum est*; *ench.* 13). Augustine uses 'nature', 'being' and 'substance' mostly interchangeably.

9 'no substance is evil' (*nulla substantia malum est*; *vera rel.* 16,32; 20,38). The same in *civ.* 11,9; *mor.* 2,2. See further *mor.* 2,3. Or: 'evil is not a substance' (*malum non esse substantiam*; *cont.* 8,21).

10 'Evil is but deprivation of good' (*Non est ergo malum nisi privatio boni*; *c. adv. leg.* 1,5,7). The same in *c. Iul.* 1,9,42; *ench.* 11; *conf.* 3,7,12; 7,12,18; *civ.* 11,22.

Psychotherapists working in forensic settings have often noted the failed or undermined acquisition and diminished possession of intellectual, emotional and volitional capacities in evildoers and their sense of being fundamentally flawed and incompetent as human beings.[11] According to both Augustine and psychotherapeutic theories, evildoers are also victims of evil. To Augustine, any disruption of nature brings about evil, which is why he calls it deprivation (*privatio*), deficiency (*defectio*), lack (*amissio*), disorder (*inordinatio*), perversion (*perversio*), corruption (*corruptio*) or incongruity (*inconvenientia*) (*mor.* 2,5; 2,7; 2,8; 2,11–12; *civ.* 11,22; 11,9; 12,6–7; *Gn. litt.* 8,14,31; *div. qu.* 6; 30). A similar language is to be found in psychotherapeutic literature: deprivation, deficiency, lack, loss, disorganization, absence are the terms used to account for the evil suffered as the developmental origin of evildoers' personality (see for instance Bowlby 1984; Winnicott 1975, pp. 306–15; de Zulueta 2006; Gilligan 1996). Those who discuss the various abuses suffered by violent offenders in early childhood in the relationships with their primary caregivers under the general term of 'deprivation' (originally coined by John Bowlby as 'maternal deprivation') are thus emphasizing the negativity of evil: it is not just something present or latent (our evil parts) but also something being absent, something we were supposed to have but failed to have due to relational and environmental failures. And it is not just privation, but deprivation, indicating that something essential and good is denied to the child, an experience called by Winnicott 'the original loss' (Winnicott 1975, p. 313).

An important difference between Augustine's concept of deprivation and the psychotherapeutic one is that the latter acknowledges only the psychological and not the ontological negativity of evil. This affects both how the damaged person is seen ('deprived, but good' in Augustine; 'bad because deprived' in therapeutic theories) and how that person is treated. Moreover, for Augustine, deprivation is something to which one submits oneself, rather than something to which one is submitted by others. These two different views impinge upon how deprived persons may be motivated to understand and relate to their experiences: 'I was an active part of something bad that happened to me' or 'something bad happened to me'. The psychotherapeutic notion of deprivation also raises the question of violent offenders' degree of responsibility for their offences, given that these emerge from lacks externally inflicted on their personalities. Still, an element of self-deprivation can be identified in psychotherapeutic accounts as well, as it is actually a double deprivation that takes place: the emotional malnutrition to which deprived children are subjected (lack of love and care) induces them to suppress their feelings (pain, rage, fear, love) and thus to emotion-

---

11 Adshead 2002, pp. 1–9; 2006, pp. 259–71. Also her BBC interviews in 2009 and 2010, http://www.bbc.co.uk/programmes/b00vw20v; http://www.bbc.co.uk/radio3/free-thinking/2009/events/event09.shtml; Gilligan 1996, pp. 118, 127, 129; Goldberg 1996, pp. 45, 70–1, 147, 240; de Zulueta 1997, p. 203; 2006, pp. 6, 12, 329.

ally deprive themselves as a means of self-protection (see, for instance, de Zulueta 2006, p. 148; Gilligan 1996, p. 53).

For good reasons, in psychotherapeutic scholarship the focus is not on self-deprivation (a term that is not used at all). Yet looking at deprivation as not only something that happened to individuals but as something to which they contributed as well may advance understanding of why not all of those who have been abused turn into abusers themselves. It also indicates that the fact that most of those not submitted to deprivation in early childhood do not turn into violent abusers in adulthood is not due just to the 'moral luck' of not having been caught in the vicious circle of violence–trauma–violence (cf. Watson 2004, pp. 244–6; Arpaly 2003, pp. 169–73; Martin 2006, p. 127). Furthermore, I think that Augustine's view on the negativity of deprivation as primarily ontological and not psychological, as well as on the connection between ontological deprivation and individual will, can prove useful for psychotherapeutic work both with perpetrators and victims of evil.

According to psychotherapeutic theories, evildoers' psychic structures are pervaded with lacks in their reasoning, moral emotions and agency, that is, in their moral identity. Their *morally* impaired identity is based on deficient patterns of relationship and action, congruent with those they experienced in infancy, which restrict their freedom to act differently and bind them to enact and perpetuate destructive behaviour (Adshead 2002, p. 3; de Zulueta 2006, pp. 150–1, 324; Goldberg 1996, pp. 143–62, 166). Augustine noted that by reiteration morally faulty actions build up a force of habit (*consuetudo*), which binds the moral agents to defective modes of operating, diminishing their capacities to break free from them (*s.* 98,6; 242; *c. Fort.* 22; *en. Ps.* 5,6; *vera rel.* 35,65; 21,41; *ord.* 1,1,3; *s. dom. m.* 1,12,34; *conf.* 8,5,10–12; 10,40,65; *civ.* 12,3). Yet Augustine would say that the lacks go deeper than what is morally formed in wrongdoers, pervading their *ontological* structure, which consists in their being, knowing and willing (*esse–nosse–velle*) (*conf.* 13,11,12). This means the lacks are not what evildoers *are*, but instead point to something still present, on which the lacks are parasitic: their good and deprived substance.

Looking through such a framework, we can say that before those capacities that are impaired in evildoers can be morally exercised they have to be first *formed* as capacities. For instance, forensic therapists usually emphasize the evildoers' inability to own their agency and experience, but regard this strictly as a moral impairment (sometimes supported by psychological defence mechanisms) and not as an ontological deficiency. Instead, for Augustine a bad will is self-negating, is a deficient will, one that expresses itself by way of what it lacks, or what it fails to be (*civ.* 12,7). That is why I would say that in Augustine the will cannot be genuinely owned in bad actions, even though all bad actions are voluntary (*civ.* 12,3; 8; 5,10; *vera rel.* 14,27; *retr.* 1,13,5; 1,15,3; *conf.* 7,3,5), because these emerge from a will falling short of itself, a self-deprived will. Wrong actions are de-forming the will as a capacity, so that although it remains ontologically good, the will cannot be exercised in morally good actions unless it undergoes further formation.[12] If we follow Augustine, even those hardened into evil habits are able to opt for a different use of the will, when their *ontological deprivation* is met with appropriate aid.

Thus, instead of working to make clients willing to accept responsibility for their faulty actions, therapists could first help them form and acknowledge their will as a faculty. Taking Augustine's line, this would entail for clients to first acknowledge a level on which their will is good (as part of human nature) and to explore that ontological goodness. For Augustine, the will as a faculty can be known (as will) outside moral contexts (*lib. arb.* 1,12,25), and to know you have a will is prerequisite for the exercise of a good will, in the pursuit of understanding and goodness. In therapeutic settings, helping clients to know and exercise their will in morally *neutral* activities may enable them to own their will *when* and *as* exercised in moral contexts as well.[13] This process is also facilitated if they learn to distinguish between the two levels of their will and, consequently, that they can rely on the ontological goodness of their will, and in fact even increase it, even when admitting to a wilful morally faulty action.

Approaching clients beyond the level of their flawed moral identity in order for them to acknowledge their ontological capacities that remain good even when de-formed, is a way to affirm clients' fundamental goodness that may constitute the first step to their forming a good and *healing* will, one that would work against self-deprivation. This approach requires therapists to recognize both the *ontological* deprivation and the *ontological* goodness that are present in their clients. This way of working can apply both to evil-doers and evil-sufferers because the defective quality of evil affects them in the same way: by deprivation, experienced as inner disorder.

Deprivation in Augustine connotes both goodness (ontological) and perversion (moral disorder). His concept of *consuetudo* reflects the interweaving and interplay between the two, and thus I consider it to give continuity to his two accounts of evil, metaphysical and experiential, which are treated separately and seen either as compatible or incompatible in contemporary scholarship (Grumett 2000, pp. 157, 159; Mathewes 2001; Miller 2011, pp. 390–7; Brachtendorf 2000, pp. 79–92; Maker 1984, pp. 149–60; Hick

---

12 It can be argued that in Augustine this formative role is played by grace, which *ontologically* builds a de-formed will, one that is consequently either subdued to habit, or divided and 'incomplete' (*non tota, conf.* 8,9,21), making it coherent and strong enough to be able to formulate and enact *morally* good choices.

13 This is not quite what Augustine would recommend as he thought that one can reach awareness of one's own will purely intellectually, irrespective of both moral or practical applications. Also it is the *moral* exercise of the will that is formative not only of one's will but of one's being. However, as I have presented his view, a previous formative intervention is required before one becomes apt to exercise a good will.

1978, pp. 53–8).[14] Perversion is indicative of the ontological deprivation (lessened reason and will) that supports it, and which is in turn generated and increased by moral failure. An act that injures or corrupts one's nature causing it to lose its corresponding integrity or goodness is a morally flawed act. Thinking with Augustine, we can say that inasmuch as evil-sufferers are in a condition where they use their reason and will deficiently, towards self-deprivation, they too are not only ontologically deprived but also *morally* flawed, lacking inner order and binding themselves to damaging habits.

Therapeutic uses of the distinction between being and action

In Augustine, therefore, evil is a bad functioning of something that is good in itself, and in fact he states that 'Only something good can be evil'.[15] As *privatio boni*, evil has secondary and dependent existence, and thus it is self-defeating: if it destroys completely the nature on which it is parasitic, then evil ceases to exist itself (*c. ep. Man.* 35,40; *nat. b.* 17; 4; 6; 9; 13; 3; 19; *ench.* 11; 12; 13; 14; *conf.* 7,12,18; *civ.* 12,3; 5; *mor.* 2,7). Its very presence proves the goodness of the nature it damages or corrupts (*civ.* 12,3; also *lib. arb.* 3,13,36), which means that the person 'totally identified with evil' (Mollon 2000, p. 71; Ivey 2002, p. 58; 2005, p. 205; Hering 1997, p. 212) from the psychotherapeutic accounts of evil is an ontological impossibility.[16] Thinking in Augustine's terms, as long as perpetrators of evil are not completely deprived of being, they remain good (*vera rel.* 13,26; *conf.* 7,12,18), in the same way that all other humans are good, and in a way that they can never be evil. Enabling them to gain awareness of this in therapy may facilitate change, because it offers clients a legitimate way to entertain their sense of being good and empowers them to explore it and use it as a resourceful ground favourable to developing their relational goodness as well. This perspective can also positively motivate them, because it assumes that their goodness of being is maintained and further formed, when they exercise goodness towards the other, and that this capacity for moral goodness is contained in the goodness of nature. This would be an alternative to the classic therapeutic approach of recognizing the evil in clients' selves

---

14 It has not been yet noticed that Augustine's two conceptions of evil (ontological and experiential) are contrasted by his two conceptions of God, which correspond to the two names he revealed to Moses (Ex. 3.14–15), the first describing what God is in himself ('I am that I am'), the second what he is for humans through his historical engagement with them, 'the God of Abraham, Isaac and Jacob' (*s.* 223/A, 5; *s.* 6,4–5). I would further add that this facilitates an argument for the coherence of his views on evil.

15 *Non igitur potest esse malum, nisi aliquod bonum* (*ench.* 13). See also *ench.* 14; *c. adv. leg.* 1,5,7; *civ.* 12,3; *c. Iul. imp.* 5,44; 41, 43.

16 'There cannot be a nature in which there is no good' (*esse autem natura, in qua nullum bonum sit, non potest*; *civ.* 19,13,2). See also *c. Iul.* 1,8,36; *c. Iul. imp.* 3,196; *mor.* 2,14; *nat. b.* 1; 17.

(substantialization) in order to help them integrate it with the good, where evil and good are both considered parts of human nature.[17]

By working with the view that nothing substantially evil exists, therapists can enable clients to de-substantialize evil by avoiding or revoking the identification of *an action* (whether done or suffered) with *a being*, whether the offender's, the victim's, or evil's presumed independent entity. This distinction between being and action benefits both therapists' approaches and clients' therapeutic progress, and it is highlighted by Augustine in his rather famous saying, 'Hate the vice and love the human being.'[18] Our evil wills do not inaugurate a different, evil nature in us, so that beyond all evil deeds there remains always our good nature, which cannot be taken away by vices (*gr. et pecc. or.* 1,19,20; 2,40,46; *mus.* 6,11,30), because these are not what constitute but what damage our being.[19] Our actions have ontological effects (they either construct or deconstruct our being) but do not replace our substance with another (*gr. et pecc. or.* 2,40,46), as 'corruption in itself is not a substance'.[20] Hence, Augustine's counsel: 'Love the human being more than you hated the error.'[21] He advises us to treat wrongdoers both by admonition and a formative type of love, which loves in them the human being who *is* good by nature, as a way to help them *do* good, amend the error, and become worthy of the love offered, leaving nothing more to be hated.[22] What one does or what one suffers is never what one is, and by

---

17 Whether we are considered to *be* evil (the 'death instinct' theory), or to *become* evil (due to deficient interactions with others), psychotherapeutic theories typically substantialize evil by making no distinction between our ontological and moral status. Ironically, the death instinct concept was criticized as a replica of the 'original sin' construct, and even linked back to Augustine's theory of original sin (de Zulueta 2006, pp. 19–33), when this in fact states that our nature remains good even though flawed (*gr. et pecc. or.* 2,33,38; 40,46).

18 *oderit vitium, amet hominem* (*civ.* 14,6).

19 *lib. arb.* 3,13,36; 38; *vera rel.* 11,21; 18,35; 19,37; 23,44; *civ.* 12,3; *doctr. chr.* 1,32,35; *c. Iul.* 1,8,36; *c. Iul. imp.* 3,206. That is why 'When the vice is healed no evil remains, because the vice was indeed in nature, but the vice was not nature.' *Sanato autem vitio nullum malum remanet; quia vitium naturae quidem inerat, sed vitium natura non erat* (*gr. et pecc. or.* 1,19,20).

20 *non enim substantia est ipsa corruptio* (*mor.* 2,7). Similarly in *en. Ps.* 68 I,5, where he also adds that 'Vices come from our will and are not substances' (*Vitia enim ex nobis et ex nostra voluntate habemus; et vitia non sunt substantia*). See *civ.* 14,6: 'Whoever is evil is evil by vice, and not by nature' (*Et quoniam nemo natura, sed quisquis malus est, vitio malus est*).

21 *Plus amate hominem, quam prius oderatis errorem* (*s.* 279).

22 *ep. Io. tr.* 7,11; *civ.* 14,6; *c. Faust.* 19,24; *ep.* 153,1,3; *trin.* 9,6,11; 8,6,9. It thus happens that 'It has to do rather with humanity than with iniquity that one prosecutes the offence in order to free the human being.' *Non est igitur iniquitatis, sed potius humanitatis societate devinctus, qui propterea est criminis persecutor, ut sit hominis liberator* (*ep.* 153,1,3). The objection of some authors who argued that it is difficult and even undesirable to distinguish between wrongdoers and their acts (Neu 2002, pp. 24–8; Murphy 2002, pp. 46–7; Martin 2006, pp. 125–7) comes from their failure to separate between a person's moral and metaphysical standing, and in the case of those who also

appreciating this distinction (whether with therapeutic assistance or not) one can take the proper actions towards what one experiences.

Drawing such a distinction allows therapists to be both *not* morally neutral and *non*-judgemental towards their clients, and to break the vicious circle in which a strictly moral approach to evil locks their work with evildoers. Both therapists' and clients' need for the former to take a moral stance towards the actions of the latter has long been pointed out, but to date it has only taken the form of 'hate the person'. In 1947, D. W. Winnicott referred to this as therapists' 'objective hate' (1975, pp. 194–203), and recently, Sue Grand argued in favour of a therapist's 'object-related hatred', which is to be balanced with 'object-related concern' (2002, pp. 97, 147–59). By these therapeutic 'twin' attitudes, the client is both recognized/known as evil and condemned/contained as such by the therapist. However, if most perpetrators of evil turned into evildoers, because in their early life they were severely deprived of love and basic human warmth, then to hate them as persons might not be the most effective therapeutic attitude. Moreover, it is difficult both to experience and convey *objective* hate. The attitude that Augustine recommends usefully separates the levels on which love and hate are offered to the same person and avoids the risk of the giver stopping at hate and condemnation without communicating love as well or of confusing the recipient as to what the love and hate are targeted at. Hating what evildoers did and affirming their value as human beings offers them a way to think of *themselves* as good that discourages their rationalizations and creation of a parallel morality meant to justify their *actions* as good, while it also responds to their intellectual concerns regarding evil.[23]

Evildoers' refusal to take responsibility for their actions as *evil* springs precisely from the identification between being and action endorsed both by psychotherapists and our general way of thinking. The same identification makes such clients flee responsibility, as a way to preserve a sense that they *are* good, and makes therapists intent on having them accept that 'what one does is what one is', or else one is 'not being the agent of one's life, one's acts' (Grand 2002, p. 67). But this is precisely what the act of taking responsibility *is not*: when I am assuming responsibility for something I have done, I am affirming that I, as a human being, am more than my actions, and therefore can rise critically above them. If I identify myself with my acts, as acted out, it means that I am *not* their agent and therefore not free to act otherwise, whether before, *during* or after any of my actions. Evildoers refuse to be trapped as *evil* in their evil actions, either by appropriating

refer to Augustine (Neu, Murphy), to acknowledge that his discourse is based on this distinction.

23 Clients do sometimes pose metaphysical questions about evil, such as 'Does it have a life of its own?' (Goldberg 1996, p. 217). These are crucial to how they see themselves and construct their actions, which is why I think therapists should recognize their speculative character and meet them with an appropriate ontological understanding of evil rather than bypassing such queries with technical approaches.

the generally accepted identification but inverted through rationalizations (my actions are good/justified, so I am good) or by disconnecting their self from their actions (these are not my actions). In both cases, therapists can motivate them to assume responsibility for evil acts by emphasizing the distinction between their self and their actions, as a way to work towards restoring the proper connection between them.[24]

Commenting on Augustine's prescribed treatment of the wicked, who are to be loved as human beings and hated for their wicked wills, Frederick Russell inferred that 'Since we should both love and hate one and the same person Augustine introduced a profound ambivalence into human social relations' (Russell 1990, p. 708). In fact, as we are not to love and hate the same person on account of the same owned quality (the first is ontological, the second ethical), I think Augustine actually indicates how we can avoid the contradictory ambivalence that therapists aspire to practise towards their clients. In psychodynamic theories this kind of ambivalence where the ethical appropriates the ontological is also regarded as a major developmental achievement: that is, to be able to love and hate the same object in its duality, where the object's function, action or relation to the subject are identified with what the object *is* (e.g. mother *is* both good and bad) (Klein 1975; Fairbairn 2001). I suggest that working with Augustine's non-contradictory ambivalence both in therapeutic settings and outside them would facilitate less conflicting modes of relating both to ourselves and the other, ward off a self-defeating sense of self and establish a connection between our self and our actions that would empower our sense of agency and call forth responsibility.

Evil as a relation and the impermanence of evil actions

In Augustine, evil is a relation between substances, which means it is an act (or activity) and not a thing or a person and actions are not substances (*vera rel.* 20,39). This idea has potential therapeutic value, because it implies that an evil act cannot subsist by itself, and if it endures and remains active to harm us, it is because we chose to substantialize and solidify it.

Augustine's metaphysical theory of evil presents our common way of understanding things with a double difficulty. First, we tend to take actions to be *something* (or things, and not relations between them). Murder or torture are to be considered evil, but they do not exist by themselves; they are activities, and depend on the relation in which two ontologically good substances are placing themselves. Second, we tend to take the words in our vocabulary (evil included) to denote things that have being, or else we would

---

24 Notably, Tangney and Stuewig (2004) have shown the importance for perpetrators of evil deeds not to infer that they are evil persons. However, despite the self-behaviour distinction they use, for the authors the self *too* is what one *does*, not what one *is*, which is what brings them to affirm that some persons *are* evil (i.e. psychopaths).

not have a word for them, or be able to speak of them. Taking Augustine's view, evil exists in such a way that we can speak of it only through that which is affected by it and not directly through what evil is, because evil is nothing, it has no being of its own.

Because it is experienced as deprivation of being, we tend to think there must be *something* that deprives us, and we then treat evil as *something* that ought not to be (substantialization) instead of an experience of there not being what ought to be there. Conveying to clients that whatever they take to be evil in them (their hurts, their dispositions) has only parasitic existence, and remains active because sustained by the good that gets damaged by it, may stimulate them to refuse to give substantial support to evil actions and feel less acted upon by these as given, fixed, autonomous and damaging realities. When they are substantializing evil both evil sufferers and evildoers are acting, passively and actively, as their own aggressors: if evil is independent and unchangeable, it means that all they can do is to be its victims. As victims, they freeze their capacity to transform their relation with the experience of evil and continue to host it and be consumed by it by submitting themselves to similar processes: they identify an act with a person or thing, substantialize that person/thing as evil, and suffer a loss of their personal agency, which is partly assigned to the evil entity. They consequently also lose in part their sense of being real and responsible, entertaining the illusion that these belong to someone/something else. When solidified an evil action is empowered with qualities it does not possess (substance, persistence, agency), and thus enhanced in its function and effects by one's action of self-deprivation.

As lack of being, or a substance falling short of its corresponding integrity, whether experienced as a loss or a failure, evil has tremendous, devastating, real effects. At the same time, also as a lack, evil depends entirely on that *something* it lives upon (either our or others' being), and in order to affect its actions we need to put ourselves in relation to that something. Following Augustine this would mean to turn our attention from the lacks to the being damaged by them, which needs to be further formed in its ontological capacities (reason and will) in order for its internal disorder to be reduced through a better use of these capacities. Therapists could support this process by facilitating a change of focus in clients from what was done to them by someone else, something they suffered in the past, to what they are actively doing in the present to keep alive that evil action inside them, and what they can do instead that would not count as a further self-depriving action. This stimulates their sense of agency, responsibility, and their co-operation in establishing an order of action that would be less dictated by deprivation, and more by a formative ordering of volitions, actions and appreciation of things in their proper value, reality and power.

The damaging dynamic of an evil action is not self-generated since evil is not an independent force, and therein lies its weakness, as well as, sometimes, its power. In substantializing it, we mistake it for the substance that allows for its power to exist, whether the one that brought it about, or the one that suffers it and increases it within.

Our response-able being and evil's weakness

Psychotherapists insist on telling their clients or their readers that there is no evil force outside, but an evil side of each of us, within ourselves (Hering 1997, p. 215; Ivey 2005, p. 204; Powell 2002, p. 9; Messler Davies 2004, pp. 728–9; Diamond 2005, pp. 189–99). But in my view, it is all the same: outside, inside, it does not matter, if evil is substantialized it navigates from inside to outside and vice versa, and we can imagine it or place it wherever, but we would still be fighting nothing, while making this nothing undefeatable.

A view that either in ourselves or others, whether suffered or enacted, evil is a lack of inner order and unity could be usefully worked with in therapy. Therapists can motivate and guide clients to replace the power within themselves by understanding evil as a non-substantial, relational, dependent and secondary reality. As a lack, even if experienced as disorder (or wrongful habituation), evil is weak: it cannot impose its being or its agency on ours because it does not have them.[25] Evil exists through our actions but we cannot create substances by them, and the defective actions of others can have over us only the power that we allow them to have, through our will and mind. Augustine reasoned that no spiritual being can have its goodness corrupted by another against its consent; the human spirit can remain unaffected by the actions of other humans even when the body cannot (*lib. arb.* 3,14,39–41). When raped, a woman can use her will to withhold its assent to the *action* forced on her and to work towards preserving her integrity of spirit and thereby fend off guilt and the need to punish herself for the violence done to her body (*civ.* 1,18). Such a focus on the responsibility for one's being and inward, free action over one's outward, imposed behaviour and the behaviour of others can be a useful tool for therapists working with trauma victims or clients suffering regular (domestic) abuse.

Augustine therefore thought that we can suffer without being damaged, and if we are, it is because we too are making it happen. Indeed, we are not simply an object of someone else's action: even at the moment when we are suffering harm we can choose either to support the deprivation inflicted on us, or to act in a way that would counter it. We are not just in a position

---

25 *Consuetudo* is supported by a constant *surrender* of *our* will to bad choices. Cochran (2006, pp. 51–72) argued that for Augustine evil as sin has both power and ontological status, although inferior to goodness, because otherwise there will be no need for it to be overcome by Christ's works. Her point disregards that in Augustine sin alters our nature but does not become a nature in itself that works within us; it still lacks *substantial* existence, and, speaking in ontological terms, our perverted nature represents something good existing in a disordered way. That is why Christ's work of salvation is not accomplished so much by defeating evil as by reforming our natures.

of 'being done-to', we can also act as 'response-able' human beings, to use a Gestalt therapy formula.[26] Augustine's viewpoint is mirrored by a therapeutic Gestalt principle which says that 'I am responsible for me and you are responsible for you'. This means that no matter what the other is doing to me, I am the primary agent of my own experience, the one determining my behaviour, and ultimately responsible for my own well-being. The same view is reflected in the rational emotive behaviour therapy principle that no one has any control over me except me, no one can control what I think, feel or am, but me.

We ourselves, a therapist, or someone who assists us in our suffering can help us become aware when we are substantializing an evil and start polarizing ourselves, guarding against it, or fearing it, keeping it alive. Once we identify what is the substantialized evil for us and inside us, we can work to de-substantialize it and thereby move out of the position of helpless victim passively aggressively suffering harm, into the position of someone who activates and supplies more abundantly their own inner resources, thus countering deprivation and its effects.

Concluding remarks

Augustine's thought introduces us to a world-view in which evil is a weak, defective activity, with dependent existence and no agency of its own, made possible, pervasive and persistent only when we give it *substantial* support. Evil is active by way of what someone is lacking in (*minus esse*, their being less), and not because of *something* powerful being present, which means it can be overcome by one's enhancement of being (*magis esse*).

The difficulties of transferring such a view into the theoretical and practical frames of various psychotherapeutic approaches assuming and working with a double ontology (human nature is both good and bad) should not be underestimated, because it would require them to adopt something contrary to their theoretical scheme and integrate it in such a way as to make it work in practice, without affecting the consistency of their method. Distinct ways of accomplishing this need to be investigated for particular psychotherapeutic orientations, but until further exploration will be undertaken I want to indicate a few reasons for which I think such an undertaking would be worthwhile.

When imported into the framework of psychotherapeutic thought and practice Augustine's theory can help therapists avoid the double substantialization of evil (in one's actions and one's being), which has so far generated ambivalent discourses on and attitudes towards the reality of evil as reflected in the experiences of clients. Operating with a joint metaphysical–ethical

---

26 The situation is different in the case of abused children, not least because they have fewer resources to operate with a distinction between what they experience (action) and their own self (being).

understanding of evil, which separates between the ontological dimension (someone's being) and the moral dimension (someone's actions), facilitates therapists' exercise of both moral and non-judgemental stances towards their clients favourable to building a good therapeutic alliance, and allows for a non-contradictory call to responsibility in clients: to know and accept themselves as agents they need not be identified with their actions. In addition, therapists can guide clients to resist a particular double substantialization of evil that hinders their healing process, and is based on the same identification of being with action (the harming person/thing is evil) and of action with being (the harming experience is solidified as evil). Promoting a clear distinction between the two, therapists can precipitate a change of focus in clients from past or passive experience, objectifying the self, to present, agentive action oriented towards self-reconstruction. Also, an understanding of evil done and suffered as indicative of *ontological* deprivation can point to therapeutic interventions centred on that which needs to be formed in clients rather than corrected or mended.

What Augustine tells us, and can be transformed into healing approaches, in professional and non-professional contexts, is that evil is devastating because it is *nothingness* penetrating inside being, and it is therefore by growing our will, our knowledge and our love that we can fill the gaps of evil and restore the powerful substance of its host: our very being.

References

Adshead, G. (2002), 'Capacities and dispositions: reflections on Good and Evil from a forensic psychiatrist', published on the Royal College of Psychiatrists 'Spirituality and Psychiatry Special Interest Group' website: http://www.rcpsych.ac.uk/PDF/adshead. pdf.

Adshead, G. (2006), 'Capacities and dispositions. What psychiatry and psychology have to say about evil', in Mason (ed.), *Forensic Psychiatry*, pp. 259–71.

Alford, C. F. (1997), *What Evil Means to Us*, Ithaca NY: Cornell University Press.

Arpaly, N. (2003), *Unprincipled Virtue: An Inquiry into Moral Agency*, Oxford: Oxford University Press.

Bowlby, J. (1984), 'Violence in the family as a disorder of the attachment and caregiving systems', *American Journal of Psychoanalysis* 44:1, pp. 9–27.

Brachtendorf, J. (2000), 'The goodness of creation and the reality of evil. Suffering as a problem in Augustine's theodicy', *Augustinian Studies* 31:1, pp. 79–92.

Burns, J. P., Goodman, D. M., Orman, A. J. (2012), 'Psychotherapy as moral encounter: a crisis of modern conscience', *Pastoral Psychology* 62:1, pp. 1–12, doi:10.1007/ s11089-012-0456-x.

Cochran, E. A. (2006), '*At the Same Time Blessed and Lame*: ontology, christology and violence in Augustine and John Milbank', *Journal for Christian Theological Research* 11, pp. 51–72.

de Zulueta, F. (1997), 'Demonology versus science?', *British Journal of Psychotherapy* 14:2, pp. 199–208.

de Zulueta, F. (2006), *From Pain to Violence: The Traumatic Roots of Destructiveness*, Chichester: Wiley and Sons.

Diamond, S. A. (2005), 'Psychotherapy, evil, and the daimonic: toward a secular spiritual psychology', in Richard H. Cox, Betty Ervin-Cox, Louis Hoffman (eds), *Spirituality and Psychological Health*, Colorado Springs CO: Colorado School of Professional Psychology Press.

Fairbairn, W. R. D. (2001), *Psychoanalytic Studies of the Personality*, New York: Routledge.

Gilligan, J. (1996), *Violence: Our Deadly Epidemic and Its Causes*, New York: G. P. Putnam's Sons.

Goldberg, C. (1996), *Speaking with the Devil: A Dialogue with Evil*, New York: Viking/Penguin.

Grand, S. (2002), *The Reproduction of Evil: A Clinical and Cultural Perspective*, Hillsdale NJ: Analytic Press.

Greig, D. (1996), 'Criminal responsibility and the concept of evil', *Psychiatry, Psychology and Law* 3:2, pp. 163–78.

Grumett, D. (2000), 'Arendt, Augustine and evil', *Heythrop Journal* 41:2, pp. 154–69.

Hall Davis, M. (2008), 'Perspectives on evil: Structures of evil encountered in pastoral counseling', *Zygon* 43:3, pp. 665–80.

Hering, C. (1997), 'Beyond Understanding? Some thoughts on the meaning and function of the notion of *evil*', *British Journal of Psychotherapy* 14:2, pp. 209–20.

Hick, J. (1978), *Evil and the God of Love*, San Francisco: Harper & Row.

Ivey, G. (2002), 'Diabolical discourses: demonic possession and evil in modern psychopathology', *South African Journal of Psychology* 34:4, pp. 54–9.

Ivey, G. (2005), '*And What Rough Beast …?* Psychoanalytic thoughts on evil states of mind', *British Journal of Psychotherapy* 22:2, pp. 199–215.

Jung, C. G. (1959), 'Christ, a symbol of the self', in *The Collected Works of C. G. Jung*, Sir Herbert Read, Michael Fordham, Gerhard Adler (eds), trans. R. F. C. Hull, vol. 9II, London: Routledge & Kegan Paul.

Khan, M. M. R. (1989), *Hidden Selves: Between Theory and Practice in Psychoanalysis*, London: Karnac.

Kinzie, J. D. (2006), 'Evil – a clinical perspective', in Mason (ed.), *Forensic Psychiatry*, pp. 249–57.

Klein, M. (1975), *Envy and Gratitude and Other Works (1943–1963)*, London: Hogarth Press.

Levine, M. (2006), 'Mad, bad, and evil: psychiatry, psychoanalysis, and evil', in Mason (ed.), *Forensic Psychiatry*, pp. 295–312.

Maker, W. (1984), 'Augustine on evil: the dilemma of the philosophers', *International Journal for Philosophy of Religion* 15:3, pp. 149–60.

Martin, M. W. (2006), *From Morality to Mental Health: Virtue and Vice in a Therapeutic Culture*, Oxford: Oxford University Press.

Mason, T. (ed.) (2006), *Forensic Psychiatry: Influences of Evil*, Towawa NJ: Humana Press.

Mason, T. (2006), 'An archaeology of the psychopath: the medicalization of evil', in Mason (ed.), *Forensic Psychiatry*, pp. 89–108.

Mason, T., Richman, J. and Mercer, D. (2002), 'The influence of evil on forensic clinical practice', *International Journal of Mental Health Nursing* 11:2, pp. 80–93.

Mathewes, C. T. (2001), *Evil and the Augustinian Tradition*, Cambridge: Cambridge University Press.

Messler Davies, J. (2004), 'Whose bad objects are we anyway? Repetition and our elusive love affair with evil', *Psychoanalytic Dialogues* 14:6, pp. 711–32.

Miller, R. B. (2011), 'Evil, friendship, and iconic realism in Augustine's *Confessions*', *Harvard Theological Review* 104:4, pp. 387–409.

Mollon, P. (2000), 'Is human nature intrinsically abusive? Reflections on the psycho-dynamics of evil', in Una McCluskey and Carol-Ann Hooper (eds), *Psychodynamic Perspectives on Abuse: The Cost of Fear*, London: Jessica Kingsley.

Murphy, J. G. (2002), 'Forgiveness in counseling: a philosophical perspective', in Jeffrie G. Murphy and Sharon Lamb (eds), *Before Forgiving: Cautionary Views of Forgiveness in Psychotherapy*, Oxford: Oxford University Press, pp. 41–53.

Neu, J. (2002), 'To understand all is to forgive all – or is it?', in Murphy and Lamb (eds), *Before Forgiving*, pp. 17–38.

Pârvan, A. (2013), 'Jung, C. G.', in Karla Pollmann (ed.), *The Oxford Guide to the Historical Reception of Augustine*, Oxford: Oxford University Press.

Patout Burns, J. (1988), 'Augustine on the origin and progress of evil', *The Journal of Religious Ethics* 16:1, pp. 9–27.

Peck, M. S. (1983), *People of the Lie: The Hope for Healing Human Evil*, New York: Simon & Schuster.

Phillips, A. (1994), *On Flirtation*, London: Faber & Faber.

Powell, A. (2002), 'Good and Evil – a psychiatrist's perspective', published on the Royal College of Psychiatrists 'Spirituality and Psychiatry Special Interest Group' website: http://www.rcpsych.ac.uk/pdf/powell4.pdf.

Prins, H. (1994), 'Psychiatry and the concept of evil. Sick in heart or sick in mind?', *British Journal of Psychiatry* 165:3, pp. 297–302.

Royston, R. (2006), 'Destructiveness: revenge, dysfunction or constitutional evil?', in Celia Harding (ed.), *Aggression and Destructiveness: Psychoanalytic Perspectives*, London and New York: Routledge.

Russell, F. H. (1990), '*Only something good can be evil*: the genesis of Augustine's secular ambivalence', *Theological Studies* 51:4, pp. 698–716.

Růžička, J. (2010), 'Psychotherapy and the concepts of good and evil', *Existential Analysis* 21:2, pp. 193–208.

Schäfer, C. (2000), 'Augustine on mode, form, and natural order', *Augustinian Studies* 31:1, pp. 59–77.

Spinelli, E. (2000), 'A person view: therapy and the challenge of evil', *British Journal of Guidance and Counselling* 28:4, pp. 561–7.

Swinton, J. (2002), 'Does Evil have to exist to be real? The discourse of evil and the practice of mental health care', published on the Royal College of Psychiatrists 'Spirituality and Psychiatry Special Interest Group' website: http://www.rcpsych.ac.uk/pdf/swinton.pdf.

Swinton, J. (2007), *Raging with Compassion: Pastoral Responses to the Problem of Evil*, Grand Rapids MI: Eerdmans.

Tangney, J. P. and Stuewig, J. (2004), 'A moral–emotional perspective on evil persons and evil deeds', in Arthur G. Miller (ed.), *The Social Psychology of Good and Evil*, New York and London: Guilford Press, pp. 327–55.

Watson, G. (2004), *Agency and Answerability: Selected Essays*, Oxford: Oxford University Press.

Wilson, P. (2003), 'The concept of evil and the forensic psychologist', http://epublications.bond.edu.au/hss_pubs/31.

Winnicott, D. W. (1975), *Through Paediatrics to Psycho-Analysis*, London: Hogarth Press.

5

Exorcism

Some Theological, Psychoanalytic and Cultural Reflections on the Practice of Christian Deliverance Ministry in the Light of Clinical and Pastoral Experience

CHRISTOPHER MACKENNA

Summary

Exorcism – now widely referred to as deliverance ministry – is amenable to interpretation from a variety of disciplinary, pastoral and theological perspectives. It is considered here in the light of the author's clinical experience as a psychoanalytically trained Jungian analyst working with religiously distressed patients and his pastoral experience within the Church of England as a diocesan adviser in deliverance ministry and the paranormal, assisting parochial clergy with their work in this area. The case studies that are put forward for consideration demonstrate the need for a multi-professional and multidisciplinary approach to practice, and raise important questions concerning the nature of the self and the power of unconscious processes.

A theological perspective on deliverance

Within contemporary Christian pastoral practice the term 'deliverance ministry' is generally used to describe religious interventions designed to free a person or a place from oppression or possession by a malign or disturbing influence, believed to be of a spiritual nature (Working Party on Healing 2000, pp. 167ff.; Perry 1996; Richards 1974; Walker 1997). From a theological point of view, it is important to recognize that this focus is narrower than the Bible's overall understanding of deliverance, which is at least equally concerned with collective issues of social justice, political oppression and care for God's creation. The tragic experience of the Christian centuries is that narrower thinking about deliverance, especially in the form of exorcism, has sometimes exercised such fascination over peoples' minds that it has led to actions that were totally opposed to the wider perspective provided by the Bible (Cohn 1993).

Central to the biblical understanding of deliverance is the belief that the God who creates the cosmos and holds it in being, the God who calls the Patriarchs and raises up a Chosen People, is also the God who hears the cries of his people and delivers them from oppression. Within the Hebrew Scriptures and the life of the Jewish people, the story of their ancestors' enslavement in Egypt and their deliverance for the journey towards freedom in the Promised Land is re-enacted, annually, in the Passover festival. In this deliverance, personal, political and spiritual freedoms are intertwined. In turn, the Passover festival, with its promise of release from human oppression, is taken up and transformed in the life, death and resurrection of Jesus, celebrated weekly, daily even, at the altars of Christendom in the Holy Communion service, which anticipates our deliverance from the ultimate enslavement of death (Dix 1945, pp. 743ff.).

These themes, present throughout the Bible, are powerfully focused in St Luke's Gospel, which begins with the prediction of the birth of the Messiah, who will be called 'Jesus' – 'Joshua' in Hebrew and Aramaic – which means 'he will save' (Luke 1.26–38). The three great canticles with which the Gospel begins – the songs of Mary (Luke 1.46–55), Zechariah (Luke 1.68–79) and Simeon (Luke 2.29–32) – are all thanksgivings for deliverances, anticipated or received. When Jesus begins his public ministry, he does so by reading a key text from the prophet Isaiah, which anticipates the deliverance associated with the coming 'year' of the Lord:

> The Spirit of the Lord is upon me, because he has anointed me to bring good news to the poor. He has sent me to proclaim release to the captives and recovery of sight to the blind, to let the oppressed go free, to proclaim the year of the Lord's favour. (Luke 4.18–19 NRSV; compare Isa. 61.1–2; the whole chapter should be read)

Luke's Gospel illustrates how this prophecy was enacted in Jesus' ministry, until he prefaces the Last Supper – which will display the inner meaning of his career – with the words, 'I have eagerly desired to eat this Passover with you before I suffer; for I tell you, I will not eat it until it is fulfilled in the kingdom of God' (Luke 22.15–16).

Deliverance, in the Bible, always has this positive intent: moving us from slavery, of whatever kind, *towards* the freedom needed for loving service to God and to our neighbour. However great the deliverance we experience, here and now, it is never more than an anticipation of that complete deliverance that always lies before us in God's kingdom. From a theological point of view it is within this wide context that Jesus' more specific works of healing and deliverance should be understood (Eve 2009).

Spirit possession, Satan and evil in the New Testament

A significant fact, emerging from accounts of demon possession in the Synoptic Gospels, is that although the activities of the demons are described as unpleasant, and physically and mentally deleterious to their sufferers, they have little to do with the moral evil we might expect from the devil and his minions. By and large, they sound more like the symptoms of mental or physical distress. There are also passages where the devil has a more clearly defined personal presence (e.g. Mark 1.12–13 and parallels), but these passages are insufficient to resolve the uncertainty that runs through Christian thinking: is Satan a 'personal' being? Or is Satan language a mythological way of speaking about the power of evil and negativity to influence us; pictured by our minds in personal terms because we experience it as if it was the action of a personal being?

St Paul speaks of 'the elemental spirits of the world' (e.g. Gal. 4.3; Col. 2.8), but these appear to be forces that, although powerful, are more structural or psychological than demonic. Indeed, in his Letter to the Romans – one of the most sustained pieces of theological thinking in the New Testament – Paul discusses the nature of evil without reference to the devil, suggesting that the evil and disorder in creation can be traced to the fact that human beings, knowing God, have refused to honour God (Rom. 1.21). In place of Satan, Paul speaks of 'the law of sin' (e.g. Rom. 7.21–25), which functions with implacable and impersonal force. This non-demonic theology of evil must find a place in our thinking about deliverance ministry.

Turning to John's Gospel, we find that although John, like Paul in places, is open to devil language, he also has his own variant on Paul's impersonal 'law of sin'. John calls it 'darkness'. Like 'the law of sin', darkness appears to be akin to wilful unconsciousness: it fuzzes our thinking and makes us unwilling to come to the Light, which will expose the meaning of our actions (e.g. John 3.19–21). John also makes a number of references to the devil. Some are metaphorical, Judas is not literally a devil (6.70), or abusive, as when Jesus is accused of 'having' a devil (10.20). Others, though, suggest some degree of agency: the devil 'puts it into Judas' heart' to betray Jesus, and 'enters into him' (13.2, 27). Do such references require us to believe in a 'personal' devil? Or are they personified ways of describing the 'action' of darkness? My own belief is that, just as the ancient Greeks personified their own virtues and vices, and turned them into gods and goddesses, so our psyche, which dreams in mythological terms, has done the same with the devil. There is good cause for this: 'the law of sin' and 'darkness' are real. They impinge on us, and we experience their action in personal terms. Personal language is the only language that does justice to what we feel; but this does not mean that the devil is a personal being.

A psychological perspective on possession and deliverance

As well as seeking to locate itself within the overall framework of the Bible, a modern Christian approach to deliverance ministry must also take account of developments in psychology and psychiatry. If people were afflicted by evil spirits in Jesus' day, it seems likely that they will be so afflicted now; but what do we mean by spirit possession? Although the Bible assumes the existence of evil/unclean spirits, it provides little information about their origin and nature. They seem to be non-physical entities, possessed of a certain consciousness and volition, and able to be addressed, which cause physical and emotional harm to their victims. Such beliefs are almost universal, and in cultures way beyond the confines of the Bible. Why then, given the universality of such beliefs, does spirit possession feature so little in textbooks of psychiatry?

Psychiatry

The reason is that psychiatry, in the course of its development and in an attempt to qualify itself as a scientific enterprise, largely dispensed with subjectivity and with anything that looked like magic or religion (Cook, Powell and Sims 2009, p. 3). Instead of trying to understand what people were saying, in terms of their subjective experience, doctors were trained to scan their patients' communications for information that would enable them to classify their patients' illnesses according to certain diagnostic criteria. Mental illnesses were assumed to have physical causes. So while the patient might feel that he was possessed by an unclean spirit or demonized by tormenting voices, the doctor would see only 'psychotic depression' or a 'schizophrenic type illness'. There is value in these psychiatric classifications. Not all mental illnesses have psychological or spiritual causes, and those that do may become so severe that psychiatric intervention is essential. Equally, as will be illustrated below, some apparent cases of demon possession are directly attributable to mental illness and need to be recognized and treated as such.

In this field, as in so many others, we are suffering from the post-Enlightenment split between the physical sciences and more intuitive and spiritually informed approaches to knowledge. The gulf between these two worlds is partially bridged, however, by the psychodynamic approach initiated by Freud and greatly enriched by Jung and others, down to the present day.

Freud

Freud has had a bad press in some Christian and psychological circles (Webster 1995). As the pioneer of a movement, rather than its perfecter, he naturally threw up many ideas that have subsequently been modified or abandoned. One of his lasting achievements, though, was to provide us with a picture of the mind that is compatible with belief in evil/unclean spirits – so long as we are not wedded to unbiblical ideas about their origin and nature.

Like Paul, who wrestled with the dilemma of not being able to do the good that he wanted to do (Rom. 7.15–23), Freud was puzzled by mental and emotional conflict. What is it that interferes with our conscious intentions, sometimes to the extent of making us physically ill, even disabled, as Freud knew from the case of 'Anna O', attended by his colleague Josef Breuer, whose emotional conflicts had sometimes produced disturbing physical symptoms: headaches, distortions of vision, contractures of limbs, partial paralyses, and loss of sensation over areas of her body (Breuer and Freud 1955, pp. 21ff.)?

By attending to his own dreams and fantasies and to those of his patients, Freud became aware that our conscious sense of self – the Ego – is only a small part of our mental apparatus. Beneath it, to use a spatial metaphor, is an unconscious realm – Freud calls it the Id – that is home to our instinctual drives and to aspects of our experience we have unconsciously repressed, or of which we have never become aware. Over the ego, to use another spatial metaphor, is the Super Ego, which is like an internalized parent; a 'moral policeman' that exerts pressure on the ego as it struggles to maintain itself between the conflicting wishes and needs of the Id and of the outside world (Freud 1961, pp. 3–66). If we are unexpectedly overwhelmed by anger, lust or sadness, which seems to come from nowhere and dictates our feelings and actions, we might reasonably fear that we are being possessed by an alien force or personality. And indeed our ego has momentarily been oppressed or possessed – by a content arising from the unconscious. The notion of ego possession by an apparently independent force, which may well feel dangerous, unclean or evil, is written into psychoanalytic thinking (Fairbairn 1952).

Jung

Jung enlarged Freud's work in a number of directions (Stephenson 2009). Working with a Word Association Test, he found that the stimulus words that interfered with the volunteer's normal capacity to respond were all charged, in some way, with unresolved conflict and emotion. Often, by looking at the conflicted words, Jung was able to group them into families: little clusters of linked themes that he called 'feeling toned complexes'. He wrote:

> [C]omplexes always contain something like a conflict, or at least are either the cause or the effect of a conflict. At any rate the characteristics of conflict – shock, upheaval, mental agony, inner strife – are peculiar to the complexes. They are the 'sore spots', the *bêtes noires*, the 'skeletons in the cupboard' which we do not like to remember and still less to be reminded

of by others. They always contain memories, wishes, fears, duties, needs, or insights which somehow we can never really grapple with, and for this reason they constantly interfere with our conscious life in a disturbing and usually harmful way. (Jung 1971, p. 528)

Instead of our conscious ego being in control of our inner worlds, Jung suggested that it is only one complex among many although, hopefully, more durable and extensive than the others. Complexes sometimes behave like splinter personalities, and are often personified in dreams. In cases of multiple personality disorder, the ego is fragile and can be pushed aside by other complexes that demand to be treated as if they were the real person. These sub-personalities can have very different characters from the ego's and may be of the opposite sex. The Gadarene Demoniac, possessed by a legion of evil spirits, fits this picture well (Charet 1993).

The idea that our ego is not in control of our inner world can be alarming but, as Jung says, the existence of a complex means that:

Something discordant, unassimilated, and antagonistic exists, perhaps as an obstacle, but also as an incentive to greater effort, and so, perhaps, to new possibilities of achievement. In this sense, therefore, complexes are focal or nodal points of psychic life which we would not wish to do without; indeed, they should not be missing, for otherwise psychic activity would come to a fatal standstill. (Jung 1971, p. 529)

Troublesome as they can be, the 'sub-personalities' represented by the complexes can also provide the impetus, and the material, for growth. Within the Bible the figure of the Satan fulfils a similarly ambiguous role (Schärf Kluger 1967).

The interpersonal psychic world

Present in Jung's thought, and evident in more recent psychoanalytic thinking, is the belief that a complex belonging to one person's mind can be projected into another's, where it may function in a harmful or disabling way (Grotstein 1985). It is not uncommon, for example, to find oneself unaccountably feeling nervous, depressed or enraged in the presence of another person who claims, and may indeed appear, to be feeling relaxed. Within the tightly drawn psychoanalytic consultation these experiences of projective identification can be recognized and explored: do the feelings belong to the therapist? Or is the therapist experiencing emotions the patient is not yet able to feel for himself? In daily life, however, where there are no clear boundaries, it can be more difficult for us to know where our thoughts and feelings come from.

Families function as open psychological systems in which one child may be designated as the 'good' one, and another singled out as the 'bad' or 'sick' one. Unconsciously, the positive qualities of the family are then 'invested' in the first child, whereas the irreconcilable and unconscious conflicts in the parents' relationship get projected into the second child, whose increasingly disturbed behaviour only confirms the initial fantasy that that child would come to no good. A tragic example of this will be given below.

Both in the first case, of feelings that get projected into us, and in the second case, of good and bad qualities being attributed to different children, we are dealing with the insertion of non-physical, alien and possibly intensely destructive psychic contents into another person. From a psychological point of view, this bears an uncanny resemblance to the traditional understanding of possession by evil spirits. In a somewhat similar way the malign potential of a curse can be associated with the phenomenon of hypnotic suggestion, where an idea is inserted into a receptive subject's mind so that it unconsciously influences his post-hypnotic behaviour.

Another significant psychological discovery is that time does not exist in the unconscious (Freud 1957, p. 159ff.). Once repressed, emotional or spiritual injuries remain unmodified in an unconscious limbo and can be transmitted to later generations. A similar process can be observed in the lives of groups. Like a family, a group that has been in existence for a number of years may now contain none of its original members; and yet traumatic events that occurred at an early stage in the group's life, which were not adequately dealt with at the time and are now unknown to its current members, may still exert an unconscious influence on the workings of the group today.[1] This process can sometimes be detected in Christian congregations that, for no obvious current reason, appear to be 'blighted'. The movement, in some Christian circles, to offer healing to the family tree is another recognition of these trans-generational difficulties (McAll 1986).

Psychological understanding can also be useful for the light it throws on psychosomatic disorders. Physical illnesses are sometimes regarded as 'real', whereas physical symptoms, perhaps an apparent heart attack that turns out to be a panic attack, are treated as unreal, 'all in the mind'. The Bible offers a more psychological view, suggesting that we are a psychosomatic unity, compounded of matter and spirit. When we are distressed, either by an overwhelming personal situation, or as a child might be if he becomes the recipient of his family's negative qualities, or as a clergywoman might be if she becomes the focus of a 'blight' afflicting her congregation, the stress may manifest in different ways. We may become physically or mentally ill. We may begin to behave in inappropriate or dangerous ways. Or as is sometimes seen in clergy families, a member of the family may become depressed or enact the distress in some disturbing way. In such circumstances, it is not altogether incorrect to suspect that a malign spiritual influence is at work.

---

1 Freud's thinking was moving in this direction when he wrote *Moses and Monotheism* (Freud 1964; Blass 2006).

These reflections indicate some of the ways in which psychodynamic thinking can bring us closer to the spirit world of the Bible. In doing so, they sometimes challenge current scientific notions about the nature of reality (Main 2004), but they do so at a time when the New Physics is revolutionizing our understanding of the world in which we live (Goswami 1995). If mental processes can influence the quantum wave, then psyche-spirit may be the ultimate medium within which we exist – an idea that would come as no surprise to Paul, who could approvingly quote a pagan author to the effect that in God 'we live and move and have our being' (Acts 17.28).

Deliverance ministry today

Psychic disturbances always involve troubled, and sometimes very frightened and disturbed people. Where there is fear there is often considerable pressure for someone to 'do something', but it is important that doctors, pastors and therapists should not be stampeded into premature action. Very often there are mundane causes for the phenomena being experienced. In one case, for example, the uncanny rattling of brass handles on a dresser and a door that appeared to be opening itself were traced to vibrations from trains passing through a tunnel, deep below the house. Pastors may also, unwittingly, become involved in political games, as when a couple, wishing to be rehoused, persuaded their parish priest that their present home was being rendered uninhabitable by evil spirits; or in dangerously manipulative relationships, where one person is using supposed spirit activity to exercise control over others.

Where complaints are genuine, they are almost always caused by a distress that has yet to find its meaning. The responsibility of the pastor or of the clinician, in these circumstances, is to try to provide a safe environment in which the underlying dynamics of the situation can emerge. Accurate assessment paves the way for whatever blend of psychiatric, psychological and spiritual intervention may be most appropriate.

From a Christian perspective the pastor needs to understand the difference between magic, which involves the manipulation of power, and religion, which is concerned with love and with deepening relationship with God. This is important, not least because troubled people often hope that a magical exorcist will arrive to do battle with the devil in a powerful but impersonal way; whereas what they may really need is a centred and prayerful priest who will find a way of bringing them, and the whole situation, into the loving providence of God.

In all of this, we need to learn from history. Some of the darkest chapters in the history of the Christian Church have been written by earnest but misguided Christians who, for multiple reasons, discerned the activity of witches or demons in their fellow men and women. The terrible events at Loudun in the 1630s (de Certeau 2000) or the tragic witch trials at Salem in

1692 (Rosenthal 2009) should be ingrained in the minds of those embarking on this work. Sadly, recent cases of child abuse and murder, linked to accusations of possession and witchcraft, demonstrate that these ancient fears and impulses survive.

Apart from the tragic story of Victoria Climbié, the case material in the following section is drawn directly from the author's clinical and pastoral experience. As far as possible, for reasons of confidentiality, it has been stripped of identifying detail, but the salient points are given.

Requests for exorcism in cases where medical help is needed

1 A priest was approached by a woman who said that she was the victim of spiritual attack by satanists. The history was that she had formed an intense friendship with a woman living in another country. To begin with, everything was wonderful, but then difficulties arose in the relationship, and she began to fear that her friend was discussing her with other people. Soon afterwards she became physically ill and 'knew' that this was because of the gossip and the spells that her former friend and her accomplices were directing at her. Since then she had discovered that they were part of a global conspiracy of satanists, of which she was the prime target.

2 A man complained of being tormented by devils. Especially at night he could overhear them laughing and talking and mocking intimate details of his life. Sometimes they would curse him and claim that God hated him and had abandoned him.

3 A woman was in torment because she knew that she had committed the unforgivable sin (although she did not know what that sin was or when she had committed it). Although she knew that prayer was useless and that nothing could save her from damnation, she still begged her priest to deliver her from her torment.

The common factor between these three people was that all were suffering intensely, and all believed that the roots of their problem were spiritual or demonic, rather than psychological. In reality, though, the first was suffering from paranoid schizophrenia, the second from a schizophrenic-type illness and the third from psychotic depression. All had profound spiritual needs, but their first need was for skilled psychiatric attention. This created particular problems for the first person who – as is frequently the case with paranoid conditions – believed she had a completely objective understanding of her situation and clung to her belief that it had nothing to do with mental illness.

Ultimately, in each case, medical attention, coupled with medication, reduced the intensity of the symptoms and enabled the sufferers to find comfort and reassurance in the ordinary practice of their faith.

4   A man came to his parish priest complaining of being haunted by faceless spiritual presences, which constantly frightened and oppressed him. So much so that a great deal of his time was spent seeking sanctuary in churches and cathedrals.

5   Another man said that he was possessed by seven spirits, each having a name and a distinct personality.

On investigation, the first man was found to be suffering from a borderline personality disorder. In cases like this, the ego is too fragile to manage the stresses and strains of emotional life – the pain of having conflicting feelings and ideas – so it tends slightly to fragment and 'loses touch with' its more troublesome components. In this case, the man suffered most from the sense of being haunted and oppressed when, for good reason, he was feeling murderously angry, although he could not experience his anger directly. Instead, his displaced anger created the terrifying sense of something awful and terribly dangerous hovering around him.

With the second man, it was found that his ego had been fragmented by repeated experiences of traumatic abuse suffered during childhood. Subsequently, his ego had managed to reconstitute itself, but in the form, as it were, of a committee, rather than as a single centre of consciousness. Understandably, he found this very exhausting.

Both of these men found considerable relief through psychotherapeutic interventions, which strengthened their egos and enabled them to achieve a more coherent sense of themselves.

6   A woman approached her parish priest asking for her house to be blessed. It had already been blessed by several Christian groups, but in each case, after a short period of time, she had been afflicted by returning feelings of anxiety and dread. Sometimes she found that furniture had been thrown around or that crockery was broken. On several occasions she had also found traces of blood on her carpets and walls. To her, this was evidence of voodoo activity.

On investigation, she was found to be suffering from an epileptic condition that was poorly controlled by drugs. At one level, she knew this, but what she did not appreciate was that, in the aftermath of a seizure, she would go into a zombie-like state in which she moved violently and erratically around – on one occasion even falling out of a window, an event that had convinced her she was the victim of demonic assault.

7 A man approached a priest, concerned that he might be Jesus. To begin with, the priest imagined the man was suffering from a psychotic illness, but his lucidity and rationality gradually convinced the priest that this was not the case. Could he be a mystic? It seemed that, from time to time, he would be caught up into a visionary state in which he was unconscious of the passing of time, or of events around him. Most often, during these visionary episodes, he would 'become' Jesus, undergoing the events of his passion. Advised by the priest to consult his GP, the man was referred to a neurologist, who discovered he was suffering from Temporal Lobe Epilepsy, which sometimes manifests in the form of pseudo-mystical experiences or auras.

In situations such as these, where mental illness, psychological distress or neurological disturbance mimic spiritual possession or oppression, there is need for sensitive co-operation between pastors, therapists and medical practitioners.

Requests for exorcism in situations where psychological and spiritual factors predominate

8 A priest was called to a flat where a souvenir bought on holiday was reportedly moving around of its own accord. This had thoroughly alarmed the couple living there, especially when the souvenir found its way into their bed. They had no explanation for its movements, but were certain that neither of them could in any way be responsible for them.

What was the priest to think? Could one of them have been moving it unconsciously or maliciously? When investigating paranormal phenomena, it is vital to eliminate natural causes before resorting to psychic or spiritual explanations. In this case, the priest was convinced of the couple's sincerity, so the question then became what might the object's movements mean if it was moving in this way?

In the culture where the object had been made and where it had been bought, it symbolized an aspect of God's unseen presence and omniscience. What might God be seeing or knowing here?

In a long and difficult conversation, the couple gradually revealed the circumstances in which they had met and their continuing obligations to others; the intractable conflicts of interest in which they were locked. Both were feeling intensely guilty. At one level, they may have hoped that if a priest came and blessed or exorcised their house, their relationship too would have been blessed and legitimated. But they knew this could not be the case. Somehow, the moving object had forced more difficult truths into the light.

In this case, as in so many others, the path to deliverance lay not immediately through a spiritual ministration but through recognizing and accepting the reality of the conflict they were in. Often, in deliverance ministry, we have to discover where the real demons lie.

9   A woman travelled to the country of her parents' birth and arranged to visit the house her parents had built when they were first married, where they had spent the happiest years of their lives before she was born. It was her first visit to this house. In the course of her visit, the current owner, who had not known her parents, laughingly remarked that the house had a ghost. Hearing this, the visitor was immediately convinced that the ghost was the unquiet spirit of her father, whose death had been complicated by the fact that he had insisted that there be no religious ceremony at his funeral. The daughter, as executor, had obeyed her father's instructions, but the emotional and spiritual vacuum at the crematorium left an abidingly painful memory.

None of this was explained to the owner of the house, but when the daughter returned to England, she arranged for a requiem Eucharist to be said for her father. Two or three years later she visited the house again and, without revealing any of this background to the owner, casually asked, 'How's the ghost?' 'Oh, that's most extraordinary,' said the owner, 'we haven't seen the ghost since your last visit.'

Something had clearly happened, but what? Was the ghost an objective, independent reality – the spirit of the father – who had been helped by the Eucharist to move on into the nearer presence of God? This is one possibility. On the other hand, knowing the daughter as I did, I knew that there had always been something achingly unresolved about her father's death. When other people close to her had died, awful as their deaths were, she had had some reassuring sense of their continuing existence. This had not happened with her father, who had simply 'disappeared'. Could it be the case, spiritually and emotionally speaking, that not having anywhere to 'locate' him in her mind she had unconsciously 'placed' him in the original family home, which had always held such a special place in the affections of her parents and older siblings, who had been born there? In this case, the long journey to the ancestral home might have been an unconscious quest to find her father. Having done this and finally feeling justified in offering the prayers that her heart had longed to offer, had she now been able to let him go? In this case, the ghost would have been a projection of her, very alive, mental image of her father. Either way, the requiem Eucharist laid her father's ghost to rest.

These speculations may strike the reader as being quite mad, but deliverance ministry, like psychodynamic thinking, not infrequently draws us into confusing places where the everyday boundaries between time and space, internal and external, subjective and objective, physical and mental are confounded (Jung 1963, pp. 270–301; Radin 2009).

10 A young couple from a Middle Eastern country were referred by a parish priest because it appeared that the woman was being possessed by the devil. At times she would lapse into a coma in which she twitched and shook, and from which she could not be roused by calling or shaking. The only antidotes to these distressing attacks were the prayers and the holy water supplied by the parish priest. When the woman recovered consciousness she would talk of being tormented by a demonic figure with terrible eyes who mocked her and told her she was now subject to his power.

The first time the diocesan adviser saw the couple, their plight seemed profoundly mysterious and frightening. Communication was somewhat difficult because, although the woman understood more English than she spoke, her boyfriend had to speak for her. At the end of that meeting the priest prayed with them, and made another appointment to see them in a few days' time. By then the situation was worse: the seizures more frequent and the demon's words even more terrible and triumphant.

The couple found it very difficult to confide what the demon was saying, but eventually it became clear that he was mocking and taunting her, telling her that she was damned eternally because of her wickedness in killing her baby. At this point the sad truth came out: some time before, finding herself alone in London, unmarried and pregnant, the young woman had undergone an abortion. In the short term, this had solved her problem, but had left her with the unbearable thought that she had killed her parents' first grandson, and the knowledge that – should they ever find out – she would be disowned or might even be in danger of her life. In her own eyes, she was beyond redemption.

In a case such as this a very sensitive psychological-cum-spiritual response is needed, which will address the issues of grief, guilt and self-hatred in a culturally acceptable way.

11 A woman in her late thirties was referred for help. She had been staying in a hotel, where she had complained of loud banging from the central heating pipes. No one else had heard the noise. In email correspondence before the first meeting, she was emphatic that the diocesan adviser should understand that her difficulties were demonic; that she needed spiritual not psychological help.

At the first meeting, the priest discovered that she had had a long history of self-harm, beginning in her teenage years. During her early twenties, she had had several compulsory psychiatric admissions for depression and attempted suicide. She had then been through a wilderness period of about eight years, when she was signed off work and simply survived, often spending days in bed.

In her early thirties, she had experienced a powerful conversion experience in a charismatic church. This had been a lifesaver and convinced her that only God could deliver her from her appalling inner torment and pain. Since then she had benefited from individual psychotherapy and from several years' membership of a psychodrama group, but she was still tormented by chaotic states of mind and demonic voices abusing and ridiculing her, intent on destroying her capacity for faith and hope and on breaking her spirit. At her worst moments, thoughts of suicide would fill her mind.

She produced a picture of the demon from which she needed to be delivered: Goya's black picture of Saturn as an old man devouring one of his children, the naked torso of a young woman grasped in his claw-like hands, her head and arms already partially dismembered. When asked if she knew who this demon was, she said he was her father. She had grown up in a constant atmosphere of ridicule, belittlement and detestation, suffering years of psychological torture (rather than physical or sexual abuse).

In retrospect, several factors about that first meeting seem to have been crucial. First, the priest believed what she told him about her experience of her father, and the demonic effect he had had on her. Then, he believed in the genuineness of her relationship with God and affirmed her conviction that she was known, loved and held by God. He also prayed with her and explained why he believed that, both psychologically and spiritually, she was on a long but very real journey of personal integration and inward separation from the abusive father who had taken possession of her being.

From a clinical point of view, I think this woman fits, very well, the picture of structural dissociation and chronic traumatization described by van der Hart, Nijenhuis and Steele in their book *The Haunted Self* (2006). As the authors say, sufferers are tormented by a terrifying and painful past that 'haunts' them (p. vii), not least because 'they do not realize that the past is not the present, and that the future is not a repeat of the catastrophic past' (p. x). She had travelled a very long way before the priest met her and had already achieved considerable insight into her condition.

Had that meeting taken place ten years earlier, Goya's picture might have had the force of a self-object, giving a picture of her as wholly in her father's clutches and on the point of dying. By the time of that meeting, though, thanks to her conversion, which had generated a powerful image of a loving God within her inner world, her inner demon had gradually diminished to the status of an internal object relation, or complex: still the source of excruciating pain and torment, but no longer representing her global condition. It is now several years since that first meeting. Her journey of inward reintegration and dissociation from the appalling father image has steadily continued, and this has happened in time with the consolidation of her inward relationship with the image of a loving God.

12 A woman was referred by a priest, who had attempted an exorcism following complaints of widespread psychic disturbances in her home. To begin with, the Diocesan Adviser believed she was suffering from an

incipient psychotic illness and sought to arrange a medical referral. But as he got to know the woman better – she was a visitor to this country and of another faith, with only an imperfect grasp of English – he sensed that she was undergoing a turbulent, violent (and potentially catastrophic) process of psychological and spiritual development.

In the country from which she came, women had no independent status apart from their menfolk. In England, she was glimpsing what it might mean for her to become her own person, which she found unthinkable, terrifying and exhilarating in equal measures. Religiously speaking, too, she had no confidence that God would, or even could, speak to a woman. But her dreams and fantasies were packed with visions and thoughts about God, so much so that they threatened to engulf her.

Again, since coming to England, she had had several positive contacts with individual Christians and Christian groups, and had visited churches that had made a profound aesthetic and spiritual impact on her. Although her commitment to her religion was more social and cultural than spiritual, the idea of converting to Christianity was unthinkable to her. It would mean the end of her marriage, the loss of her family, and might lead to her death; and there was no one with whom she could share these overwhelmingly powerful thoughts and emotions.

In this spiritual emergency, the best way forward was to establish an on-going relationship that provided sufficiently frequent opportunities for the woman to talk and think as her experience unfolded – something between psychotherapy and spiritual direction. The aim was to provide a secure enough container within which this accelerated process of development could work its way through, until she came to whatever adjustment to life and faith might prove beneficial for her.

13 A highly educated West African woman referred herself, because she believed she was possessed by the spirit of a dog. On a recent trip to visit her family in Africa, she had attended a celebration at which a dog had been sacrificed by some non-Christian members of her community. In the course of the ceremony, which she was trying to avoid, she had been splashed with the dog's blood. Since then, she had felt possessed by the spirit of the dog.

A priest from the same part of Africa was consulted – in culturally specific situations, local knowledge is often essential for understanding the language of distress. His immediate reaction was, 'The spirit of a dog means lust. She must confess the sin of attending a pagan ritual – even if she did not intend to be caught up in it – and receive absolution. Then the spirit of the dog must be told to depart, and she must be cleansed with holy water, and sealed with holy oil to heal and protect her. Then she must make her communion.'

If we think about this advice in Jungian terms, we can imagine that the 'spirit of the dog' is an enormously powerful archetypal image – stronger than the woman's ego that it had invaded. The fact that, in her culture and belief, the spirit of the dog symbolized unbridled lust meant that, once her ego boundaries were breached by the archetypal invasion, she was exposed to unmodified Id drives. The rite suggested by the African priest was tremendously powerful, both at a spiritual and at a psychological level, because it re-drew the boundaries between her ego-self and the archetype, thus repairing her psycho-spiritual defences against unbridled incursion from her Id.

14   There have been several tragic cases in which systematic child abuse, even murder, have been linked to belief in witchcraft and possession by evil spirits. Eleanor Stobart's government-sponsored research report followed several high-profile cases, most prominently the death of Victoria Climbié, on 25 February 2000. Stobart writes:

> Research suggests that when a family experiencing problems has a child who exhibits a behaviour that the family views as problematic, difficult to understand or outside family norms; this, combined with a change in family dynamics may increase the risk of the family accusing the child of harbouring some 'evil' force such as 'witchcraft' or 'possession'. (2006, p. 20)

In these situations, we need to understand that the carer may genuinely believe that the child has been taken over by the 'devil'. In the perpetrators' minds, any violence, which may include beating, burning, cutting, semi-strangulation, starvation or more general neglect and threats of abandonment (p. 16), is not going to affect the child, because the child is effectively not there any more. The violence is directed at the devil (p. 24). This course of action may be advised and supported by the perpetrators' spiritual advisors, who share the same religious and cultural understanding of the problem.

Such behaviour looks very different from a western perspective. HM Government has issued an advisory document, *Safeguarding Children from Abuse Linked to a Belief in Spirit Possession* (2007), which advises what should be done in cases of abuse or neglect linked to belief in spirit possession; or if there are concerns about the beliefs and practices of a place of worship. In every case, statutory services must be informed, while the wider Church may have a role in attempting to intervene with the family's spiritual advisers.

From a psycho-spiritual perspective, we can see that the child's initial distress, which causes it to behave in difficult and apparently inappropriate ways, is actually an expression of the distress being suffered by the whole family as it tries to adjust to adverse circumstances. In these situations there is an understandable tendency to say, 'Something is wrong, therefore someone must be to blame.' Once a child is identified as the cause of the family's ills it may become the target for increasingly violent and desperate attempts to rectify the situation.

Other experiences

15 A man who took up dowsing to assist his professional work found himself making contact with all sorts of apparently spiritual forces and presences, some of which reacted in destructive ways.

16 In the course of a psychotic breakdown, a woman had a number of telepathic and clairvoyant experiences which, unnervingly, gave her accurate information about the private lives of two of the medical team who were caring for her.

17 A group of teenagers playing with a ouija board were terrified when the 'spirits' took hold of them and prevented them from stopping. Subsequently, one lad suffered a psychotic breakdown.

18 A priest attempted to deliver a man who had suffered from severe depression and consequently had a depressive breakdown herself, which put her off work for nearly a year.

19 A warm and effusive woman, who believed she had a gift of healing and could not bear anyone to be in pain, rushed, uninvited, to lay hands on a distressed person and was flung across the room by the psychic force that erupted from them.

Experiences like these suggest that the ego-self we think of as 'me' is like a little boat, floating on a sea of unconscious processes. Some of these unconscious processes belong to us – they are part of our personal unconscious – but Jung suggests that the personal unconscious opens out into a much wider domain, which he called the 'collective unconscious' (Jung 1968, 1969; Bernstein 2005; Gieser 2005). Collective, because we are all rooted in it; and in the collective unconscious there is neither time nor space. This is the domain of angels, demons and all other spiritual-cum-psychic entities. Ultimately, I believe, it is grounded in God, in whom we 'live and move and have our being'.

Both from psychological and spiritual points of view, we need to find wise spiritual practices that will support our ego-self, and enable it to maintain appropriate boundaries and fluent working between its different parts. At the same time, the ego needs to find ways of being open to the external and internal worlds that lie beyond it. From the Christian point of view, this means growing in the life of prayer, meditation and contemplation, so that we become more open to God and the spiritual world without losing our own internal boundaries.

Where there are psychic eruptions, such as those described above, the ego-self has been breached, or overwhelmed, by deeper forces. This explains why the Bible is so hostile to mantic or occult practices, designed to 'open the doors of perception' (Huxley 1994). Certain drugs create similar dangers. In such situations, appropriate pastoral care will involve the search for an adequate psychiatric, or psychological-cum-spiritual, understanding of the phenomena experienced, plus the development of a wise and viable spiritual discipline.

Conclusion

This essay has offered a theological and pastoral perspective on the subject of deliverance, and has suggested ways in which psychiatric, psychoanalytic and spiritual understandings may all be important in seeking to understand the suffering, and to meet the needs of those who appeal for exorcism or for deliverance from apparently spiritual forces that are threatening to upend their lives. A multidisciplinary approach has been recommended, with flexible medical, therapeutic and spiritual interventions, designed to meet the physical, emotional, spiritual and cultural needs of the individuals concerned.

References

Bernstein, J. S. (2005), *Living in the Borderland: The Evolution of Consciousness and the Challenge of Healing Trauma*, London and New York: Routledge.

Blass, R. B. (2006), 'Beyond Illusion: psychoanalysis and the question of religious truth', in David M. Black (ed.), *Psychoanalysis and Religion in the 21st Century: Competitors or Collaborators?*, Hove: Routledge.

Breuer, J. and Freud, S. (1955), 'Fräulein Anna O', reprinted in *The Standard Edition of the Complete Psychological Works of Sigmund Freud*, vol. II, London: Hogarth Press and the Institute of Psychoanalysis.

Charet, F. X. (1993), *Spiritualism and the Foundations of C. G. Jung's Psychology*, Albany NY: State University of New York Press.

Cohn, N. (1993), *Europe's Inner Demons: The Demonization of Christians in Medieval Christendom*, London: Pimlico.

Cook, C. C. H., Powell, A. and Sims, A. (eds) (2009), *Spirituality and Psychiatry*, London: Royal College of Psychiatrists Press.

de Certeau, M. (2000), *The Possession at Loudun*, Chicago and London: Chicago University Press.

Dix, Dom G. (1945), *The Shape of the Liturgy*, London: Dacre Press.

Eve, E. (2009), *The Healer from Nazareth: Jesus' Miracles in Historical Context*, London: SPCK.

Fairbairn, W. R. D. (1952), 'The repression and the return of bad objects', in W. R. D. Fairbairn (ed.), *Psychoanalytic Studies of the Personality: The Object Relations Theory of Personality*, London and Boston: Routledge & Kegan Paul.

Freud, S. (1957), 'The unconscious', reprinted in *The Standard Edition of the Complete Psychological Works of Sigmund Freud*, vol. XIV.

Freud, S. (1961), 'The Ego and the Id', reprinted in *The Standard Edition of the Complete Psychological Works of Sigmund Freud*, vol. XIX.

Freud, S. (1964), 'Moses and Monotheism', reprinted in *The Standard Edition of the Complete Psychological Works of Sigmund Freud*, vol. XXIII.

Gieser, S. (2005), *The Innermost Kernel, Depth Psychology and Quantum Physics: Wolfgang Pauli's Dialogue with C. G. Jung*, Berlin, Heidelberg: Springer Verlag.

Goswami, A. (1995), *The Self-Aware Universe: How Consciousness Creates the Material World*, New York: Penguin Putnam.

Grotstein, J. S. (1985), *Splitting and Projective Identification*, New York & London: Jason Aronson.

HM Government (2007), *Safeguarding Children from Abuse Linked to a Belief in Spirit Possession*, www.dcsf.gov.uk/everychildmatters/resources-and-practice/IG00220/.

Huxley, A. (1994), *The Doors of Perception, and Heaven and Hell*, London: Flamingo.

Jung, C. (1963), *Memories, Dreams, Reflections*, London: Collins and Routledge & Kegan Paul.

Jung, C. (1968, 2nd edn), 'The archetypes of the collective unconscious', reprinted in *C. G. Jung The Collected Works*, vol. IX. I, London: Routledge & Kegan Paul.

Jung, C. (1969, 2nd edition), 'The structure and dynamics of the psyche', reprinted in *C. G. Jung The Collected Works*, vol. VIII.

Jung, C. (1971), 'A psychological theory of types', reprinted in *C. G. Jung The Collected Works*, vol. VI.

Main, R. (2004), *The Rupture of Time: Synchronicity and Jung's Critique of Modern Western Culture*, Hove: Brunner-Routledge.

McAll, K. (1986), *Healing the Family Tree*, London: SPCK.

Perry, Michael (ed.) (1996, 2nd edn), *Deliverance, Psychic Disturbances and Occult Involvement*, London: SPCK.

Radin, D. (2009), *The Noetic Universe*, London: Corgi.

Richards, J. (1974), *But Deliver Us from Evil: An Introduction to the Demonic Dimension of Pastoral Care*, London: Darton, Longman & Todd.

Rosenthal, B. (ed.) (2009), *Records of the Salem Witch-Hunt*, New York: Cambridge University Press.

Schärf Kluger, R. (1967), *Satan in the Old Testament*, Evanston: Northwest University Press.

Stephenson, C. E. (2009), *Possession: Jung's Comparative Anatomy of the Psyche*, Hove: Routledge.

Stobart, E. (2006), 'Child abuse linked to accusations of "possession" and "witchcraft"', Department for Education and Skills Research Report RR750.

van der Hart, O., Nijenhuis, E. R. S. and Steele, K. (2006), *The Haunted Self*, New York and London: Norton & Co.

Walker, D. (1997), *The Ministry of Deliverance*, London: Darton, Longman & Todd.

Webster, R. (1995), *Why Freud was Wrong: Sin, Science and Psychoanalysis*, London: Harper Collins.

Working Party on Healing (2000), *A Time to Heal: A Report for the House of Bishops on the Healing Ministry*, London: Church House Publishing.

6

The Human Being and Demonic Invasion

Therapeutic Models in Ancient Jewish and Christian Texts

LOREN T. STUCKENBRUCK

Summary

Attempts to find common ground between the ancient practice of exorcism in the New Testament Gospels and contemporary practices of psychotherapy have often been wrong-footed. The need to find something 'normative' in Jesus' ministry has led many interpreters to emphasize differences in world-view between the ancient religious texts that had conceptual and practical space for demonology and contemporary therapeutic practice, especially in western cultures, which reject the value and practice of exorcism. This chapter argues that these very real differences cannot hide the fact that the Gospels, shaped by a Jewish apocalyptic way of understanding the world, and many psychotherapists today share something of a perspective. That perspective is illustrated in the analysis of Jesus' and his followers' dealings with the demonic world that presuppose a realistic understanding of exorcism as essentially a 'relocation' rather than a 'destruction' of evil power.

Introduction

The expression 'mental health' is used today to refer to a state of well-being while, in negative terms, it is sometimes associated with the lack of a mental illness or disorder.[1] On the one hand, mental wellness ideally involves the

---

1 This is not to imply that mental health is merely the absence of mental illness. It is thus appropriate to draw attention to the often cited definition of the World Health Organization for mental health in 2001: '... a state of well-being in which the individual realizes his or her own abilities, can cope with the normal stresses of life, can work productively and fruitfully, and is able to make a contribution to his or her community'. See the World Health Organization Factsheet no. 220 (2010) and further *The World*

ability to adapt to new situations, to engage in appropriate social behaviour, to handle conflicts and to make considered decisions. On the other hand, discourse about mental illness or mental disorders draws attention to a bewildering variety of problems and, increasingly, to a wide range of diagnoses that characterize a dysfunctional mind. Conditions associated with mental illness have included some of the following designations: psychosis, depression, attention deficit disorder, agoraphobia, paranoia, bulimia, bipolar disorder, Alzheimer's disease, Asperger's syndrome, autism, a diverse set of learning disabilities and all sorts of addictions.[2] These and similar challenges have been regarded as disorders that impact clinical, developmental, personal and psychosocial dimensions of an individual's life and, as is increasingly recognized, often relate closely to the physical condition of those affected. The above-named disorders, which themselves are fluid and complex, present issues that, however they are classified, affect people in all parts of the globe. Moreover, they illustrate how difficult it can be to define a particular form of 'mental illness' with precision.

If one turns to the Gospel traditions in the New Testament, the closest analogy to what today passes for mental illness and its treatment may be found, respectively, in the dire circumstances ascribed to the destructive activity of demons and Jesus' effective handling of them.[3] One of the most obvious comparisons has to do with social arrangement: there is the specialist exorcist and psychotherapist on the one hand, and the suffering patient on the other. In addition, those being treated, whether through exorcism or psychotherapy, are thought to live with harmful conditions that call for relief. We have already noted a number of possible diagnoses related to mental disorders in the previous paragraph. Turning to the Synoptic Gospels composed nearly two millennia ago, we observe that a number of detrimental states or symptoms are attributed to demonic beings.[4] When expressly mentioned, demons can be said to convulse (Mark 1.16; Mark 9.20; Luke 9.39, 42), seize (Mark 9.18; Luke 9.39), throw down (Mark 9.18; Luke 4.35; cf. Matt. 17.15; Mark 3.11; Luke 8.28), trouble (Luke 6.18), isolate (Mark 5.3; Luke 8.27, 29), strike dumb (Mark 9.17, 25; Matt. 9.32–33; 12.22; Luke 11.14), make deaf (Mark 9.25), inflict bodily harm on (Matt. 17.15; Mark 5.5; 9.22), make naked (Luke 8.27; cf. Mark 5.15 par. Luke 8.35), incapacitate (cf. Mark 7.30), render ritually unclean (Mark 1.23, 26, 27; 3.11, 30; 5.2, 8, 13; 6.7; 7.25; 9.25; Matt. 10.1; 12.43; Luke 4.33, 36; 6.18; 8.29; 11.24) and generally worsen the state of (Matt. 12.45 par. Luke 11.26) their victims. These texts assume that a proper or ideal response to the conditions described involves the removal or mitigation of

---

Health Organization Report 2001. Mental Health: New Understanding, New Hope (2001), pp. 3–4.

2 See e.g. *Diagnostic and Statistic Manual of Mental Disorders* (2000).

3 Diamond 1996 and 2012.

4 For the terminology used in the Gospel traditions, see below, under the section 'God, demons and humans in the Jesus tradition'.

demonic activity, just as mental illness is thus classified because it is a condition in need of treatment.

That said, the analogy between ancient exorcism and contemporary psychotherapy is a very complex one, and those who look for discontinuity between the two need not look far. References to demonic entities in accounts of Jesus' activity reflected a way of looking at the world that is very different from that adopted by many therapists today who seek to help their patients. For example, demonic attribution posits the invasive ontological existence of *another* being while strategies devised to deal with mental disorders in the modern sciences are more inclined to focus on issues that reside within the individual him- or herself.[5] Correspondingly, whereas the former is more likely to take the victimization of the person as a point of departure, the latter is more likely to stress a person's agency in his or her return to well-being. To make matters even more complicated, the differences between language of the Gospels and that adopted by psychotherapists are not always clear-cut: a number of texts in the Gospels move discourse about demons in a metaphorical direction,[6] while psychotherapists can use the term 'demons' – or 'daimons' – to denote something real (i.e. destructive mental states within a person).[7] Finally, we may note that the Gospel accounts make relatively little attempt to 'get to the bottom' of problems of individuals being treated by Jesus and thus tend to streamline and simplify their diagnoses (e.g. as ontologically demonic or as physical illness, without showing an interest in distinguishing clearly between the two), while, by contrast and as intimated in the opening paragraph above, mental health sciences today have developed a discourse that works with a number of possible classifications in the process of treating patients.

There is thus no doubt that for many Christian interpreters of biblical writings – in the present case, we are considering the Gospels – the recognition of demonic influence within human beings brings with it a hermeneutical challenge. How does one relate a religiously 'normative' tradition to problems that in many parts of the world today are discussed on other terms? Forging links between contemporary illnesses and demon-induced maladies encountered by Jesus within the context of the ancient world is fraught with difficulty. This discontinuity is, for example, seen by those psychiatrists who, regardless of their religious or non-religious affiliations, regard 'Jesus'

---

5 It should be acknowledged that both academics and practitioners in the fields of psychology and psychiatry frequently engage in discourse about 'demons' as well. Here the term, especially under the influence of Sigmund Freud, is metaphorical and is made to refer to aspects of the individual to be treated. See Freud 1950, pp. 18–74, 75–99, esp. 65, 92, and e.g. Ribi 1990, Mäyrä 1999, esp. pp. 51–80, and R. Harris 2006, pp. 2–8.

6 The most notable example of this is the Gerasene demoniac episode, in which the demoniac presence is called 'Legion' (Mark 5.1–20, pars. Matt. 8.28–34 and Luke 8.26–39).

7 See n. 5 above.

and religion as factors that contribute to mental illness rather than being resources for therapeutic treatment.[8]

Is it fair, then, to ask what, if anything, we can learn from Jesus' activity in relation to mental illness, especially since what Jesus did involved dealing straightforwardly with the demonic while we have many more alternative diagnoses at our disposal? In an effort to read the Gospels constructively, notwithstanding these and other difficulties, I would like to suggest in what follows that a meaningful conversation is indeed possible, especially if one recognizes the important role ancient Jewish apocalyptic tradition played in shaping the theological contours of Jesus tradition in the New Testament.

Coming to terms with Jesus' exorcisms: contemporary interpretations

Before addressing the activity of Jesus within the Synoptic Gospels and his Jewish context directly, we may find it helpful to note how many interpreters have attempted, on hermeneutical grounds, to make contemporary sense of what the Gospels state about Jesus' confrontations with the demonic world. One option, followed by many Christians in the developing and western world (among them, for example, Pentecostals), has simply been to 'take the Gospels at their word': if Jesus dealt with problems by exorcizing demons, then the world-view that accompanies what Jesus did must be true as well, even if it needs to be qualified.[9] Problems people face today can thus also reflect the existence of demonic powers. This perspective finds something normative in the world-view behind Jesus' exorcistic activity, coming as it does from 'Scripture', so that the Church should be able to factor it into life and practice.

Other interpreters, especially those who take analytical methods developed in the West as their point of departure, find it difficult to adopt straightforwardly the world-view of Jesus' time and therefore prefer symbolic interpretations of Jesus' exorcisms.[10] Accordingly, scholars of ancient

8 See S. Harris 2004, Hitchens 2007.

9 See the widely disseminated books by Basham 1972, MacNutt 1974, pp. 189–210, and 1995. For a more recent exegetical attempt to give place within New Testament theology for the notion of exorcisms as deliverance from the demonic, see Bell 2007, who uses the notion of myth to forge a link between Jesus' exorcisms and salvation from the realm of Satan in Pauline tradition. In contrast to Bell's approach, the present discussion focuses on the contribution of Jewish tradition to the theological context of exorcism.

10 Many think it necessary to explain how Jesus could have expelled demons, almost as if it was an embarrassing aspect of his activity. A frequent response to Jesus' exorcisms assumes that one is obliged to find or retain something normative that does not rest on the exorcisms *as such*: since there are many people today (i.e. in the West) who do not believe in the existence of demons, one is to regard Jesus' activity as an exorcist as an accommodation to beliefs at the time, an accommodation that no longer needs to be made. So, for example, Langton 1949, esp. pp. 147–83, 219–25, Blanch 1988, pp. 56–66.

Christianity, theologians, priests and pastors in the Church often look for ways to make such texts easier for contemporary readers to access. In this vein, readings of Jesus' exorcisms have gone in several directions, and sometimes several of these views are held at the same time. Before offering a perspective that I think is commonly overlooked, I would like to mention some of the more common ways Jesus' exorcisms have been and are being understood.

One way of construing Jesus' demonic encounters is to think of demons as metaphors for political oppression. This perspective emphasizes that Jesus was actively engaged, on a symbolic level, in a war of resistance against the economic and political domination of Rome. Getting rid of demons was, on his part, a way to subvert the control of Rome and proclaim boldly the overarching reality of another kingdom, that of God. Thus, for example, the successful exorcism of 'Legion' from the Gerasene demoniac (cf. Mark 5.1–20; pars. Matt. 8.28–34, Luke 8.26–39) reflects the conviction that in Jesus' ministry, God's rule manifests itself so strongly that it can vanquish the military might of Rome.[11]

Second and closely related to the interpretation just mentioned, the expulsion of demonic beings by Jesus is taken to be concerned with portraying Jesus as the one who fulfils the ultimate hopes of the covenant people of Israel. In such a series of small-scale episodes, Jesus is acting out a much grander narrative: by ridding people of evil spirits, he puts God's restorative power for Israel on display, so that, free from enslavement and oppression, Israel can become the covenant faithful people they were meant to be.[12]

Third, Jesus' exorcisms are sometimes taken as evidence that, in very general terms, establishes that Jesus was acting as a Jew. His exorcisms can be compared with the activities of a number of Jewish miracle-workers who, like Jesus and according to tradition, were based in Galilee. This comparison means that Jesus was simply doing the kind of thing that a Galilean 'charismatic' *ḥasid* would have done.[13]

Fourth, and in a different sense, many use a comparison of Jesus' activities with those of contemporary healers and exorcists to emphasize how much Jesus is different and is essentially without meaningful parallel in his contemporary world. It is held that this 'uniqueness' of Jesus holds true

---

11 As argued by, e.g., Eitrem 1966, p. 70, Horsley 1987, pp. 184–90, Myers 1988, pp. 191–4, Waetjen 1989, pp. 81–3, 113–19; and Crossan 1991, pp. 313–18.

12 Cf. N. T. Wright 1996, pp. 193–7, 226–9. Referring to Jesus' logion in Luke 11.20/ Matt. 12.28 ('if by the finger of God I cast out demons, then the kingdom of God has come upon you'), Wright concludes that Jesus' exorcisms are 'clear signs' that the God of Israel is beginning to defeat the enemy that has 'held Israel captive' (p. 228).

13 Vermes 1973, pp. 58–82, Borg 1988, esp. pp. 30–2, and Ehrman 1999, pp. 197–8. Smith 1978 has a similar approach, though presses his presentation of Jesus into the category of 'magician'. Crossan 1991, pp. 142–58, takes up a position that ends up mediating between the views of Vermes and Smith, arguing that traditions about the originally 'magical' Ḥoni and Ḥanina were eventually domesticated when we meet them in early literature that mentions them (e.g. *m. Ta'an.* 3.8 and *t. Ta'an.* 2.13).

whether comparisons are drawn with sources from the Ancient Near East, with non-Jewish and non-Christian pagan sources, or with Second Temple Jewish literature.[14] Driven by prior theological convictions centred around Christology, interpreters who adopt this position focus on the character of Jesus' exorcisms as miraculous. The exorcisms are to be read alongside the stories of Jesus' healing and nature miracles as interventive acts of God. There was no equal to what Jesus did. The result of this approach is to render Jesus' activity *itself* as remote, while symbolic interpretations (see the first and second above and the fifth and sixth) are made to bridge the gap between the accounts and contemporary experience.

Fifth, exorcisms could also be interpreted as symbolic in relation to individuals themselves. They are, in effect, stories that signify how Jesus' proclamation of God's rule agitates for a more just society; Jesus' ministry is essentially a matter of reintegrating marginalized or excluded people into the life and activity of social and religious institutions. Jesus' exorcisms have to do with those who on account of illness or some condition were without social honour, dispossessed of dignity and, within the Jewish context, ritually 'unclean'. The effect of an exorcism on afflicted and unclean individuals is their full inclusion within the worshipping community.[15]

Sixth, exorcisms are sometimes comprehended as stories, again in a symbolic sense, about the salvation of people who are, on a profound level, delivered from evil and its effects. This soteriological interpretation is bound up with an understanding of Jesus as the essential way to salvation. When Jesus' disciples perform exorcisms, they do so in Jesus' name and so continue that ministry of salvation through Jesus to others. Exorcisms show how Jesus' ministry brings God's salvation about within a world that is otherwise hostile to God.[16]

Seventh, and a less symbolic interpretation, exorcism (and healing) stories in the Gospels illustrate that Jesus was 'a physician before his time'. With remarkable success, he was in effect able to treat people with mental disorders which sometimes manifested themselves through physical symptoms or illness. Thus language about demons was a way to talk about psychosomatic, mental illness. Jesus brought wholeness and hope to the mind, with the result that physical symptoms could be alleviated.[17]

---

14 See Twelftree 1993, e.g. pp. 157–74, for whom Jesus is different in the connection he established between his own expulsion of demons and the dawning rule of God; see further Twelftree 2007, Stegemann 1998, pp. 237–8, Eve 2002, and Söding 2003, pp. 519–49.

15 E.g. Patterson 1998, pp. 69–73, Ehrman 1999, pp. 187–8, Klutz 1999, pp. 156–65, cf. Crossan 1994, pp. 81–2.

16 So, for example, Noack 1948.

17 See Capps 2008, Ellens 2008, pp. 1–14, and, in another vein, Meggitt 2011, pp. 17–43. Meggitt, rather than attempting a psychosomatic reading, draws on the function of a 'placebo' in medical practice and emphasizes the role of both faith (in Jesus) and self-healing (human agency) in the Gospel healing and exorcism narratives. Aside from the general points made below, the difficulty with these interpretations of

Good reasons have been put forward for each of the interpretations just described. However, they each lose some of their force to the extent that they make Jesus' exorcisms illustrate *something else* than what they claim to be: Jesus dealing with people who suffer from invasive demonic control. The argument that follows shall move, therefore, in a somewhat different direction.

An attempt to focus on Jesus' activity as confrontation with the demonic may meet with resistance among interpreters who are shaped by modernist sensibilities. I hope, nonetheless, that by focusing on the demonic world in the Gospels per se, we find ourselves in a better position to recover some fundamental insights. For ancient readers of the Gospels the metaphorical and symbolic power of stories about the defeat of demonic evil (so the first and second, and fifth and sixth interpretations above) gain their force if they could assume that Jesus of Galilee had actually been effective in deal-ing with individuals in the way the Gospel accounts claimed. If one does not reach too quickly for sociological, political, psychological or even some theological interpretations, it may be possible to hear once again what some of the Gospel traditions about Jesus convey about several basic issues. These issues include the following questions: What is the power and nature of evil itself? How do the harmful effects of evil manifest themselves in people? What is the place of human beings within the created order? Within what larger framework of time and space does conflict with evil occur? And what role might a life of faith have in coping with the stubborn persistence of evils that intrude into life and often cannot be fixed?

One reason why Jesus' exorcisms are considered problematic within some religious circles has to do with the following question. Many ask, 'Can or should exorcisms be performed today and, if so, what can be learned for this purpose from the New Testament Gospels?' This question misses the point; it is misguided because it looks for something normative in a particu-lar world-view. It is precisely a response of 'No!' to this question that has led to some of the interpretations we have reviewed above. On the other hand, for those who would answer the question with a 'Yes!' (that exor-cism is a valid religious practice for today) there is the burden of coming up with a 'right' diagnosis.[18] A diagnosis that includes an ontological demonic element more often than not stands in tension with approaches to illnesses adopted in medical professions shaped by western education. Despite the stark contrast in these positions, however, it is possible that advocates of exorcism as a legitimate practice and those who a priori have no place for

---

problems suffered by people in Jesus' day is that, while they look for language to describe what may have actually been the case, they attempt to recover what is inaccessible and, more importantly, do not adequately seek to understand what was happening in the framework and terms set by the ancient sources themselves.

18 See the different approaches by Basham 1972, MacNutt 1995 and the more thoroughgoing treatment in Thomas 1998.

it have something to learn from one another. Indeed, the question about the validity or non-validity of exorcism can be replaced by a more germane one: What fundamental *perspective* on demonic power, on the human being and on Jesus' activity in relation to people do exorcism passages of the Gospels convey? What understanding of the world and God's activity within the world can one reasonably discern?

This refocus of the issues puts us in a position to reconsider the conflict between Jesus the exorcist and the demonic world. After reviewing the Gospel traditions briefly, I shall focus on selected passages that may contribute to a fresh reading of Jesus' exorcisms.

Jesus' ministry against the demonic: an overview

References in the Synoptic Gospels for the practice of exorcism are not wanting. In fact, the presentation of activity that expels demons is preserved among each of the main literary sources in and behind the Gospels.[19]

- *tradition in Mark alone* – two times
  Mark 3.13–15 (omitted in par. Luke 6.12–13) – Jesus' commissioning of his disciples;
  Mark 6.13 (omitted in par. Luke 9.6) – summary of the disciples' deeds;
- *tradition shared by Mark and Matthew* – once
  Mark 7.24–30, par. Matt. 15.21–28 – the Syrophoenician woman;
- *tradition shared by Mark and Luke* – three times
  Mark 1.23–28, par. Luke 4.33–37 – exorcism of a man in the synagogue;
  Mark 3.11–12, par. Luke 6.18 – summary of Jesus' deeds at the sea;
  Mark 9.38–41, par. Luke 9.49–50 – the 'strange' exorcist;
- *tradition shared by Mark with Matthew and Luke* – five times
  Mark 1.32–34, pars. Matt. 8.16–17 and Luke 4.40–41 – summary of Jesus' activity;
  Mark 3.22–27, pars. Matt. 12.24–30 and Luke 11.15–23 (perhaps an overlap of Mark and 'Q') – accusation of Jesus' collusion with Beelzebul;
  Mark 5.1–20, pars. Matt. 8.28–34 and Luke 8.26–39 – exorcism of the Gadarene man (two men in Matt.);
  Mark 6.7, pars. Matt. 10.1 and Luke 9.1 – Jesus' commissioning of his disciples;
  Mark 9.14–29, pars. Matt. 17.14–21 and Luke 9.37–43 – exorcism of a boy;

---

19 The categories set forth here do not strictly follow the 'four-source hypothesis', though omissions of references to exorcisms within parallel passages in some literary relationship are noted. The presentation below, which does not presume a particular direction in literary dependence, bears the advantage of reflecting the proclivities of each Gospel while noting where the parallel pericopes occur.

- *tradition in Matthew alone* – three times
  Matt. 7.21–23 (omitted in pars. in Luke 6.46 and 13.25–27) – saying about inauthentic followers of Jesus;
  Matt. 9.32–34 – exorcism of a mute man;
  Matt. 10.7–8 (omitted in par. Luke 10.9) – Jesus' commission of his disciples;
- *tradition in Luke alone* – four times
  Luke 7.18–23 (omitted in par. Matt. 11.2–6) – Jesus' response to John the Baptist;
  Luke 10.17–20 (cf. Mark's longer ending, 16.17–18) – the return of the 70 disciples;
  Luke 13.10–17 – exorcism of a crippled woman in the synagogue;
  Luke 13.32 – summary of Jesus' activity;
- *tradition shared only by Matthew and Luke* – two times
  Matt. 12.22–23, par. Luke 11.14 – exorcism of a blind and mute man;
  Matt. 12.43–45, par. Luke 11.24–26 – return of an evil spirit.

This listing is, in the first instance, revealing. It provides evidence for the multiple attestation of the exorcism tradition in the Synoptic Gospels, not only in relation to a documentary hypothesis (if one accepts categories such as the 'triple tradition', 'Q', 'special Matthew', 'special Luke'), but also in relation to identifiable tendencies of the Gospels each of which alone refers to the tradition at particular points.

A look at these passages as a whole allows us to make several further observations. First, exorcistic activity in the Gospels is preserved in different forms. Far more than simply being the subject matter of Jesus' encounters in narrative form, exorcisms are referred to in a number of Jesus sayings as well as among more general summaries of Jesus' or his disciples' activity. Second, it is significant that successful exorcisms in the Synoptic Gospels are not only attributed to Jesus alone. Not only are exorcisms performed by Jesus' disciples (Mark 6.7, 13–15; Matt. 10.1, 7–8; Luke 9.1; 10.17–20),[20] they are also assumed to be a condonable activity practised by those who are not among Jesus' immediate followers. This is, for instance, the case with the so-called 'strange' exorcist mentioned in Mark 9.38–41 (par. Luke 9.49–50) as well as with Jesus' rhetorical question which assumes that his Jewish contemporaries were likewise able to exorcize demons (Matt. 12.27, par. Luke 11.19: 'by whom do your sons cast out?'). The latter episode, which is tucked away in a passage that focuses on Jesus' response to an accusation that questioned the source of his power, admits that an analogy exists between the exorcisms of Jesus and those performed by the 'sons' of his interlocutors (the 'Pharisees' in Matthew and 'scribes' in Luke). In other

---

20 See, however, the lack of success to exorcize by the disciples in Mark 9.18, par. Luke 9.40, and Mark 9.28–29, par. Matt. 17.19–20. This presentation of the disciples' inability makes Jesus as the expert exorcist stand out in sharp relief.

words, Jesus' encounters with the demonic world are located by the Synoptic Gospels within a religious climate in which exorcisms were considered a legitimate, if not effective, way to combat evil. According to the Gospels, Jesus, as an exorcist, participated in a world-view in which exorcism makes sense. For all the wish of the Gospel writers to accentuate Jesus' prowess and expertise in this area, Jesus would have shared some fundamental assumptions with his contemporaries on how such activity works and what it signifies for both practitioners and those deemed to be under demonic sway. Third, both the multiple attestation in the Gospels and their recognition of exorcism as an effective practice among non-devotees of Jesus strengthen the likelihood that we have to do with the preservation of early tradition that was at least circulating during the time of Jesus' ministry. Contemporaries of Jesus believed that he was, controversially or not, engaging in open conflict with demonic beings. However much individual pericopae, especially exorcism episodes, were shaped by conventional oral and literary forms, there is no reason to doubt that any reconstruction of Jesus' life and ministry that does not include the claim (by others and by Jesus himself) that he expelled evil spirits omits something essential. Likewise, since each of the Gospel writers wished to emphasize the unprecedented magnitude of Jesus' life, teaching and ministry,[21] there is no compelling reason why a post-Easter community would have generated stories that acknowledged the performance of exorcisms by his contemporaries.

Both on the level of their respective presentations and in the traditions they variously preserve, the Synoptic Gospels leave us with a portrait of Jesus who, as a pious Jew of his time, believed he was effectively able to confront and gain control over demonic power.[22]

---

21 So e.g. Mark 1.22; 1.27b (par. Luke 4.36); 2.12b; 4.41 (pars. Matt. 8.27 and Luke 8.25); Matt. 7.29; 9.33; Luke 5.26. Of these texts, the depiction of Jesus' superior ability in performing exorcisms occurs in Mark 1.27b (par. Luke 4.36) and Matt. 9.33.

22 For a discussion that stresses inter alia the importance of multiple attestation as a criterion, see Telford 1999, pp. 88–103. Here the study is limited to the Synoptic Gospels precisely because the Gospel of John does not preserve any account of an exorcism performed by Jesus. This does not mean, however, that the Fourth Gospel completely ignores this aspect of the Jesus tradition; traces of it are, instead, reconfigured to reinforce characteristic Johannine interests: (a) The language of casting out (ἐκβάλλειν) demonic power is taken up in John 12.31, according to which Jesus' death is the event that marks the decisive defeat of 'the ruler of this world'; (b) the accusations of 'having a demon', which in the Synoptic Gospels are linked to the performance of exorcisms (cf. Mark 3.22–30, par. Matt. 12.24–32, Luke 11.15–23) and also involve John the Baptist (Matt. 11.18; Luke 7.33), are more widespread in John (7.20; 8.48–49, 52; 10.20–21), where they are made to function as labels in order to exercise social control over religious threat from opponents. The motif of 'having a demon' is thus reminiscent of, and perhaps grew out of, accusations surrounding Jesus' exorcistic activity as attested in the Synoptics. For an excellent discussion and overview of the Johannine tradition, see Piper 2000, pp. 252–78.

God, demons and humans in the Jesus tradition

Within the Gospel traditions about Jesus' exorcisms, three features stand out with regularity. They add up to a world-view that integrates God's activity, the nature of evil and the nature of humanity.

First, we note that Jesus' exorcisms are associated with the beginning of God's rule. As acts of power, they manifest and proclaim the royal power of the God of Israel. In addition to his healing miracles, Jesus regarded his expulsion of demons from people as concrete demonstrations that God's rule is breaking into this world, dispossessing evil forces from the foothold they have on people in the present age. However, none of the exorcism *stories* in the Gospels actually affirms the connection between what Jesus was doing, on the one hand, and God's kingship or rule, on the other. For this link the Gospels steer our attention to the sayings of Jesus.

In this respect, most scholarly attention has focused on the 'Q' tradition in Luke 11.20 (par. Matt. 12.28). According to the Lucan version, Jesus claims, 'But if by the finger of God I cast out demons, then God's rule has come upon you.'[23] The saying assumes that a vacuum that arises within a person dispossessed of demonic power is filled by the protective power of God's rule. For those who have been exorcized, Jesus' ministry signals the beginning of a process of deliverance. Similarly, Jesus' declaration upon the return of the 70 disciples in Luke 10.18 that he 'saw Satan fall from heaven like lightning' is offered as an explanation of why the disciples could be portrayed as successful exorcists.[24] Exorcisms result from a power struggle in which demonic power is being overcome.

Though the link between exorcisms and God's rule may be traced back to Jesus,[25] how unique a link is it? Is Twelftree correct, for instance, when he concludes that 'it was Jesus himself who made this connection between exorcism and eschatology', as if such a link had no real precedent in Jesus' environment?[26] Was Stegemann, similar to Twelftree, correct when he concluded that the notion that God's reign is beginning to vanquish Satan's rule is to be found 'neither in the Qumran texts nor in other Jewish literature, at

---

23 Instead of 'the finger of God', Matthew's version has 'the Spirit of God', a phrase that reflects editorial interests (cf. Matt. 12.18, 32). Thus, despite the allusion here to Ex. 8.9, Luke's wording is to be preferred.

24 See Becker 1998, pp. 107–10.

25 The historicity of this or that episode of exorcism attributed to Jesus is less important than the more general point that it played a vital role in demonstrating his proclamation of God's kingship. On this, see Meier 2001, pp. 646–8.

26 So Twelftree 1993, p. 220. N. T. Wright 1996, p. 195, advocates a similar point of view: 'The exorcisms are especially interesting, in that they formed a part neither of the regular Old Testament predictions, nor of first-century Jewish expectations, concerning healing and deliverance associated with the coming of the kingdom; nor were they a major focus of the life and work of the early church. They therefore stand out, by the criterion of dissimilarity, as being part of a battle in which Jesus alone was engaged.'

least where these surely stem from pre-Christian times'?²⁷ We will address this claim below.

Second, we note that in the Gospels 'demons' always refer to evil or unclean spirits. Another feature belonging to the tradition about Jesus has to do with the consistent presentation of 'demons' as evil powers. In the Synoptic Gospels the following designations occur, sometimes as a single term and sometimes in combination with one or more qualifying adjectives:

(a) 'demon' – δαίμων or δαιμόνιον (Mark 1.34 *bis*, 39; 3.15, 22; 6.13; 7.26, 29, 30; 9.38; Matt. 7.22; 9.33, 34; 10.8; 11.18; 12.24 *bis*, 27, 28; 17.13; Luke 4.33, 35, 41; 7.33; 8.2, 27, 30, 33, 35, 38; 9.1, 42, 49; 10.17; 11.14 *bis*, 15 *bis*, 18, 19, 20; 13.32)

(b) 'evil spirit' – πνεῦμα πονηρόν (Luke 7.21; 8.2; cf. Acts 19.12, 13, 15, 16)²⁸

(c) 'unclean spirit' – ἀκάθαρτον πνεῦμα (Mark 1.23, 26, 27; 3.11, 30; 5.2, 8, 13; 6.7; 7.25; 9.25; Matt. 10.1; 12.43 (Q); Luke 4.36; 6.18; 8.29; 11.24 (Q))

(d) 'spirit of an unclean demon' – πνεῦμα δαιμονίου ἀκαθάρτου (Luke 4.33 [cf. Mark 1.23])

(e) 'spirit of weakness' – πνεῦμα ... ἀσθενείας (Luke 13.11)

(f) 'dumb' or 'deaf-and-dumb spirit' – πνεῦμα ἄλαλον (Mark 9.17), ἄλαλον καὶ κωφὸν πνεῦμα (Mark 9.25)

(g) 'spirit' – πνεῦμα (Matt. 8.16; 9.20; Luke 9.31 [cf. Mark 9.17], 38)

Three points are noteworthy from this list of terms. First, in the Gospel narratives, the expressions 'demon' and 'unclean spirit' are used interchangeably (cf. Matt. 10.1, 8; Mark 3.22, 30; Luke 8.27, 29). To be impure was to have a demon and to have a demon was to be impure.²⁹ While this might signify that exorcism functioned as a means of reintegrating someone 'impure' into society, the function of exorcisms related, in the first instance, to the well-being of individuals.³⁰

---

27 See Stegemann 1998, p. 233. Throughout his chapter on 'Jesus' (pp. 228–57), Stegemann draws too much of a distinction between Jesus and his Jewish context. As far as exorcism in relation to God's rule is concerned, he stresses differences in technique and methods between Jesus and his contemporaries, but fails to consider the wider theme of God's rule in relation to the defeat of evil in Second Temple texts.

28 The restricted distribution of the expression within Luke–Acts suggests that it is a Lucanism.

29 Klutz 1999, p. 161, who regards this as the 'demonization of impurity'.

30 As we shall see below, this becomes clear when *1 En.* 6–16 and its early influence are taken into consideration. This point contrasts with the emphasis of Suter 1979, pp. 115–35, for whom the myth of rebellious angels who breed illegitimate offspring through women functions as a protest against priests who were thought to be falling prey to reprehensible incursions of Hellenistic culture. For a critique, see A. T. Wright 2005, pp. 46–7.

Second, it is well known that in the ancient world outside of Judaism and Christianity, the term δαίμων was, on the whole, neutral. It referred to intermediary beings capable of having good as well as harmful effects on humans.[31] However, in the Gospels – indeed, in the New Testament as a whole – the term acquires a categorically negative meaning.[32]

The third point to note is the remarkable distribution and frequency of the designation 'unclean spirit'. As far as I am able to ascertain, this expression is without parallel in non-Jewish literature from pre-Christian times. Here, at least as far as the Synoptic Gospels are concerned, we find ourselves on unmistakably Jewish soil with which Jesus and those who spoke and wrote about him would have been familiar. This language extends back to Zechariah 13.2, where in an association with idolatry, the 'unclean spirit' (רוח הטמאה, τὸ πνεῦμα τὸ ἀκάθαρτον) describes Judah and Jerusalem in an imperilled state of religious unfaithfulness; correspondingly, the removal of this spirit by God is envisioned on a national scale. The next references, preserved among the Dead Sea Scrolls, bring us closer to the climate of the Gospels in that 'spirit of uncleanness' pertains to a state of being from which *individuals* seek deliverance or relief (cf. 11Q11 xix 15; 4Q444 1 i 8; 1QS iv 22; perhaps also 4Q458 2 i 5).[33] The expression here suggests that the effect of the bad spirit is to make its victim ritually unclean and therefore unable to participate in the religious life of Israel. While the origins of such spirits can be contemplated by considering the larger context of the Dead Sea Scrolls and their reception of Enochic tradition (see Excursus B below), the Gospels offer very little information about what it is that made the exorcized spirits unclean;[34] instead, the impurity of such spirits is taken for granted and, in addition, it is taken for granted that the effects of such spirits is injurious to human well-being.

---

31 To be sure, there are occasional instances in which δαίμων or a related verb denotes inimical powers as e.g. in Hippocratic school's criticism of those who think they (δυσμενέες δαίμονες) lie behind illnesses such as epileptic seizures ('the sacred disease') and related conditions (so *On the Ailments of Young Women* 8.466); Plutarch's view that the notion of 'evil demons' (φαῦλοι δαίμονες) derives from Heracleon, Plato, Xenocrates, Chrysippus and Democritus (*Def. orac.* 419A); and the vilifying rhetoric used by orators in Athenian law courts (e.g. Aeschines, *In Ctesiphontem* 157; Dinarchos, *In Demosthenem* 91; Isocrates, *Areopagiticus* 73). However much *daimones* could be regarded as harmful to humans, their malevolence was not addressed by means of exorcistic practices in Greek and Roman culture. On their essential neutrality in early folk traditions, Homeric and post-Homeric literature, the philosophical literature (esp. Plato), Neopythagorean thought, Philo, Plutarch, Lucian, Apuleius and Philostratus (on Apollonius of Tyana), see Brenk 1986, pp. 2068–145, Sorensen 2002, pp. 75–117 and Albinus 2005, pp. 425–46.

32 See Sorensen 2002, p. 121.

33 See Alexander 1998–99, pp. 331–53, esp. 349–50, Lange 2005, pp. 254–68 and Wahlen 2004, pp. 41–7.

34 The accounts of the exorcisms of the Gerasene demoniac (Mark 5.1–20 and pars.) and the possessed boy (Mark 9.14–29 and pars.) include descriptions of the harm inflicted by the unclean spirit on their victims without, however, indulging in any explanation of how these spirits became impure to begin with.

Third, we note that demonic possession involves entry into the human body. Despite the many passages in the Gospels that refer to the exorcisms of Jesus, his disciples and others in the Gospels, there is an extraordinary uniformity when it comes to the way demons are described in relation to their human victims. Almost all the texts portray exorcism as a *disembodiment* of spirits: they are 'cast *out*' (ἐκβάλλειν) of the victims they have possessed.[35] The image of exit from within is reinforced by the notion of evil spirits either 'entering' (εἰσέρχομαι)[36] into individual human beings or 'departing' (ἐξέρχεσθαι)[37] from them. Underlying this language is the twin assumption that people can be victimized by demons when the demons inhabit their bodies and that such affliction occurs when the inner equilibrium of a person is out of balance.

Among the sayings of Jesus, this understanding of exit and entry is most clear in a passage from tradition shared by Matthew and Luke (Matt. 12.43–45 par. Luke 11.24–26), often referred to as 'the return of the spirit'. The less redacted version, which is found in Luke,[38] reads as follows:

(24) When an unclean spirit departs (ἐξέλθῃ) from a person, it passes through dry places seeking rest; and when it does not find (it), it says, 'I will return to the house from whence I left'. (25) And it goes and finds it swept and put in order. (26) Then it goes and takes seven other spirits more evil than itself and they enter and dwell there. And the last state of that person is worse than the first.

The saying simply concludes with a warning (v. 26b) without any accompanying exhortation. In its present form, this *logion* is remarkably open about the danger that, we may assume, follows an exorcism: the 'last state' is not presented as a potential condition, but rather as what can be expected to happen if, presumably, further measures are not undertaken. The scenario depicted here is that of an exorcism that is ultimately ineffectual; no attempt is made in the saying to specify whether the exorcist was Jesus, one of his disciples or others exorcizing in Jesus' name. For this reason a number of interpreters regard this tradition as one that neither Jesus' disciples nor the early Church would have been likely to create; the thrust of the saying, especially in the Lucan version, is counter-intuitive to the portrait provided in the Gospels of Jesus, whose exorcisms would more ideally have been portrayed as successful.[39] If this saying can be traced back to Jesus, it is significant that, consistent with the exorcism stories, Jesus presupposes

---

35 So in Mark 1.34, 39; 3.15, 22, 23; 6.13; 9.18, 28; Matt. 7.2; 8.16, 31; 9.33, 34; 10.1, 8; 12.24, 26, 27 *bis*, 28; 17.19; Luke 9.40, 49; 11.14, 15, 18, 19 *bis*, 20; 13.32.

36 Mark 3.27; 5.12, 13; 9.25; Matt. 12.29; Luke 8.30, 32, 33; 22.3.

37 Mark 5.13; 7.29, 30; Matt. 12.43 (Q); Luke 8.2, 33; 11.14, 24 (Q).

38 At the end of the pericope Matthew (12.45) adds a comparison that awkwardly makes the saying refer to the 'perverse generation' at the end-time.

39 A. T. Wright 2005, pp. 455–6.

that the human body can serve both as a demon's 'house' (v. 24b,[40] cf. the metaphorical use of 'house' in Mark 3.25, 27, Matt. 12.25, 29) and as the natural place to which it can return (v. 26a).

The uniformity of demonic corporeal indwelling in the Synoptic Gospels stands out, given that it is relatively rare in Jewish sources that pre-date the New Testament writings.[41] Far more widespread in Graeco-Roman antiquity is language that depicts demonic activity more in terms of affliction or attack rather than as entry per se.[42]

Excursus A: Jewish sources, demonic affliction and demonic embodiment

The distinction between demonic attack and demonic entry introduces to us a semantic problem. Thus, before noting a few analogies in Jewish sources for demonic possession, we may draw attention to several texts that have sometimes been misleadingly understood as references to 'possession' in the strict sense. First, in the book of Tobit, there are the fatal attacks by the demon Asmodeus against the seven would-be husbands of Sarah, as well as the threat this poses for Tobias (Tob. 3.8; 6.8, 14–15; 8.2). Here the means undertaken to gain control of the demon (i.e. the smoking of a fish's heart and liver) are protective and do not formally amount to any expulsion from a body. Second, there is the well-known account in the Aramaic document *Genesis Apocryphon* (1Q20 xx 16–29), which relates to the biblical story of Abraham and Sarah in Egypt (Gen. 12.10–20). Although Pharaoh and his household are made to suffer physical sores from a plaguing spirit, the trouble is described more in terms of an affliction (as in Gen. 12.17) than as possession. In line with this, the evil spirit, when Abram lays his hands on Hyrqanosh,[43] is not so much 'expelled' or 'driven out' as it is 'banished' or

---

40 The metaphorical use of 'house' corresponds to the saying in Mark 3.25, 27 (cf. Matt. 12.25, 29), though has got lost in its Lucan redaction at 11.17. This further strengthens Luke's preservation of a tradition that ultimately derives from another source.

41 Meier overstates the matter when he asserts that 'demonic possession as well as obsession became a frequent theme in the Jewish literature of the intertestamental (*sic!*) period' (Meier 2001, p. 405). The instances that Meier cites as evidence (i.e. *Genesis Apocryphon* and 4QPrayer of Nabodinus) relate more to what he calls 'obsession' than to 'possession' in the strict sense, and he cites with approval the conclusion of Hull 1974, pp. 62–3, to maintain that despite considerable evidence for exorcism in the Ancient Near East before the Common Era, actual stories of such encounters remain relatively rare (cf. Meier 2001, pp. 460 n. 30).

42 It remains possible that writers thought demons could inhabit bodies, while not choosing to depict demonic affliction in precisely this way. However, it is conspicuous that the language of corporeal habitation that characterizes the Gospel traditions is not as widespread as one might be led to assume.

43 See Eve 2002, pp. 177–82.

'driven away' (רעגהא, line 29).[44] A third example can be observed in the fragmentary *Apocryphal Psalms* text from Qumran Cave 11 (11Q11), which includes a version of Psalm 91 in the final column vi. The psalms of the text, one of which is called an 'in]cantation' (11Q11 v 4: לֿ[שׁ),[45] were a collection of short pieces to be sung or recited for the purpose of warding off demonic attacks. Again, there is no evidence that the demonic powers in view are being thought to 'possess' the human body.[46] The same is true in a fourth document that has come to be called *Songs of the Maskil* (4Q510–511; 4Q444); in the text, the Maskil's proclamation in praise of the splendour of God's radiance is intended 'to frighten and terrify' malevolent powers who might strike without warning to lead people astray (4Q510 1.4–6, par. 4Q511 10.1–3; 4Q511 8.4; 35.6–9; 48+49+51 ii 2–3).[47] Fifth and finally, it is the 'afflicted' (i.e. not necessarily the 'possessed') for whom David is said in 11Q5 xxvii 9–10 to have composed four songs.[48]

Less clear in distinguishing between affliction and possession is the text of *Jubilees* 10.7–14. According to this passage, the angels of the presence give instructions to Noah on how, for example, to use herbs to combat the malevolent effects of the remaining evil spirits (a tenth of their original number) who, following the Great Flood, were allowed to engage in seductive activities and to cause illnesses. It is not clear whether the text assumes that the revealed herbal remedies have exorcistic effects (in dealing with physical ailments within the body), are prophylactic and simply ward off the evil spirits, or – as most likely the case – both.

There are, in any case, only a few Jewish sources outside the New Testament and composed before the end of the first century CE that, analogous to the Synoptic Gospels, communicate demonic effects in terms of the inhabitation of demons within the human body. Perhaps the most well known instance of an exorcism is the story of 'a certain Eleazar' recounted by

---

44 For a similar use of the verb רעג, without any concern for the interiority of evil within humans, see the Hebrew *War Rule* at 1QM xiv 10: 'you (i.e. God) have driven away from [us] the spirits of [de]struction'.

45 According to 11Q11 v 4–5, this incantation may be 'spoken at any time to the heavens when a demon comes to you during the night'.

46 Wise, Abegg and Cook 1996, p. 454, García Martínez and Tigchelaar 1999, pp. 1179, 1203, and Lange 1997, pp. 377–435, esp. 379–84 and 431–3.

47 Though at times casually referring to 'exorcism', Nitzan 1994, pp. 227–72, esp. p. 238, has emphasized the apotropaic nature of 4Q510–511 and designated them broadly as a variety of 'anti-demonic songs'.

48 Within the collections of psalms in 11Q5 as a whole, it is important to note that the twin notions of exorcism, on the one hand, and possession, on the other, are not necessarily absent by virtue of not being explicitly mentioned. For language that comes closer to that of exorcism, see e.g. the petition (or perhaps self-exorcism?) in the prayer for deliverance in 11Q5 xix 15–16, especially if both parts of the petition are to be read as synonymously parallel: 'Do not let Satan rule over me, nor an unclean spirit; let neither pain nor evil inclination take possession of my bones.'

Josephus who illustrates the continuing potency of exorcistic cures attributed to Solomon (*Ant.* 8.42–49).[49]

Three more examples from the Dead Sea Scrolls may offer further evidence for the embodiment of evil power. The first of these comes to us from the *Damascus Document*, a portion of which is unattested among the later materials recovered from the Geniza of the Ezra Synagogue in Cairo: 4Q266 = 4QD^a 6 i 5–7 (with more fragmentary parallels in 4Q269 = 4QD^d 7; 4Q272 = 4QD^g 1 i–ii; and 4Q273 = 4QD^h 4 ii).[50] The text describes with precision a condition located 'under the hair' (4Q266 6 i 7 + 272 i 15), attributed to a spirit that has 'entered the head or the beard, taking hold of the blood vessels' (4Q266 6 i 6–7) and has rendered the person 'unclean' (4Q266 6 i 11).[51] As the text focuses on the establishment by a priest of when the diseased person is cured, no procedure of dealing with the spirit (such as exorcism, prayer or purification ritual) is described in the text. The cure is deemed to have taken effect when the priest can observe (a) that there are no further living hairs beyond the dead ones after seven days (4Q266 6 i 11–12), (b) that the artery is filled with blood again (line 12), and (c) that the 'spirit of life' ascends and descends in it (line 12). While it seems that the cure is effected by the removal of the disease-causing spirit, the text implies that the 'spirit of life' can either co-exist with it or replaces it within the person once the malevolent spirit is gone. I find it plausible, then, to regard this text as an instance of 'possession', though perhaps a softer expression such as 'habitation' is preferable.

A second text to note occurs within the *Treatise of the Two Spirits* preserved within the *Community Rule* at 1QS iii 13 – iv 26. At first glance it might not seem clear that the *Treatise* refers to 'possession'. After all, in 1QS iv 9–12 'the spirit of deceit' (חור הלוע, line 9) is co-ordinated with or thought to underlie a number of vices; moreover, according to the text the influence of this spirit leads to 'abundance of afflictions' (בור סיעוגנ) brought about by 'all the angels of destruction' (לוכ יכאלמ לבח, line 12) for those who fall sway to its rule. Though the precise relation of this spirit of deceit to human beings is not apparent, towards the end of the *Treatise* such a notion becomes apparent: at the appointed time of divine judgement, the deeds of humans will be purified from all wrongdoing, and God will 'finish off every spirit of deceit from the inward parts of his (the human's) flesh' (1QS iv 20–21 – הלוע ימכתמ ורשב מתהל לוכ חור), an act further described in the following phrase as a cleansing from every wicked deed through the spirit of holiness. The *Treatise* thus portrays eschatological judgement in terms of a global exorcism (cf. John 12.31) that is anthropologically focused: anything that remains from the spirit of deceit within humanity will be completely annihilated. In the present age, the spirit of deceit indwells human

---

49 Thackeray and Marcus 1938, pp. 594–5.
50 See Baumgarten 1996, pp. 52–3.
51 See further Baumgarten 1990, pp. 153–65.

beings, though not alone; the text declares that both 'the spirits of truth and deceit contend (against one another) in the hearts of man' (1QS iv 23: וביררי יחוד תמא לועו בבלב רבנ) in an attempt to control a person's actions. The language of possession does not occur and the habitation of the spirit of deceit is not exclusive; nonetheless, such a spirit, in so far as it is pitched in conflict with the spirit of truth, manifests itself within the human being as the cause of reprehensible deeds and attitudes (1QS iv 9–11).

Whereas the last two texts only approximate the idea of possession as we meet up with it in the New Testament Gospels, a third offers the clearest example thereof among the Dead Sea materials. The source in question consists of two small Aramaic fragments bearing the numerical designation 4Q560.[52] The incompletely preserved text refers to male and female poisonous beings that invade the human body and its parts: they gain 'e]ntry into the flesh' (1 i 3: [ללע ארשבב) where, presumably, their activities become the cause of 'iniquity and guilt', on the one hand, and of 'fever, chills, and heart of the heart', on the other (1 i 4: ואוע עשפו אשא הירעו תשאו בבל ...).[53] Column ii of the fragment (lines 5–6) preserves the beginning of an adjuration formula in which a malevolent spirit is directly addressed by an exorcist ('I, O spirit, adjure' – הנא חור המומן] and 'I adjure you, O spirit' – [כתימוא אחורי, respectively) who by such means is to bring the spirit (along with its effects) under control. To be sure, the text does not explicitly refer to expulsion; however, one may infer that the formula to be recited by the practitioner was intended to reverse what occurs when the spirit has invaded the body.

While the last three examples do not provide evidence for practices that immediately underlie episodes recorded in the Gospels, they do preserve language that conceives of demonic influence in terms of corporeal invasion or habitation. On the basis of the texts reviewed thus far, we may at least conclude that they enhance the plausibility of the theological anthropology assumed in the Synoptic Gospels within a Jewish setting.

The Synoptic Gospels draw together the motif of God's reign as king, the belief that *daimones* are evil and unclean and the view that they affect humans by gaining entry into their bodies. Taken together, these three beliefs may probably be understood as reflecting *what* Jesus thought his exorcisms *signified, how demons affect* the human body and *what is going on when they are expelled*. This puts us in a better position to ask how the ministry of Jesus participates in the world-view of his environment and

---

52 Puech 2009, pp. 291–302; see Penney and Wise 1994, pp. 627–50, Naveh 1998, pp. 252–61, and Beyer 2005, p. 168.

53 Following the interpretation of Puech 2009, p. 298, *contra* Penney and Wise 1994, pp. 631–2, 640, who are too quick to assign the phrase 'iniquity and guilt' to a citation of Ex. 34.7 and Num. 14.18 (which contain the Heb. cognates וזע עשפו). In addition, as initially suggested by Naveh 1998, pp. 256–7, and followed by Puech 2009, pp. 296, 299, the text at 1 i 5 refers to demonic entry 'into the tooth' (אשב), while Penney and Wise read the expression as denoting a time during which the demonic attack can take place, i.e. 'during sleep'.

what an understanding of Jesus in relation to his environment has to tell us about demonic discourse, on the one hand, and mental health, on the other.

The demonic and mental health in apocalyptic perspective

It is at this point where we can recognize the value of considering early Enochic traditions – especially the *Book of Watchers* (*1 En.* 1–36), the *Book of Giants* and the *Book of Dreams* (*1 En.* 83–90). These texts, composed by pious Jews during the third and second centuries BCE, have become the focus of increasing attention during the last several decades for a number of reasons, including what their authors had to say about the introduction of evil into the world.[54] In these texts, which in turn influenced many others, discourse about the origins of evil focused on rebellious angelic beings who, related to 'the sons of God' in Genesis 6.1, are blamed for having disseminated unacceptable knowledge and practices to humanity and, through the women of the earth, produced a large race of 'mighty men' (or 'giants'; cf. Gk. to Gen. 6.4) who enslaved humans and brought destruction to the natural world during the days before the Great Flood.

Unlike Genesis 6—9, the early Enochic traditions draw heavily on an interpretation of the Great Flood as a decisive act of divine punishment carried out in response to the evils committed by the fallen angels and their giant offspring. Significantly, motifs and imagery associated with the Flood[55] contribute to the way the Enochic authors attempted to describe God's ultimate triumph over and annihilation of evil. Perhaps the most influential form of this tradition is preserved in the *Book of Watchers* (hereafter *BW*), which, as a whole, dates to the third century BCE. The earliest extant copy of *BW*, 4Q201,[56] already combines the once separate strands of tradition in *1 Enoch* chapters 6–11 and 12–16.[57] The resulting narrative, if one reads chapters 6–16 as a unit, focuses on the reprehensible instructions given to

---

54 Since the seminal research in the 1970s by Dimant (e.g. 1974), Delcor 1976 and Milik 1976, a significant number of studies have focused on the significance of the fallen angels myth within Second Temple Judaism and in relation to the New Testament. In addition to numerous articles published in journals such as *Dead Sea Discoveries*, *Journal of Biblical Literature*, *Henoch*, *Revue de Qumran*, and *Journal for the Study of the Pseudepigrapha*, a representation of these studies may be found in the following works: Sacchi 1990, Reeves 1992, Davidson 1992, VanderKam 1996, Stuckenbruck 1997, Jackson 2004, Auffarth and Stuckenbruck 2004, Bhayro 2005, Yoshiko Reed 2005, A. T. Wright 2005, Boccaccini and Ibba 2009. Though none of the Discoveries in the Judean Desert series volumes have as yet presented the Enochic materials together in edited form, the *Book of Giants* fragments constitute an exception; see Stuckenbruck 2000 and Puech 2001.

55 See *1 En.* 10; 83–84; 91.5–10; 93.1–3 and 93.12–15; 106.13–107.1; *Book of Giants* at 4Q530 2 ii + 6–7 + 8–12, lines 4–20.

56 See Milik 1976, pp. 140–1.

57 Newsom 1980, pp. 310–29.

humanity during the period before the Flood by the wayward angelic beings (*1 En.* 7.1; 8.3; 9.6–8a; 13.2b; cf. Eth. to 16.3), as well as on the violent activities of their progeny, the giants, who correspond to the 'mighty men' and 'Nephilim' in Genesis 6.4. In contrast to Genesis 6, which makes no direct mention of the giants' involvement in the events leading up to the Flood, the giants in *BW* are prominent among those who are held accountable for the increase of oppression and suffering on the earth (*1 En.* 7.3–6; 9.1, 9–10). So it is in response to the cries of the giants' human victims (8.4–9.3; cf. 7.6) that divine judgement is set in motion (ch. 10). The giants are then punished through either infighting among themselves (7.5; 10.9, 12)[58] or, though less clearly, through the Great Flood (10.15; *Jub.* 7.21–25).[59]

The emphasis placed by *BW* and, subsequently, the *Book of Giants*, on divine judgement of the giant offspring of the rebellious angels was not simply based on the violence and oppressiveness of their deeds. More fundamentally, there was something inherently wrong with the very form of their existence. According to one strand of the narrative associated with the angel Shemihazah, the giants were the product of the illicit sexual union between the angels as heavenly beings and the human women as earthly beings (*1 En.* 6.1–4; 7.1–2; 9.7–8; 10.9, 11; 15.3–7, 12; cf. *Book of Giants* at 4Q531 1). In *1 Enoch* 15.3–7, the main reason why this union is so objectionable is given: the giants are a mixture of spirit and body that derives from acts of defilement in which beings, angels and humans, assigned to essentially separate spheres in the cosmos (i.e. heaven and earth) had come together. By definition, then, the giants embodied a violation of the created order (15.4, 9–10; cf. *Jub.* 7.21). As the offspring of such an illegitimate union, they were neither fully angel nor fully human.[60] Hence they are called 'bastards' in *1 Enoch* 10.9 (Cod. Panopolitanus reads τοὺς μαζηρέους, a transliteration from Hebrew or Aramaic אירממ/ד). They are misfits and have no proper place.

Both *BW* and the *Book of Giants* make it clear that through an act of divine intervention the giants had to be categorically and decisively held to account.[61] Nonetheless, although the giants are not spared, neither is it the case that they are completely annihilated; though not escaping divine wrath, they end up surviving in a radically altered state: they are 'evil spirits' (*1 En.* 15.8–9). The preserved textual witnesses to *1 Enoch* 15 do not state how this alteration of existence has occurred, but it is possible to reconstruct

---

58 See also *Jub.* 5.9; 7.22; and the *Book of Giants* at 6Q8 1 and 4Q531 7.

59 Within the early Enochic tradition, punishment of the giants through the deluge is clearest in the *Animal Apocalypse* at *1 En.* 89.5. In service of paradigmatic interests, the Flood soon became the primary, if not only, means for the giants' destruction in Second Temple literature from the second century on. So esp. 4*QExhortation Based on the Flood* (= 4Q370) i 6; *Damascus Document* (CD A ii 19–20); Ecclus. 16.7(?); Wisd. 14.6; 3 *Macc.* 2.4; and 3 *Bar.* 4.10.

60 See Stuckenbruck 2005b, pp. 318–38, and A. T. Wright 2005, pp. 143–51.

61 See Stuckenbruck 2004, pp. 87–118.

an etiology[62] behind the existence of demons based on 15.3—16.3 and the *Book of Giants* that may have been elaborating on parts of *1 Enoch* 10. When the giants came under God's judgement, their physical nature was destroyed while their spirits or souls emerged from their dead bodies. In this disembodied state, they continue to exist until the final triumph of God at the end of history as we know it (16.1). After the Great Flood they engage in the sorts of activities that they had previously done. In particular, as before, they wished to afflict human beings (15.12). Why? We may infer that they were jealous of humanity who had managed to escape the deluge with their bodies intact. *The spirits who came from the giants, then, are misfits and have no sanctioned place within the created order. It is this kind of being that lies behind the physical and mental afflictions that people suffer* (*1 En.* 15.12—16.1a).

Excursus B: The giants' spirits as demonic beings in ancient Judaism and early Christianity

This storyline explains how it is that the giants could become identified as demons, not only among the Dead Sea Scrolls but also at a later stage. Among the Dead Sea materials several references to demonic beings reflect the direct influence of the Enochic tradition and have the giants' post-diluvian existence in view. According to *Songs of the Maskil* at 4Q510 1.5, the expression 'spirits of the bastards' (רוחי ממזרים) occurs within a longer catalogue of malevolent forces. This also avails in the same document at 4Q511 35.7; 48+49+51.2–3 and at 4Q444 2 i 4, where they are beings who need to be brought under control by the hymns directed by the Maskil to God.[63] Furthermore, in the above mentioned *Apocryphal Psalms* text (section D.3), at 11Q11 v 6, the demon visiting during the night is, if the text is correctly restored, addressed as 'offspring of] Adam and seed of the ho[ly] ones'.[64] This explanation of demons as disembodied spirits emanating from the giant offspring of the fallen angels continues in later Christian literature, picked up in *Testament of Solomon* (5.3; 17.1), the *Pseudo-Clementine Homilies* (8.12–18: giants designated as 'bastards' and 'demons'), Tertullian's *Apology* (22), Lactantius' *Institutes* (2.15) and Commodianus' *Instructions* (3).[65]

---

62 An etiology is a story that explains how what we experience has come about.

63 Lange 1997, pp. 383, 402–3, 430–3; see Stuckenbruck 2005a, pp. 55–73.

64 For the expression 'holy ones' as referring to the fallen angels, see also *Genesis Apocryphon* (1Q20) ii 1, vi 20 and *Book of Watchers* at 4Q201 1 i 3.

65 VanderKam 1996, pp. 76–9, and Yoshiko Reed 2004, pp. 141–71.

Jewish apocalyptic perspective and the Gospel traditions: what this means for understanding mental illness

Before stating what our consideration of the Gospels and Jewish traditions can contribute constructively to understanding pastoral implications of Jesus' ministry, I think it appropriate to acknowledge a couple of points for the sake of caution. We acknowledge, first, that none of the Enochic traditions contains any of the more technical language such as 'kingdom of God' which in the Gospels plays such a prominent role in Jesus' proclamation and which, as we have seen, is related to Jesus' exorcism ministry. Second, not a single instance among the Gospels openly identifies a demon as a giant living in a postdiluvian state of existence. Nevertheless, what might the early Enochic traditions and the trajectory of development they set within the Dead Sea documents (see Excursus A and B)[66] contribute to what Jesus the exorcist is seen to accomplish in the lives of people according to the Synoptic Gospels?

In relation to a better understanding of the ministry of Jesus in the Gospel tradition, the story of the giants could function in a number of ways. First, although it is hard to show that the origin of bodiless giants was conscious to the Gospel writers themselves, the story does help to explain why it is that demons were so intent on *entering* the bodies of human beings. Demonic entry is understood as an attempt to recover a form of existence the giants had lost and to make humans suffer since, as a species, they came through the Great Flood unscathed. When present inside humans, these spirits interfered with and upset the balance of humans whom God had created to have a body and spirit of their own.

Second, the story serves to locate the problem of demonic evil within an apocalyptic-eschatological framework. On the one hand, the giants' punishment during the period of the Flood is regarded as a decisive, indeed definitive, act of God in the past. On the other hand, although the giants were allowed to survive after the Flood as disembodied spirits, their newly altered state as spirits was accompanied by a consciousness on their part that they are powers that have already, in essence, been defeated. Thus, even the demonic world knows that it is fighting a battle that it will ultimately lose. The Flood is portrayed and retold as a proleptic episode out of the sacred past. Accordingly, imagery from the Flood narrative is adapted in *1 Enoch* 10 as the text looks forward to an eschatological judgement when evil will be destroyed once and for all (10.13—11.2). The meantime – that is, between the time God's rule became manifest in the Flood and the time when evil will be eradicated – is an age during which evil spirits that came from the giants can operate under restriction (cf. *Jub.* 10.7–9), knowing their time to wreak havoc on humanity is limited (*1 En.* 16.1; *Jub.* 10.7–9;

---

66 See my forthcoming book, *The Influence and Reception of the Fallen Angels Tradition in Ancient Judaism and Early Christianity*, Tübingen: Mohr Siebeck.

see Matt. 8.29 – 'have you come to torment us before the time?' (pars. Mark 5.7; Luke 8.28); cf. also Mark 1.24, par. Luke 4.34 – 'have you come to destroy us?' – and James 2.19). In this sense the Gospels present us with a world order that, as in Jewish apocalyptic tradition, temporarily falls under 'the dominion of wickedness'[67] or, similarly, 'the dominion of Satan' (cf. Matt. 4.8, par. Luke 4.5–6; Luke 22.31–32; Matt. 12.26, par. Luke 11.17–18; cf. also John 12.31; 14.30; 16.11).[68] Jewish contemporaries of Jesus who undertook means to curb the influence of demons could, against such a background, proceed with a certain measure of confidence. In relation to the discourse about the demonic world, then, Jesus does not so much introduce the notion of an eschatological tension between the 'already' and 'not yet' as much as he intensifies it through his ministry.

Third, God's act of delivering humanity and God's punishment of evil at the time of the Flood is associated with royal power (cf. Ps. 29.10). The divine response happens following complaints of murdered souls in which the archangels address God *inter alia* as 'King of kings' (*1 En.* 9.4).[69]

Fourth, in view of the framework outlined here, one may then well ask: what do the Gospel stories of exorcisms performed by Jesus and others think happens to demonic powers when they have been expelled? *Those who understood themselves to live in a world inhabited by demons would not have thought exorcism is a matter of extermination or of total destruction.* Through exorcism, *spiritual forces are not destroyed, they are relocated.* This is the view affirmed in Luke 11.24–26 (par. Matt. 12.43–45; cf. the section above under 'God, demons and humans in the Jesus tradition') and is presumed by all the accounts of Jesus' confrontation with malevolent spirits. Even the Gadarene demoniac episode provides another case in point, with its two-stage exorcism that builds on the presumption (articulated by 'Legion' in Mark 5.12, 'send us into the swine so that we may enter into them') that this is what customarily happens.[70] Therefore, despite the

---

67 Among the Dead Sea materials, see esp. 4Q510 1.6–7, par. 4Q511 10.3–4.

68 Cf. 1QS i 23–24, ii 19; 1QM xiv 9–10, par. 4QMa = 4Q491 8–10 i 6–7; 4Q177=4QCatena[a] iii 8; 4Q390 2 i 4.

69 Moreover, if it is correct to read one of the *Book of Giants* fragments (4Q203 9) as a petition (by Enoch?) that God intervene to punish the fallen angels and giants, then the reference in the prayer to 'your great rule' (תוכלם הכתובר) suggests that God's kingship was being understood to have manifested itself in the past in the deluge (cf. also *1 En.* 9.4–11). Indeed, Enoch's petition in the *Book of Dreams* (*1 En.* 84.2–6), which also appeals to God's kingship, anticipates – and is followed by – the punishment of antediluvian evil. The presence of royal power in curbing or dealing with the effects of demonic power may also be implied in the *Songs of the Maskil* mentioned under Excursus A above. The writer of the songs holds two convictions in tension: a belief that one now lives during a time of 'a dominion of wickedness' during which 'the sons of light' can be expected to suffer and be 'plagued by iniquities', and a belief that despite this the threats posed by such evil powers, which are temporary in any case, can be neutralized until the present age is brought to an end (cf. 4Q510 1.6b–8, par. 4Q511 10.3b–6).

70 See Konradt 2007, pp. 60–1, and bibliography in n. 240.

story's attempt to highlight the distinct authority with which Jesus takes control over the situation, the drowning of two thousand swine indwelt by the spirits (5.13) does not mark the end of those spirits. Whatever early storylines of this tradition may have contained, on the level of the Marcan narrative (so also Luke 8.33), the drowning signifies the end of demonic power on this person, though an eschatological act of complete subjugation lies ahead.[71] The same applies to Jesus' expulsion of a father's son plagued since childhood by a demon in Mark 9.14–29. To be sure, Jesus' address to the demon includes the command 'Do not enter him again!' (9.25). Again, however, the conclusion of this episode underscores the effectiveness of the exorcism itself, rather than claiming anything about the destruction of the demon (cf. Tob. 6.8; 8.3). Moreover, it reflects a view that 'possession' can be momentary or sporadic as well as sustained.

Fifth, and following from the last point, the 'return of the spirit' saying in Luke 11.24–26 acknowledged, as we have seen, that exorcized powers can return and do so in such a way that the person's condition is worse than before. This reflects an outlook that evil power, once extricated from the human body, needs to be kept at bay, negotiated, or managed in order for the person to remain in an improved state of being. *Being exorcized is not a static condition, but is a mode of being within a fluid life process.* If this is so, then Jesus' exorcisms are not simply to be understood as 'miracles' in a remote or unusual sense. It is important to say this, since many mental health professionals think that the Bible presents us with a worldview that is essentially irrelevant to today. Jesus is imagined as one who offered 'quick or sudden solutions' for people's problems. *Our evidence in the Gospels, informed by the Enoch tradition, paints a much more realistic portrait of life. People suffering from problems we might refer to today as mental illnesses were being helped, and we are not to assume that cures were automatically permanent.* Exorcism – and we may include healing (whether through medicine or prayer or both) – is, even in Jesus' ministry, *a temporary expedient.* From the perspective of the Gospel tradition, it illustrates that the physical, spiritual and mental problems that beset people are evils that, under the eyes of faith, have already been defeated. From the perspective of the Gospel tradition, it also illustrates that such problems cannot simply be wished away. It is in this respect that the world of the psychiatrist – even one who is not a Christian – is not so completely remote. Psychiatrists and psychologists rely on their patients to have hope that they can improve; equally, they know that even with medication mental illness does not simply vanish into thin air. For too long the mental health profession and the world of the Gospels have been held apart when, in reality, they are not so completely disconnected.

Sixth and finally, the very idea that exorcism is needed at all is not actually built around an understanding of a person as someone invaded by evil.

---

71 Cf. Williamson 2009, p. 104.

The Enochic tradition and a number of texts that drew upon it regarded demonic powers as inherently out of place in and alien to the world as God has set it up to be.[72] *The notion of possession, instead of undermining the dignity of this or that individual, could have functioned to preserve it.* Whatever their problems, *humans are not 'metaphysically evil', but are and remain integral to the created order.* This is fundamental both to the Enoch tradition and in the ministry of Jesus.

Conclusion

The Synoptic Gospels underline the success of Jesus as one whose power is superior to that of demonic powers in the present age (Matt. 9.34, par. earlier form of the tradition in Luke 11.14; Mark 1.27; cf. Mark 5.20). Jesus' prominence as an exorcist par excellence is also reflected in the effectiveness attributed to the use of his 'name' by others (Matt. 7.22; Mark 9.38; Luke 9.49; 10.17).[73] There is every reason to think, then, that the presentation of Jesus in the Gospels stressed the 'miraculous' character of his deeds.

At the same time, the counter-demonic manoeuvres described in the Gospels fit logically into the framework of an apocalyptic world-view that Jesus shared with some, if not many, of his pious Jewish contemporaries. Our consideration of the Second Temple context may provide one way of getting past the hermeneutical conundrum associated with Jesus' exorcisms. In parts of the contemporary world, readers of the Gospels have stressed the dramatic, spectacular character with which the descriptions of these episodes are invested in the text. While such a reading rightly picks up on the significance being attached to the person of Jesus, it may serve to make Jesus more remote or bifurcate readers around the misleading question of whether or not there is a place at all in religious communities today for such or similar activity. By contrast, we have attempted here to refocus the problem to being one that is primarily *a matter of perspective.* It is possible to regard a hermeneutically, cosmologically and sociologically controversial part of Jesus' activity in combating demonic forces not only as miracle (with its attendant symbolic interpretations) but also as – perhaps surprisingly so – a realistic approach, informed by his Jewish context. Read more specifically in relation to an apocalyptic world-view, the accounts of exorcisms performed by Jesus and others, for all their 'success' as depicted in the Gospels, presuppose the recognition of two things: that (i) however one treats it, evil is a persistent reality that cannot be conveniently ignored or removed from human experience, and that (ii) from a standpoint of faith, the wholeness of individual and collective humanity is assured through anticipation

---

72 Stuckenbruck 2009, pp. 191–208.

73 The scope for successful exorcisms in Acts 19.13–16 is implicitly narrowed to Jesus' followers, though the sons of Sceva are presented as having wrongly assumed that their use of Jesus' name would be effective.

of God's ultimate victory, which can, though not necessarily, be already experienced in this life.

Against this background, the notion of having a mental disorder, therefore, should not be regarded as 'taboo'. In the community of faith, whether one attributes problems to the demonic or to chemical imbalance, the suffering person, created in the image of God, has an undeniable dignity that is to be cultivated and preserved. Those standing in a Christian or Jewish tradition might not be able to 'get rid' of or do away with problems in others or within themselves. The above discussion, however, gives place to exorcisms in the Gospels alongside other practices – these include petitionary prayer, community support, the worshipping life of the assembled church or synagogue – through which it is possible to gain perspective on the sometimes irretrievable suffering people face. The confession and proclamation of evil that has already in principle been overcome opens up a vision for the value of personhood that signals the possibility of restoration to come.

References

Albinus, L. (2005), 'The Greek δαίμων between Mythos and Logos', in A. Lange, H. Lichtenberger and K. F. D. Römheld (eds), *Die Dämonen – Demons*, Tübingen: Mohr Siebeck, pp. 425–46.

Alexander, P. (1998–99), 'The demonology of the Dead Sea Scrolls', in P. W. Flint and J. C. VanderKam (eds), *The Dead Sea Scrolls after Fifty Years: A Comprehensive Assessment*, 2 vols, Leiden: Brill, vol. 2, pp. 331–53.

Auffarth, C. and Stuckenbruck, L. T. (eds) (2004), *The Fall of the Angels*, Themes in Biblical Narrative 6, Leiden and Boston: Brill.

Basham, D. (1972, repr. 2005), *Deliver Us from Evil*, Washington Depot CT: Chosen Books.

Baumgarten, J. M. (1990), 'The 4Q Zadokite fragments on skin disease', *Journal of Jewish Studies* 41:2, pp. 153–65.

Baumgarten, J. M. (1996), *Qumran Cave 4 XIII: The Damascus Document (4Q266–273)*. Discoveries in the Judaean Desert, XVIII, Oxford: Clarendon Press.

Becker, J. (1998), *Jesus of Nazareth*, trans. J. E. Crouch, New York: Walter de Gruyter.

Bell, R. H. (2007), *Deliver Us from Evil: Interpreting the Redemption from the Power of Satan in New Testament Theology*, WUNT, I/216, Tübingen: Mohr Siebeck.

Beyer, K. (2005), *Die aramäischen Texte vom Toten Meer*, vol. 2, Göttingen: Vandenhoeck & Ruprecht.

Bhayro, S. (2005), *The Shemihaza and Asael Narrative of 1 Enoch: Introduction, Text, Translation and Commentary with Reference to Ancient Near Eastern and Biblical Antecedents*, AOAT 322, Münster: Ugarit-Verlag.

Blanch, S. (1988), *Encounters with Jesus*, The Jesus Library, London: Hodder & Stoughton, pp. 56–66.

Boccaccini, G. and Ibba, M. (eds) (2009), *Enoch and the Mosaic Torah: The Evidence of Jubilees*, Grand Rapids MI: Eerdmans.

Borg, M. (1988), *A New Vision*, San Francisco: Harper & Row.

Brenk, F. E. (1986), 'In the light of the moon: demonology in the early Imperial period', in Wolfgang Haase (ed.), *Aufstieg und Niedergang der römischen Welt* II.16.3, Berlin: Walter de Gruyter, pp. 2068–145.

Capps, D. (2008), *Jesus the Village Psychiatrist*, Louisville KY and London: Westminster John Knox Press.

Crossan, J. D. (1991), *The Historical Jesus: The Life of a Mediterranean Jewish Peasant*, San Francisco: HarperSanFrancisco.

Crossan, J. D. (1994), *Jesus: A Revolutionary Biography*, San Francisco: HarperSanFrancisco.

Davidson, M. J. (1992), *Angels at Qumran: A Comparative Study of 1 Enoch 1–36, 72–108 and Sectarian Writings from Qumran*, JSP Supplements 11, Sheffield: Journal for the Study of the Old Testament (JSOT) Press.

Delcor, M. (1976), 'Le myth de la chute des anges et de l'origine des géants comme explication du mal dans le monde dans l'apocalyptique juive histoire des traditions', *RHR* 190:1, pp. 3–53.

Diagnostic and Statistic Manual of Mental Disorders (2000), 4th edn, Washington DC: American Psychiatric Association.

Diamond, S. (1996), *Anger, Madness, and the Daimonic*, Albany: State University of New York Press.

Diamond, S. (2012), 'The devil inside: psychotherapy, exorcism, and demonic possession', http://www.psychologytoday.com/blog/evil-deeds/201201/the-devil-inside-psychotherapy-exorcism-and-demonic-possession.

Dimant, D. (1974), '"The Fallen Angels" in the Dead Sea Scrolls and in the apocryphal and pseudepigraphic books related to them', Ph.D. Dissertation: Hebrew University (in Hebrew).

Ehrman, B. D. (1999), *Jesus: Apocalyptic Prophet of the New Millennium*, Oxford: Oxford University Press.

Eitrem, S. (1966), *Some Notes on the Demonology in the New Testament*, Symbolae Osloenses Fasc. Supplet. 20, 2nd edn, Oslo: Universitetsforlaget.

Ellens, J. H. (2008), 'Biblical miracles and psychological process: Jesus as psychotherapist', in J. H. Ellens (ed.), *Miracles: God, Science, and Psychology in the Paranormal*, Westport CT: Praeger.

Eve, E. (2002), *The Jewish Context of Jesus' Miracles*, JSNT Supplements 231, Sheffield: Sheffield Academic Press.

Freud, S. (1950 [1913]), *Totem and Taboo: Resemblances between the Psychic Lives of Savages and Neurotics*, trans. James Strachey, London: Routledge, pp. 18–74 ('Taboo and emotion ambivalence') and 75–99 ('Animism, magic, and the omnipotence of thoughts').

Freud, S. (1961 [1922]), 'A seventeenth-century demonological neurosis', *The Standard Edition of the Complete Psychological Works of Sigmund Freud. Volume XIX: The Ego and the Id and Other Works*, trans. James Strachey et al., London: Hogarth Press, pp. 72–105.

García Martínez, F. and Tigchelaar, E. J. C. (1999), *The Dead Sea Scrolls Studies Edition*, 2 vols, Leiden: Brill.

Harris, R. (2006), 'Embracing your demons: an overview of acceptance and commitment therapy', *Psychotherapy in Australia* 12:4, pp. 2–8.

Harris, S. (2004), *The End of Faith*, New York: W. W. Norton.

Hitchens, C. (2007), *God Is Not Great: How Religion Poisons Everything*, New York: Warner.

Horsley, R. A. (1987), *Jesus and the Spiral of Violence: Popular Jewish Resistance in Roman Palestine*, San Francisco: Harper & Row.

Hull, J. M. (1974), *Hellenistic Magic and the Synoptic Tradition*, Studies in Biblical Theology, 2.28, London: SCM Press.

Jackson, D. R. (2004), *Enochic Judaism: Three Defining Paradigm Exemplars*, Library of Second Temple Studies 49, London: T & T Clark International.

Klutz, T. E. (1999), 'The grammar of exorcism in the ancient Mediterranean world', in C. C. Newman, J. R. Davila and G. S. Lewis (eds), *The Jewish Roots of Christological Monotheism*, JSJ Supplements 63, Leiden/Boston/Köln: Brill, pp. 156–65.

Konradt, M. (2007), *Israel, Kirche und die Völker im Matthäusevangelium*, WUNT 215, Tübingen: Mohr Siebeck.

Lange, A. (1997), 'The Essene position on magic and divination', in M. Bernstein, F. García Martínez and J. Kampen (eds), *Legal Texts and Legal Issues: Proceedings of the Second Meeting of the International Organization for Qumran Studies, Cambridge, 1995: Published in Honour of Joseph M. Baumgarten*, STDJ 23, Leiden: Brill, pp. 377–435.

Lange, A. (2005), 'Considerations concerning the "spirit of impurity" in Zech 13:2', in A. Lange, H. Lichtenberger and K. F. D. Römheld (eds), *Die Dämonen – Demons*, Tübingen: Mohr Siebeck, pp. 254–68.

Langton, E. (1949), *Essentials of Demonology: A Study of Jewish and Christian Doctrine: Its Origin and Development*, London: Epworth Press.

MacNutt, F. (1974), *Healing*, New York: Bantam Books and Ave Maria Press, esp. pp. 189–210 ('On deliverance and exorcism').

MacNutt, F. (1995, repr. 2009), *Deliverance from Evil Spirits: A Practical Manual*, Grand Rapids MI: Chosen Books.

Mäyrä, F. I. (1999), *Demonic Texts and Textual Demons*, Tampere: Tampere University Press, esp. pp. 51–80 ('The demonic in the Self').

Meggitt, J. (2011), 'The historical Jesus and healing: Jesus' miracles in psychosocial context', in Fraser Watts (ed.), *Spiritual Healing: Scientific and Religious Perspectives*, Cambridge: Cambridge University Press, pp. 17–43.

Meier, J. P. (2001), *A Marginal Jew: Rethinking the Historical Jesus*, vol. 2: *Mentor, Message, and Miracles*, Anchor Bible Reference Library, New York: Doubleday.

Milik, J. T. (1976), *The Books of Enoch: Aramaic Fragments of Qumrân Cave 4*, Oxford: Clarendon Press.

Myers, C. (1988), *Binding the Strong Man: A Political Reading of Mark's Story of Jesus*, Maryknoll NY: Orbis.

Naveh, J. (1998), 'Fragments of an Aramaic magic book from Qumran', *Israel Exploration Journal* 48:3–4, pp. 252–61.

Newsom, C. A. (1980), 'The development of 1 Enoch 6–19: cosmology and judgment', *Catholic Bible Quarterly* 42:3, pp. 310–29.

Nitzan, B. (1994), *Qumran Prayer and Religious Poetry*, STDJ 12, Leiden: Brill.

Noack, B. (1948), *SATANÁS und SOTERÍA: Untersuchungen zur neutestamentlichen Dämonologie*, Copenhagen: G. E. C. Gads Forlag.

Patterson, S. J. (1998), *The God of Jesus: The Historical Jesus and the Search for Meaning*, Harrisburg PA: Trinity Press International.

Penney, D. L. and M. Wise (1994), 'By the power of Beelzebub: an Aramaic incantation formula from Qumran (4Q560)', *Journal of Biblical Literature* 113:4, pp. 627–50.

Piper, R. A. (2000), 'The absence of exorcisms in the Fourth Gospel', in David G. Horrell and Christopher M. Tuckett (eds), *Christology, Controversy, and Community: New Testament Essays in Honour of David R. Catchpole*, NovTest. Supplements 99, Leiden/Boston/Köln: Brill, pp. 252–78.

Puech, É. (2001), '4Q530–533, 203 1. 4QLivre de Géants[b-c] ar', in *Qumrân Grotte 4 XXII. Textes araméens, Première Partie: 4Q529–549*, Discoveries in the Judaean Desert XXXI; Oxford: Clarendon Press, pp. 9–115.

Puech, É. (2009), '560. 4QLivre magique ar', in É. Puech, *Qumrân Grotte 4 XXVII: Textes Araméens Deuxième Partie. 4Q550–4Q575a, 4Q580–4Q587 et Appendices*, Discoveries in the Judaean Desert XXXVII, Oxford: Clarendon Press, pp. 291–302.

Reeves, J. C. (1992), *Jewish Lore in Manichaean Cosmogony: Studies in the Book of Giants Traditions*, MHUC 14; Cincinnati OH: Hebrew Union College Press.

Ribi, A. (1990), *Demons of the Inner World: Understanding Our Hidden Complexes*, trans. M. Kohn, Boston: Shambhala.

Saachi, P. (1990), *Jewish Apocalyptic and its History*, trans. William Short, JSP Supplements 20; Sheffield: Journal for the Study of the Old Testament (JSOT) Press.

Smith, M. (1978), *Jesus the Magician*, London: Gollancz.

Söding, T. (2003), '"Wenn ich mit dem Finger Gottes die Dämonen austreibe ..." (Lk 11,20): Die Exorzismen im Rahmen der Basileia-Verkündigung Jesu', in A. Lange, H. Lichtenberger and K. F. D. Römheld (eds), *Die Dämonen – Demons*, Tübingen: Mohr Siebeck, pp. 519–49.

Sorensen, E. (2002), *Possession and Exorcism in the New Testament and Early Christianity*, WUNT II.157, Tübingen: Mohr Siebeck.

Stegemann, H. (1998), *The Library of Qumran: On the Essenes, Qumran, John the Baptist, and Jesus*, Leiden: Brill.

Stuckenbruck, L. T. (1997), *The Book of Giants from Qumran*, Texts and Studies in Ancient Judaism 63, Tübingen: Mohr Siebeck.

Stuckenbruck, L. T. (2000), *Qumran Cave 4 XXVI. Cryptic Texts and Miscellanea, Part 1*, Discoveries in the Judaean Desert XXXVI, Oxford: Clarendon Press, pp. 8–94 ('1Q23, 1Q24, 2Q26, 4Q203, 6Q8').

Stuckenbruck, L. T. (2004), 'The origins of evil in Jewish apocalyptic tradition: the interpretation of Genesis 6:1–4 in the second and third centuries B.C.E', in C. Auffarth and L. T. Stuckenbruck (eds), *The Fall of the Angels*, Themes in Biblical Narrative 7, Leiden and Boston: Brill, pp. 87–118.

Stuckenbruck, L. T. (2005a), 'Pleas for deliverance from the demonic in early Jewish texts', in R. Hayward and B. Embry (eds), *Studies in Jewish Prayer*, JSS Supplements 17, Oxford: Oxford University Press, pp. 55–73.

Stuckenbruck, L. T. (2005b), 'Giant mythology and demonology: from the Ancient Near East to the Dead Sea Scrolls', in A. Lange, H. Lichtenberger and K. F. D. Römheld (eds), *Die Dämonen – Demons*, Tübingen: Mohr Siebeck, pp. 318–38.

Stuckenbruck, L. T. (2008), 'Jesus' apocalyptic worldview and his exorcistic ministry', in J. H. Charlesworth and G. S. Oegema (eds), *Pseudepigrapha and Christian Origins: Essays from the Studiorum Novi Testamenti Societas*, Jewish and Christian Texts in Context and Related Studies 4, London: Continuum, pp. 68–84.

Stuckenbruck, L. T. (2009), 'The eschatological worship by the nations: an inquiry into the early Enoch tradition', in K. D. Dobos and M. Kőszeghy (eds), *Wisdom Like a Robe: Festschrift in Honour of Ida Fröhlich*, Sheffield: Sheffield Phoenix Press, pp. 191–208.

Suter, D. W. (1979), 'Fallen angel, fallen priest: the problem of family purity in 1 Enoch', *Hebrew Union College Annual* 50, pp. 115–35.

Telford, W. R. (1999), *The Theology of the Gospel of Mark*, New Testament Theology, Cambridge UK and New York: Cambridge University Press.

Thackeray, H. St. J. and Marcus, R. (1938), *Josephus. Jewish Antiquities V: Books V–VIII*, Loeb Classical Library, 281, Cambridge, MA: Harvard University Press.

Thomas, J. C. (1998), *The Devil, Disease and Deliverance: Origins of Illness in New Testament Thought*, JPT Supplements 13, Sheffield: Sheffield Academic Press.

Twelftree, G. H. (1993), *Jesus the Exorcist: A Contribution to the Study of the Historical Jesus*, Peabody MA: Hendrickson.

Twelftree, G. H. (2007), *In the Name of Jesus: Exorcism among Early Christians*, Grand Rapids MI: Baker Academic.

VanderKam, J. C. (1996), '1 Enoch, Enochic motifs, and Enoch in early Christian literature', in J. C. VanderKam and W. Adler (eds), *The Jewish Apocalyptic Heritage in Early Christianity*, CRINT III.4, Assen, Netherlands: Van Gorcum, and Minneapolis MN: Fortress Press, pp. 33–101.

Vermes, G. (1973), *Jesus the Jew: A Historian's Reading of the Gospels*, Philadelphia PA: Fortress Press.

Wahlen, C. (2004), *Jesus and the Impurity of Spirits in the Synoptic Gospels*, WUNT II.185, Tübingen: Mohr Siebeck.

Waetjen, H. C. (1989), *A Reordering of Power: A Sociopolitical Reading of Mark's Gospel*, Minneapolis MN: Augsburg Fortress Press.

Williamson, L. (2009), *Mark*, The New Testament Library, Louisville KY: Westminster John Knox Press.

Wise, M., Abegg, M. and Cook, E. (1996), *The Dead Sea Scrolls*, London: HarperCollins.

World Health Organization Report 2001: Mental Health: New Understanding, New Hope (2001), Geneva: The World Health Organization.

World Health Organization Factsheet 220 (2010), http://www.who.int/mediacentre/factsheets/fs220/en.

Wright, A. T. (2005), *The Origin of Evil Spirits: The Reception of Genesis 6:1–4 in Early Jewish Literature*, WUNT II.98, Tübingen: Mohr Siebeck.

Wright, N. T. (1996), *Jesus and the Victory of God*, London: SPCK.

Yoshiko Reed, A. (2004), 'The trickery of the fallen angels and the demonic mimesis of the Divine: aetiology, demonology, and polemics in the writings of Justin Martyr', *Journal of Early Christian Studies* 12:2, pp. 141–71.

Yoshiko Reed, A. (2005), *Fallen Angels and the History of Judaism and Christianity: The Reception of Enochic Literature*, Cambridge and New York: Cambridge University Press.

7

Religion and Mental Health

The Case of Conversion with Particular Reference to William James's *The Varieties of Religious Experience*

MARK WYNN

Summary

This chapter notes a particular kind of mental un-ease, that consists in a sense of life having lost its purpose or direction and that is manifest in a correlative presentation of the everyday, sensory world. Drawing on William James's account of conversion experience, Mark Wynn examines how a person's religious orientation may contribute to the resolution of this predicament. In particular, he considers how the subjective feel of our relationship to the sensory world may be ordered by the emotions considered as forms of salient experience; by concept-infused forms of seeing; by kinaesthetic experience tied to an assessment of the practical potentialities of the world; and by certain fundamental feelings of the body that condition a person's sense of reality. Drawing on this scheme, he considers some of the ways in which religious commitments and practices may contribute to an enlivened experience of the sensory world and how they may address thereby certain kinds of existential disorientation. On the view defended here, mental health consists in part in the realization of an appropriate match between a person's fundamental values and beliefs and the appearance of the sensory world.

Introduction

In his 1901–02 Gifford Lectures, subsequently published as *The Varieties of Religious Experience*, William James famously distinguishes between two kinds of religious temperament – what he calls the healthy-minded and sick-souled religious personalities (Lectures IV–VII). It is the second of these that I shall be concerned with here, and it is this variety of religious sensibility that James himself clearly considers the deeper from a spiritual point of view, not least because a person of this religious orientation will need to have reckoned seriously with the trials and challenges of a human life.

As the term 'sick' soul suggests, this mode of religiousness has its roots in a kind of un-ease or disease. James is interested in particular in those people whose sense of the worthwhileness of human life has been put at risk by their sensitivity to the vulnerability of human beings and their projects to frustration and reversal. So in discussing sick-souled religion, James is concerned with what we might call the existential dimension of mental health – he is concerned with the capacity of human beings who feel deeply the limitations of a human life to come to terms with those limitations and to live creatively in the face of them.

Characteristically, James's discussion is grounded in a review of particular real-life examples of the condition that he is investigating. One of his focal examples concerns Leo Tolstoy and his experience of a state of 'arrest' (James 1911, p. 152) – of life having lost its usual flow and directedness – at around the age of 50. James comments that for Tolstoy, 'Life had been enchanting, it was now flat sober, more than sober, dead' (p. 152). This 'arrest' in the flow of his life was not brought on by any obvious change in Tolstoy's condition in the world. As Tolstoy himself says:

> All this took place at a time when so far as all my outer circumstances went, I ought to have been completely happy. I had a good wife who loved me and whom I loved; good children and a large property which was increasing with no pains taken on my part. I was more respected by my kinsfolk and acquaintance than I had ever been; I was loaded with praise by strangers; and without exaggeration I could believe my name already famous ... Moreover ... I possessed a physical and mental strength which I have rarely met in persons of my age. (James 1911, p. 155)

So Tolstoy's arrest does not appear to derive from any change in the world, considered in itself; nor is it brought about by his coming to acquire some new piece of empirical information. It is the product, rather, of his growing sense that not only would he die – this was a truth he had known for many years – but that death would rob the defining commitments of his life, and his day-to-day activities, of their point. Hence he asks insistently:

> What will be the outcome of what I do today? Of what I shall do to-morrow? What will be the outcome of my life? Why should I live? Why should I do anything? Is there in life any purpose which the inevitable death which awaits me does not undo and destroy? (p. 155)

Tolstoy, then, suffers from a kind of mental un-ease, or perhaps we could say disease, which leaves him incapacitated in the face of the world; and this incapacity is bound up with a pervasive change in his experience of the world, since the world in his experience has now become, as James says, 'flat sober, more than sober, dead'. There is clearly a sense in which Tolstoy's unease is fundamentally a spiritual problem – it is an existential kind of un-ease. In this paper, I am going to try and address the wider theme of 'spirituality, theology and mental health' by considering two questions. How are we to understand the condition of Tolstoy and of others like him? How might we understand the role of spiritual reorientation or religious conversion in effecting a resolution of such conditions? I am going to approach these matters in dialogue with William James's treatment of conversion experience in his work *The Varieties of Religious Experience*.

It is implied in James's account that Tolstoy's condition is not a matter of some purely inward or mental turmoil or disorientation, though clearly something of that kind is involved. His condition is also bound up with a change in the appearance of the sensory world. In particular, the patterns of salience that had once lit up the world and sustained his interest in it have now fallen away, so that everything has taken on the appearance of being 'flat'. This same sense of the world, as divested of significance, or as monochrome or lacking in relief, emerges in the accounts of a number of James's other sources. And he notes that in general, for the melancholiac, '[t]he world now looks remote, strange, sinister, uncanny. Its color is gone, its breath is cold, there is no speculation in the eyes it glares with' (James 1911, p. 151). One of his sources remarks that 'I see everything through a cloud ... things are not as they were, and I am changed'; and another, 'I touch, but the things do not come near me, a thick veil alters the hue and look of everything.' Or again: 'Persons move like shadows, and sounds seem to come from a distant world'; and, 'I weep false tears, I have unreal hands: the things I see are not real things' (p. 152). These reports are not obviously of precisely the same condition, but they have in common a kind of un-ease that consists in a sense of having lost touch with the outer world, that no longer comes into clear focus, or whose reality seems in some way to have been diminished.

Unsurprisingly, then, the resolution of Tolstoy's predicament, and of other predicaments of broadly this kind, will require new life to be breathed into the sensory world. Of course, Tolstoy's own malaise is resolved when he undergoes a religious conversion (p. 185). And James notes that a revitalization in the appearances is, in fact, a common theme of conversion narratives. He notes:

> When we come to study the phenomenon of conversion or religious re-generation, we ... see that a not infrequent consequence of the change operated in the subject is a transfiguration of the face of nature in his eyes. A new heaven seems to shine upon a new earth. (p. 151)

Again, James gives a number of examples of the phenomenon. A particularly striking case concerns Jonathan Edwards, the American divine, who reports that at his conversion:

The appearance of everything was altered; there seemed to be, as it were, a calm, sweet cast, or appearance of divine glory, in almost everything. God's excellency, his wisdom, his purity and love, seemed to appear in everything; in the sun, moon, and stars; in the clouds and blue sky; in the grass, flowers, and trees; in the water and all nature; which used greatly to fix my mind. (James 1911, p. 249)

In a similar spirit, another convert writes of his experience: 'I remember this, that everything looked new to me, the people, the fields, the cattle, the trees. I was like a new man in a new world' (p. 249). And another says: 'Natural objects were glorified, my spiritual vision was so clarified that I saw beauty in every material object in the universe …' (p. 250). Or again: 'how I was changed, and everything became new. My horses and hogs and even everybody seemed changed' (p. 250).

So there is a kind of mental or existential un-ease or disease that consists in part in a changed appearance of the sensory world, and that in some cases anyway, can be brought to an end in the experience of religious conversion, which brings with it, or perhaps in part just consists in, a revitalization of the appearances. To try and understand better what this malaise consists in, and how it might be addressed by religious or spiritual means, we can begin by turning to James's own account of these matters.

James's account of this condition of spiritual un-ease

It may be that many people will deny ever having experienced such a pervasive shift in the character of the sensory world. Even so, we might take these phenomena, as reported by James, to suggest that in general the appearance of the world owes something to the underlying state of mind of the person, whether or not they are conscious of this, and whether or not they have ever undergone a transformation of this kind. Certainly, this is what James thinks. He remarks:

Conceive yourself, if possible, suddenly stripped of all the emotion with which your world now inspires you, and try to imagine it *as it exists*, purely by itself, without your favorable or unfavorable, hopeful or apprehensive comment. It will be almost impossible for you to realize such a condition of negativity and deadness. No one portion of the universe would then have importance beyond another; and the whole collection of its things and series of its events would be without significance, character, expression, or perspective. Whatever of value, interest, or meaning our respective worlds appear endued with are thus pure gifts of the spectator's mind. (James 1911, p. 150)

So on James's view, our emotions help to constitute the world as experienced, since variations in emotion make for variations in the appearance of the sensory world. And we might conclude that a bundle of emotions, or an emotion or 'mood' of particularly broad compass, such as a generalized apprehensiveness of things, will be able to contribute pervasively to the appearance of the world. And accordingly, a shift in these emotional commitments might explain a global shift in the appearances of things of the kind that seems to be experienced by Tolstoy and other figures in James's discussion. Clearly, on this approach, we should not think of the emotions as simply attitudes towards some perceived content; instead, the emotions enter into that content, by structuring the appearance of the sensory world (Goldie 2000, pp. 59–60).[1]

One straightforward way of filling out this account is by supposing that the emotions constitute patterns of salience. For me to be afraid of a large, fast-advancing dog is among other things, under normal circumstances, for the dog to assume a degree of salience within my perceptual field, so that it 'stands out', while various other items are consigned to the periphery of my awareness.[2] This perspective on the contribution of the emotions to our experience fits very directly with James's account of Tolstoy's predicament. Tolstoy's world is 'flat', James says, and we could put this point by saying that it lacks salience; and given this account of the emotions, we can understand this feature of his experience in terms of his emotional disengagement from the world. So in response to our first question, about the nature of conditions such as that of Tolstoy, which involve some generalized shift in the appearance of the world, so that it becomes flat or monochrome, we might say: at least in part, such conditions are brought on by, or in some respects perhaps they simply consist in, a loss of affective engagement with the world.

Turning to our second question, we might ask how religious commitments in particular might contribute to the structure of the experienced world, on this understanding of the emotions. Most simply, we might suppose that

---

1 James does not think of the emotional contribution to experience as easily prised apart from what is there independently of the human perspective. He notes: 'the practically real world for each one of us, the effective world of the individual, is the compound world, the physical facts and emotional values in indistinguishable combination' (1911, p. 151). However, James does think of the experience of melancholia in terms of a withdrawal of our emotional engagement, rather than as a kind of negative engagement, and to this extent he is open to the thought that we can, in principle, grasp what the world would look like when stripped of our emotionally engaged contribution to its appearance. It is worth noting that this account of our emotional engagement with the world, which takes the emotions to be world-directed, is rather different from one rather standard understanding of James's approach, which associates him with the view that emotional feelings are simply ways of registering changes in the body. For discussion of this point, see Ratcliffe 2008, ch. 8.

2 Compare James's comments on the idea of 'fields of consciousness'. He notes: 'As our mental fields succeed one another, each has its centre of interest, around which the objects of which we are less and less attentively conscious fade to a margin so faint that its limits are unassignable' (1911, p. 231).

some world-directed emotions may have their roots in religious teaching. And these emotions, like others, may be able to contribute pervasively to the structure of the world as experienced. For example, if God is thought to have condemned or, equally, commended certain activities or objects, then the believer's emotional response to these activities and objects may be shaped accordingly, with the result that the experienced world is informed by a new pattern of salience.

As well as assuming new salience in a person's experience of the world, the experience of such things may also take on a new hedonic tone. My experience of a thing may come to be shot through with revulsion, for example, if I come to understand that it is the object of a divine prohibition. Compare the case where I am told that the meat I am eating derives from my pet rabbit. In this case, under normal circumstances, the meat will assume new salience in my experience – I will become focally aware of what I have been chewing. But my experience of the meat will also change in terms of its intrinsic phenomenal quality – the meat will now be experienced as revolting. Allowing for the importance of this case, I am going to concentrate hereafter on salience, but it should be acknowledged that variations in salience are typically accompanied by variations in the 'colouring' of the perceptual field.

Given his comments on the role of the emotions in constituting the world as experienced, I take it that James would be content with an account of broadly this kind. On this view, we can understand the capacity of a religious conversion to effect a transformation in the world as experienced, or we can understand it to consist, at least in part, in such a transformation, by supposing that when converted, the subject takes on a new set of religiously informed emotions, with the result that the experienced world is pervasively restructured. Let's call this picture of religious conversion, and the role of the emotions in such conversion, the 'simple picture'. In the remainder of the paper, I want to elaborate on this picture in three respects.

Elaborating on James: the case of thought-infused experience

The simple version of the Jamesian approach, as I have just presented it, invites us to suppose that first of all we encounter a world that has been carved up in various ways, so that it is taken to include dogs and various kinds of activity, for example, and that a degree of emotional significance is then attached to the things and activities that have been picked out in this way, with the result that these things acquire a corresponding salience in our experience of the world. James himself would suppose, I take it, that this picture is too simple, because the emotions are relevant not only to our tendency to assign a certain significance to a particular dog on a given occasion, but also to the fact that we possess a particular set of general concepts, such as the concept *dog*, in the first place. In other words, they are relevant to our predisposition to carve up the world in certain ways conceptually, before we come to consider, in a particular case, what significance to attach to the various objects that emerge given some such way of configuring the data of experience.

Whether or not we suppose that the emotions are the key to our possession of certain general concepts, this elaboration of the simple picture suggests a way in which we might extend our account of what is involved in the case of religious conversion. On the simple picture, what matters is the religiously informed attitude that the convert brings to various things or activities, which in turn shapes the degree of salience that those things or activities are afforded in the perceptual field. To put the point briefly, things in which we have, for religious reasons, a significant emotional investment will be assigned a relatively high degree of salience. But in addition to this sort of consideration, we should also note the capacity of religious concepts to shape which objects and activities are presented to us in the appearances, where these objects can then be arranged in varying patterns of salience according to the nature of our emotional engagement with them.

As an example of this possibility, consider Roger Scruton's comments on how the appearance of Gothic churches can be shaped according to the concepts that a person brings to bear in their experience of them. He notes:

> [I]t is clear from Abbot Suger's account of the building of St Denis ... that the architects of the Gothic churches were motivated by a perceived relationship between the finished church and the Heavenly City of Christian speculation. Sir John Summerson has further suggested that the Gothic style aims at a certain effect of accumulation. Each great church can be considered as a concatenation of smaller structures, of aedicules, fitted together as arches, chapels, windows and spires, and so can be seen as an assembled city, rather than as a single entity minutely subdivided ... But the 'interpretation' here is not a 'thought' that is separable from the experience – it is there *in* the experience, as when I see the dots of a puzzle picture as a face, or the man in the moon. (1979, pp. 74–5)

We have seen how the emotions can enter into the ordering of a perceptual field, so that those things that matter most, in which we have the greatest emotional investment, come to be assigned a relatively high degree of salience. In the case that Scruton describes in this passage, we are again dealing with the ordering of the perceptual field, but the key to his example is, I take it, the application of a concept, rather than, in any direct way, the evaluation of a thing with the result that it is afforded a new degree of salience within the perceptual field. As Scruton shows, a religious thought, in particular the thought of the heavenly Jerusalem, can enter into the appearance of the Church, so that the content of the thought comes to be rendered in that appearance. The result is that the relevant perceptual gestalt can serve as an image of the heavenly city.

It may be that Jonathan Edwards's account of his conversion experience can be interpreted in broadly these terms. As we have seen, Edwards writes that following his conversion:

> The appearance of everything was altered; there seemed to be, as it were, a calm, sweet cast, or appearance of divine glory, in almost everything. God's excellency, his wisdom, his purity and love, seemed to appear in everything; in the sun, moon, and stars; in the clouds and blue sky; in the grass, flowers, and trees; in the water and all nature. (James 1911, p. 249)

In this passage, Edwards is not evidently proposing or presupposing that he has taken on a new, emotionally informed attitude towards these natural phenomena, with the result that they have now acquired a different appearance; if anything, it is rather that the new appearance of things leads him to evaluate them differently. So we might do better to understand his new experience of the world as a matter of his coming to see how the thought of the world as an image of God's wisdom, purity and love can be inscribed in the appearances of the natural world, so that the resulting perceptual gestalt images God's nature in these respects. If read in these terms, then Edwards's experience of the world's imaging of God is formally like that of the person who comes to see a Gothic church as imaging the heavenly city, by allowing the thought of the heavenly city to enter into the appearance of the church.

However hard it may be to understand the idea, the thought that the world in some sense images the divine nature is stubbornly rooted in various strands of the major theistic traditions. (For a classic formulation of the idea, see Aquinas *Summa Theologiae* 1a. 47. 1.) No doubt, Edwards subscribed to this idea before his conversion. What happens in his conversion, we might suppose, following the reading of his remarks that I have just proposed, is that he comes to see how this idea can be rendered in experience. James notes that when someone is converted, 'religious ideas, previously peripheral in his consciousness, now take a central place ...' (p. 196). And one way in which a religious idea may come to take a central place in a person's experience of the world is, I take it, by inhabiting the appearances of sensory things. Moreover, once it is rendered in experience, this idea is likely to gain a new purchase on the person's affections and motivations, given various familiar truths concerning the power of images, as distinct from verbal abstractions, to engage the will. (Compare Newman's distinction between a 'notion' and a 'real image' (1979, p. 108).)

We have been considering the possibility that the idea of the world as an image of God may come to be inscribed in the appearance of sensory things. While I do not have the space to explore other possibilities here, we might speculate that other religious concepts are also capable of entering into the appearance of the sensory world, and structuring the phenomena accordingly.

So here is a first point at which we might extend the simple picture of conversion with which we began. The human mind can indeed contribute to a reordering of the realm of appearances, and this may have to do with our acquiring a new pattern of interests or a new set of emotional engagements, which then comes to be written into the realm of appearances; but it may also have to do with our coming to apply relevant concepts within our experience of the sensory world, with the result that the appearances fall together in a new way. And in turn, these concepts may then acquire a new hold on the imagination, and a new capacity to motivate action. These two accounts are not in simple opposition to one another. The first begins with an attitudinal shift, and supposes that this shift can be written into the appearances; the second begins with a person's newfound capacity to inscribe a concept in the appearances, and this development may then engender an attitudinal shift. For example, the person who comes to 'see', in Scruton's thought-infused sense of 'seeing', how the world images God may find that their appreciation of the world is thereby deepened.

Elaborating on James: the case of kinaesthetic feelings

I am going to move now to a second respect in which we might seek to extend what I have called the simple picture. I shall begin with a few prefatory remarks.

So far we have been concerned with the case of visual experience. We have considered the experience of a fast-advancing dog, or the experience of a Gothic church as an assembled entity rather than a single thing subdivided; and these examples suggest that the visual field can be variously organized, according to differing patterns of salience. No doubt we could make a similar sort of case for other sensory modalities. For example, a person's auditory field can presumably be structured according to different patterns of salience. Whatever sensory modality it involves, any such account will take the form of a snapshot of the sensory world at a particular time: its constituent parts, in our experience of them, will be organized according to a particular pattern of salience at that time. This way of putting the matter throws the emphasis upon the spatial ordering of various elements in the perceptual field in the present. But of course this ordering will also be keyed to the person's sense of the past and the future: it is because it has been approaching fast, and because it poses the threat of future harm, that the dog is assigned a certain degree of salience in the perceptual field.

There are other ways too in which the content of current experience can register our sense of the world's potentialities. Most obviously, the expressive posture of the body in a particular context can involve a judgement about the practical potentialities that are afforded by the situation; and this posture, in so far as it involves the tensing of various muscles, for example, can in turn be registered in states of feeling. So to return to our earlier example, the judgement that the fast-approaching dog is dangerous can be registered experientially both in a certain organization of the perceptual field and also in the felt recognition of the body's making itself ready for self-protective action. (Compare Solomon's idea of feelings as 'activities' (2003); Pickard (2003) explores some related themes.) In this case, we might suppose, bodily feelings are not simply brute sensations, but participate in the world-directedness that is implied in the body's practical stance. So kinaesthetic feelings, feelings by means of which we keep track of the body's movement and its orientation in a given space, provide a further way of understanding how the content of current experience may partake in some assessment of the possible course of future experience.

In this way, we can understand how two objects that present exactly the same sensory profile from a person's current vantage point may nonetheless be differently experienced. For example, a table and a balsa replica of the table may look exactly the same, in terms of their dimensions, colour and so on. But our experience of these objects may be very different even so, in so far as they are associated with different sets of practical potentialities, which in turn are registered in differing organizations of the perceptual field and differing kinaesthetic feelings.

Returning to the predicament of Tolstoy, it is striking that his present experience of the world, as flat and lifeless, seems to be connected to a new assessment of its future possibilities. He asks himself: 'What will be the outcome of what I do today? Of what I shall do to-morrow?' So Tolstoy has come to a new sense of the restrictions on his capacity to have any enduring impact upon the world; and this new sense of the world's potentialities, or its lack of certain potentialities, comes to be inscribed, we could say, in his current experience, in so far as that experience is 'flat' and lifeless. In this way, we might understand how Tolstoy and a fellow nineteenth-century Russian might be presented with the same world, from a purely sensory point of view, but might even so experience it very differently, according to their different assessments of its future.

As Matthew Ratcliffe has noted, if we cease to associate an object with a set of practical potentialities, then the object may come to appear as in some way unreal. He comments:

> Consider experiencing a table without co-included possibilities like seeing it from another angle, moving it or sitting on a chair in front of it. Without the possibilities of its being accessed from different perspectives or acted upon, it would appear strangely distant, intangible and incomplete. (2008, p. 156)

And we might suppose similarly that the world can come to seem unreal in the experience of the person who suffers some generalized sense that things have lost their practical potentialities. This case seems to fit a number of the examples James presents in *The Varieties*. As we have seen, he notes how in one individual's experience: 'Persons move like shadows, and sounds seem to come from a distant world'; or again, he cites the report: 'I weep false tears, I have unreal hands: the things I see are not real things.'[3] Perhaps we can understand such experiences of the diminished reality of things as a generalized case of what happens when I lose my sense of the practical potentialities that are afforded by a particular object, where this loss is registered in, for example, a change in kinaesthetic feeling. (Compare Ratcliffe's discussion of the Cotard delusion (2008, ch. 6).)

Once again, we might wonder whether the experience of religious conversion in particular might be understood in similar terms. Some forms of religious belief do seem to involve an expanded or, in some cases, a contracted sense of human possibilities. For example, to take a case that is directly relevant to Tolstoy's account of his predicament, in some faiths it is supposed that the life of the human person does not end with physical death. And on this basis, it might be supposed, for example, that our relationship with other human beings will extend into an indefinite future. We might ask ourselves: might this expanded sense of our practical possibilities be registered in the appearances of things, with the result that new life is breathed into our experience of the world and into our experience of other people in particular?

An objector might say that it is hard to see how a belief concerning the post-mortem future of another person could make a difference to our kinaesthetic experience in the present. My belief that another human being is, for example, a potential conversation partner can, no doubt, shape my bodily interactions with them very directly in the present, but it seems much harder to associate, for example, the belief that he or she is potentially a companion in some post-mortem state with a particular practical stance in the world here and now. By contrast with this view, some theologians have thought that the belief in the human person's capacity to survive physical death should condition quite profoundly our assessment of their significance, and our sense of the fittingness of various kinds of interaction with them in the present. Similarly, some have thought that differences of view about the ultimate fate of the material order, on varying accounts of divine providence, can make a substantive difference to our sense of the kinds of practical interaction with the natural world that are permitted or mandated here and now. It is partly for this reason that eco-theology is such a contested subject matter. Given the liveliness of such debates, there is, I suggest, some prospect of our being able to understand the experience of religious conversion, at least in part, in these terms – that is, as a new, kinaesthetic registering of various possibilities for interaction with material things, where this felt appreciation of these possibilities affords a heightened or enriched sense (or, in some cases, perhaps it will be a diminished sense) of the reality of those things.

---

3 James also notes this case: 'There is no longer any past for me; people appear so strange; it is as if I could not see any reality ...' (1911, p. 152). Here it seems to be a sense of the past's loss of its potentiality, or a diminished sense of the past's reality, which is associated with, or perhaps realized in, such experience.

What I have been calling the 'simple picture' of conversion, or of human experience more generally, holds that the sensory world's appearance is given structure or salience by virtue of our emotional engagement with it. So far, I have extended this picture on two points. First, I have suggested that this account can be further refined by taking stock of the capacity of concepts, as well as of evaluations or emotional commitments, to inhabit the appearances of things; and second, we have seen that this picture can be expanded by allowing for the role of kinaesthetic experience in registering the possibilities for future experience that are afforded by a thing. I have also offered some comment on how these extensions of the simple version of the Jamesian picture may be worked out in the case of religious conversion in particular.

Extending the simple picture: the case of 'existential feelings'

I am going to mention just one more respect in which James's scheme may be extended. The presiding theme of Matthew Ratcliffe's book *Feelings of Being* is the idea that in addition to those emotional feelings that are directed at particular objects in the world, there are other emotional feelings that constitute a person's 'sense of reality' (2008, p. 3). These feelings he terms 'existential feelings' (p. 38). Ratcliffe gives various examples of such feelings. He writes:

> For all of us there are times when the world can *feel unfamiliar, unreal, unusually real, homely, distant or close*. It can be something that one feels apart from or at one with. One can feel like a participant in the world or like a detached, estranged observer, staring at objects that do not seem to be quite *there*. All experiences have, as a background, a changeable sense of one's relationship with the world. (2008, p. 7)

Let me give an example drawn from my own experience. As I write these words, I am still feeling the effects of a trip I have just made from Australia. It is not that my jet-lagged state has led me to acquire any new beliefs about the objects in my immediate environment; but because of my condition, these things do, even so, strike me differently in certain respects, and this difference is registered, it seems plausible to say, in various kinaesthetic and visceral experiences, rather than in, say, a restructuring of the items in my perceptual field according to some new pattern of salience. Moreover, in keeping with Ratcliffe's account, this feeling involves a kind of all-encompassing sense of my material context, one that conditions the way in which objects in general present themselves or could present themselves, and the kinds of desire or emotion or practical engagement that they are able to elicit. For this reason, we might say that my feeling involves a sense of reality as such, rather than being concerned simply with some narrowly delimited sphere of experience. On Ratcliffe's account, all of us have all of the time some such sense, mediated in bodily terms, of our being in the world. But often enough, we are not conscious of the role of bodily feelings in constituting such a sense of things; and it may only be when we undergo some change of existential feeling (as for example when we experience jet lag) that we become aware of the sense of being that is presupposed in our ordinary, everyday dealings with the world.

This account suggests a further respect in which we might elaborate upon the 'simple picture'. We can agree with James that the world is structured by or lit up by our emotional engagement with particular things; but we can now add that this sort of emotional engagement presupposes an already established orientation within the world, by virtue of which we feel at home in the world, or estranged from it, or whatever it might be, where this orientation is given in bodily feeling. It is, we might say, only in the light of this background orientation that our emotional engagement with particular objects of experience can take shape, since how those objects strike us – the practical opportunities that we take them to afford, and our attitude towards those opportunities, for example – will depend upon this pre-established orientation.

Given this account, we can present a further perspective on the experiences that James presents in *The Varieties*. As we have seen, James characterizes the experience of melancholiacs in these terms: 'The world now looks remote, strange, sinister, uncanny. Its color is gone, its breath is cold, there is no speculation in the eyes it glares with.' Feelings of reality as 'remote' or 'sinister' or 'strange' or 'uncanny' all seem to be, potentially, cases of existential feeling in Ratcliffe's sense. Similarly, if a person finds that the world is flat or distant or in some way unreal, in some all-encompassing way, we might conclude that their condition is rooted not so much in a particular emotion, which has as its object a particular object or circumstance, but in some broader sense of reality, which is realized in an existential feeling. Drawing on our earlier discussion, we might add that if a particular existential feeling is somehow caught up into a diminished sense of the practical possibilities afforded by the world, then it may equally involve some sense of the world as not fully real.

The notion of existential feelings seems to lend itself fairly readily to theological application. Indeed, on a theological reading, it might be supposed that existential feelings involve something like an experience of God. After all, theologians commonly suppose that God is to be conceived not so much as an individual entity or being, but as being or reality without restriction; and rather than giving us access simply to the reality of this or that individual thing, existential feelings seem to consist in a sense of what reality as such is like. (Ratcliffe's examples are concerned more exactly with the world, but so far as I can see, there is nothing to prevent this broader reading of the import of a particular existential feeling.) So providing that a given sense of being, communicated in a given existential feeling, is broadly appropriate in theological terms, might we not take it to involve a kind of apprehension of God?

Moreover, faith traditions typically offer some generalized assessment of the nature of reality, and of the place of the human person within it. And if some such sense of the significance of the human person in their material context could be made experientially accessible, in the form of an existential feeling, then that would be of considerable interest from a theological point of view. For this reason, too, a shift in existential feeling, and a correlative shift in the phenomenology of our experience of the sensory world and in our sense of its reality, may lend itself fairly readily to theological interpretation; and when this shift has the right shape from a theological point of view, it may well be appropriate to think of it as a case of, or as in some way bound up with, religious conversion.

We have been considering how we might extend the 'simple picture' of conversion and of our experience of the world more generally with which we began. That picture supposes that the appearance of the world is a function of our emotional commitments, because these commitments introduce varying patterns of salience into the perceptual field, or perhaps in part just consist in such patterns of salience. We have taken note of three ways in particular of building upon this picture. In brief, the world as experienced will also be shaped by the concepts that we bring to bear, and by our expectations concerning the future course of experience, where these expectations are registered kinaesthetically, and by those 'existential' feelings that consist in a background sense of the world's reality. These various ideas are also applicable, we have seen, to the question of how religious thoughts or commitments in particular may enter into the appearance of the sensory world; and in turn, therefore, they can be applied to the question of how we might understand the shift in the appearances of things that can arise in cases of religious conversion.

Spiritual practice and spiritual health

This general picture of the mind's contribution to our experience of the sensory world suggests a view of the nature of spirituality and of spiritual formation. When people speak of 'spirituality', they typically have in mind a commitment to certain ideals that is not reducible to the giving of sincere verbal assent to those ideals. On this view the spiritual person is distinguished by the fact that these ideals have taken root in their practical and experiential relationship to the world. The account we have been developing provides one perspective on how this might be. The spiritual person, we could say, is one whose ideals are rendered in their experience – by virtue of their emotional commitments and their capacity to inscribe certain thoughts or ideals into the appearances of things, by virtue of their practical stance in relation to the world, where this stance is registered kinaesthetically and by virtue of the background feeling of reality that provides the context for these more particular commitments. I do not say, of course, that this is all that is involved in the leading of a 'spiritual life', but at any rate this seems to be a central part of what is involved.

In turn, this account lends itself to a certain view of the nature of spiritual formation. Spiritual formation, we might say, is a matter of cultivating relevant emotions, thoughts, practical dispositions and background feelings, so that these emotions, thoughts and feelings enter into the person's lived, or experiential, relationship to the sensory world. It would be interesting to consider various traditions of spiritual formation from this vantage point, and to ask how the practices that are embedded in such traditions might be understood in these terms – that is, as contributing to a certain pattern of emotional engagement with the world that can then be inscribed in the sensory appearances, or as enabling certain ideas to become 'real' by rendering them in experience or by shaping a person's practical stance in the world, or by trying to reform their background sense of reality.

There is no time to undertake such a task here. But I will mention just one example of a religious practice that suggests the potential fruitfulness of such an approach.

An example of a materially mediated spiritual practice

Most faith traditions have recognized the existence of 'sacred sites', and the practical appropriation of such sites has often been associated with experiences of religious transformation. The literature in the phenomenology of religion suggests that sacred sites have certain recurring features across cultures. Typically, they are rather hard to access. For example, they may be set on an island or mountainside; and even when the pilgrim arrives at the site, they may find they have to negotiate various thresholds that pose a degree of physical challenge. For example, the site may be surrounded by a threshold wall or it may be dimly lit. Moreover, there is a common tradition of conceiving of such sites as presenting a kind of *imago mundi* – so that the site bodies forth the nature of reality more broadly, by exemplifying that nature in paradigmatic form.

We might suppose that the tradition of venerating sacred sites counts as one example of a spiritual practice. And we might ask, then, whether the efficacy of this practice can be understood in the terms of the account that we have been developing. First of all, it is clear that such sites are not available for casual inspection. Getting to them requires a certain seriousness of purpose – given the demands that are imposed by their remoteness or inaccessibility, for example. So the design of such sites suggests that if the believer is to grasp their meaning aright, then she or he will need to approach them in the right emotional spirit. And given our account, we may say that this is to be expected, because only the person who approaches the site with the right emotional demeanour will be able to adopt the right mode of salient viewing. The casual observer will not have access to the same experiential world as the person who approaches the site in a spirit of focused reverential seriousness.

Moreover, the physical challenges of the site also demand a certain response of the body: the dim lighting, or the overwhelming scale of the building, or whatever it may be, require the body to adopt a stance of caution, or to crouch in recognition of its own smallness, and so on. And such kinaesthetic responses, we might suppose, are also folded into the experiential recognition of the significance of the place. Moreover, if the believer takes the site to be an *imago mundi*, or thinks of it on other grounds as bodying forth the nature of reality, then she is invited to treat her experiential acknowledgement of the character of this place as a recognition of the nature of things more broadly. So her felt response to the place assumes, to this extent, the status of an existential feeling. Moreover, in so far as much of her sense of the place is registered in the brute impact of the physical space on the body, by virtue of the physical challenges that are presented by the place, then we could suppose that the place is designed to shape an existential feeling in the more precise sense that Ratcliffe has identified. Finally, the point of the sacred site is presumably to afford a setting within which the believer's adherence to various doctrines and teachings can be cast in experiential form. The site is not typically a space for formal doctrinal instruction; it is rather a space where already formed doctrinal commitments are confirmed in or, we might wish to say on the basis of our discussion, rendered in experience.

In these ways, I suggest, a relatively familiar and straightforward practice of spiritual formation can be brought into clear focus using the categories that we have been developing in this essay. And to the extent that the pilgrim's felt sense of the world is indeed shaped by the encounter with the sacred place, then we might suppose that, by the standards of her tradition anyway, she will be in a better state of mental health, for the experienced world of such a person will be shot through with her tradition's core beliefs and values, and accordingly it will be very far from being 'flat' or lacking in reality.

Concluding thoughts

We have been considering how spiritual practice may be integral to the cultivation of a certain kind of mental health, or to the resolution of the kind of existential un-ease that Tolstoy reports. From a theoretical point of view, I have been arguing, we can understand this possibility using the notions of emotional salience; thought-infused seeing; a sense of reality that is tied to kinaesthetic feeling; and the idea of 'feelings of being'. A person whose perceptual world bears the imprint of her tradition's values and sense of reality in these various ways enjoys a particularly deep kind of mental-and-bodily health. For such a person, the ideals of religion, or equally a certain conception of what really matters in a human life, are available not only in abstractly discursive form – these ideals can also be contemplated, and reckoned with, in her or his dealings with the everyday sensory world, since they are inscribed in the sensory appearances. For such a person, experience is enlivened by thought, and appearance tracks reality.

References

Aquinas, T. (1964–74), *Summa Theologiae*, ed. T. Gilby, 60 vols, London: Eyre & Spottiswoode.

Goldie, J. (2000), *The Emotions: A Philosophical Exploration*, Oxford: Clarendon Press.

James, W. (1911), *The Varieties of Religious Experience: A Study in Human Nature*, London: Longmans, Green & Co.

Newman, J. H. (1979), *An Essay in Aid of a Grammar of Assent*, Notre Dame IN: University of Notre Dame Press.

Pickard, H. (2003), 'Emotions and the problem of other minds', in A. Hatzimoysis (ed.), *Philosophy and the Emotions*, Cambridge: Cambridge University Press, pp. 87–103.

Ratcliffe, M. (2008), *Feelings of Being: Phenomenology, Psychiatry and the Sense of Reality*, Oxford: Oxford University Press.

Scruton, R. (1979), *The Aesthetics of Architecture*, Princeton NJ: Princeton University Press.

Solomon, R. (2003), 'Emotions, thoughts and feelings: What is a "cognitive theory" of the emotions, and does it neglect affectivity?', in A. Hatzimoysis (ed.), *Philosophy and the Emotions*, Cambridge: Cambridge University Press, pp. 1–18.

Some suggestions for further reading

Abram, D. (1997), *The Spell of the Sensuous: Perception and Language in a More-than-Human World*, New York: Vintage Books.

Cooper, D. (2002), *The Measure of Things: Humanism, Humility and Mystery*, Oxford: Clarendon Press.

Cottingham, J. (2005), *The Spiritual Dimension: Religion, Philosophy and Human Value*, Cambridge: Cambridge University Press.

Hadot, P. (1995), *Philosophy as a Way of Life: Spiritual Exercises from Socrates to Foucault*, ed. A. I. Davidson, trans. M. Chase, Oxford: Blackwell.

Kohák, E. (1984), *The Embers and the Stars: A Philosophical Inquiry into the Moral Sense of Nature*, Chicago IL: University of Chicago Press.

Wynn, M. (2013), *Renewing the Senses: A Study of the Philosophy and Theology of the Spiritual Life*, Oxford: Oxford University Press.

8

Transcendence, Immanence and Mental Health

CHRISTOPHER C. H. COOK

Summary

The concept of transcendence has featured in debates about spirituality and psychiatry both as a core defining feature of what spirituality might be considered to be and also as a significant point of contention. However, it is amenable to interpretation within both psychological and theological frameworks of reference and provides a possible common point of reference to professional and academic discourse. Properly understood, transcendence should be seen in a close relationship with immanence, rather than in opposition to it. A clearer analysis of the relationship between immanence and transcendence in spiritual traditions and practices has potential to clarify some of the present controversies in this field.

Theology, transcendence and mental health

Recent controversies concerning the place of spirituality in psychiatry have touched on a variety of academic, ethical and professional questions (see Chapter 1). These have been directed at the proper interpretation of the research evidence base, the nature of the concept of spirituality, the nature and management of proper professional boundaries and the nature of the relationship between science and religion, among other things. However, relatively little theological attention has been given to these controversies, or indeed to the topic of mental health more generally. This might be thought surprising, given the way in which this professional debate touches upon some important theological concerns and also given the important relationships between mental and spiritual well-being (Cook 2011, pp. 151–202; Koenig et al. 2012, pp. 123–44). Simon Dein, Harold Koenig and I have suggested elsewhere (Dein et al. 2012) that critical theological engagement with the various issues at hand might well shed some useful light on the present controversies and on the nature of the relationship between spirituality and mental health more generally.

As an example of the kind of engagement that I think could be helpful, this chapter will focus on the theological concept of transcendence as illuminative of the relationship between spirituality and psychiatry, although this will necessarily touch on a number of other important themes and disciplines with relevance to the topic at hand, including the nature of the secular context within which the present debate has been located. But first, why might transcendence be a theme worth examining in more detail, and why select this rather than any one of a number of other potentially promising starting points? For example, the nature and concept of spirituality itself is a matter in which sociologists, theologians and others have shown great interest, reflected in a significant literature (Flanagan and Jupp 2007; Roof 1999; Jones et al. 1986; Principe 1983; Sheldrake 2010), which is often not adequately attended to in scientific publications. In many ways, this might seem a more logical starting point. It might also lead to some illuminating insights into the scientific and clinical literature, and more attention to such things is surely needed. However, there are a number of reasons why transcendence would seem worthy of particular attention.

First, transcendence is a central concept to the present debate, both in the minds of protagonists and antagonists. This alone might make it a worthy topic for further theological attention. Second, however, it also provides a useful way in to beginning to think about some of the important theological issues at stake, and it provides a helpful terminology for doing this. Third, and perhaps most importantly, I think it also has utility for finding a way forward in terms of a more constructive, coherent and clinically relevant debate from within which some greater measure of agreement might emerge.

Transcendence as a central concept

There are significant references within the present debate about spirituality and psychiatry to the concept of transcendence, all of which might suggest that this is an important issue. It would seem that many people do in fact have transcendence in mind as a core concept when they speak about spirituality (Cook 2004; Zinnbauer et al. 1997). In the field of addiction, the 'power greater than ourselves' referred to in the Twelve Steps of Alcoholics Anonymous provides a good example of the incorporation of a concept of transcendence into a programme of recovery (Cook 2009). In mental health generally, it is often a transcendent relationship (i.e. with God) that is understood as being at the heart of whatever it is that appears to many to be beneficial about spirituality in conferring resilience towards and improved recovery from mental disorders. For example, Ellermann and Reed refer to spirituality as 'a self-transcendence whereby personal boundaries are expanded transpersonally to connect one to a higher power or purpose greater than the self' (Ellermann and Reed 2001). It is thus a term that, along with cognate terms, is commonly employed by clinicians and scientists, users of mental health services, members of mutual help groups and others as being meaningful in reference to the relationship between spirituality and mental health.

Harold Koenig, in the second edition of the *Handbook of Religion and Health*, refers to transcendence as central to his definitions both of spirituality and of religion:

> Religion involves beliefs, practices, and rituals related to the transcendent, where the *transcendent* is God, Allah, HaShem, or a Higher Power in Western religious traditions, or to Brahman, manifestations of Brahman, Buddha, Dao, or ultimate truth/reality in Eastern traditions. (Koenig et al. 2012, p. 45; original emphasis preserved)

> Spirituality is distinguished from all other things – humanism, values, morals, and mental health – by its connection to that which is sacred, the *transcendent*. The transcendent is that which is outside of the self, and yet also within the self – and in Western traditions is called God, Allah, HaShem, or a Higher Power, and in Eastern traditions may be called Brahman, manifestations of Brahman, Buddha, Dao or ultimate truth/reality ... Thus, our definition of spirituality is very similar to religion, and there is clearly overlap. The one common element, the minimal requirement to call something religious or spiritual is its connection with the transcendent, however understood. (Koenig et al. 2012, p. 46; original emphasis preserved)

Koenig finally concludes his section on the definition of spirituality with a recommendation that 'for the sake of conceptual clarity researchers not include personal beliefs that have nothing to do with the transcendent under the term spirituality' (p. 47).

In a not dissimilar fashion, although employing the 'sacred' rather than the transcendent as the core category, Pargament points out that definitions of spirituality 'without a sacred core' create a boundary problem. Definitional boundaries that are expanded and ill-defined potentially 'include virtually any pathway leading to virtually any valued destination' (Pargament 1999). Once this happens the concept becomes more or less useless in research, easily confounded with psychological variables, vulnerable to fragmentation and at least potentially is completely meaningless.

Whether most researchers have in the past, when choosing and constructing measures of spirituality for their research, observed such clarity in their thinking as exhorted by the injunctions of Koenig, Pargament and others is clearly doubtful (Cook 2004). However, it behoves researchers to pay more attention to such things, and transcendence, as a concept, would appear to be the closest thing that we have to something that is widely acknowledged as being both distinctive and characteristic of spirituality.

As Koenig points out, the extension of the concept of spirituality to psychological states and beliefs not concerned with transcendence is both unnecessary and unhelpful. Psychological language and concepts are adequate for such things and people clearly find (for example) meaning and purpose in life outside of what might usually be considered 'spiritual' in any strict sense. When I have asked my own patients, in the course of clinical practice, what matters most to them or what confers purpose to their lives, they frequently refer to family and loved ones. In a sense, these are 'spiritual' conversations, but it is not necessary to use the language of spirituality in such clinical practice (unless of course that is the language preferred by the patient), and it is confusing to do so in research.

This is not to deny that in published writing spirituality often is concerned with such things as meaning and purpose, relationships with loved ones, morality and a range of other concepts that do not require the language of spirituality. Furthermore, these other things that are often included under the umbrella of spirituality usually do relate directly or indirectly to transcendence, in one form or another (Cook 2004). Such things might be considered a part of what Kenneth Pargament refers to as the 'sacred ring', that is, a realm of life within which things become sacred (we might say here, transcendent or spiritual) through association with a sacred 'core' (Pargament 2011). However, if we are to be clear about what is really at the heart of the concept, about how it is to be distinguished from variables more easily defined in purely psychological terms and about how it is to be operationalized in research, Koenig's recommendation that we focus on transcendence would seem to be an important one to heed.

Transcendence also emerges as a point of contention. For example, Rob Poole states that 'The insistence that even nonbelievers have a spiritual life shows a lack of respect for those who find meaning within beliefs that reject the transcendent and the supernatural' (Poole et al. 2008). It is not necessarily the case, although it might be a reasonable assumption, that the assertion that 'nonbelievers have a spiritual life' means that those who do not self-identify as spiritual nonetheless (in the eyes of those who do) have a life in relation to transcendent reality. Some definitions of spirituality maintain an ambiguity about the place of transcendence, or even explicitly exclude the necessity for it (e.g. Goddard 1995). However, it is clearly the case that there are those who do and those who do not assert the existence of some kind of transcendent reality, and that for both transcendence may indeed be the crucial dimension of what spirituality is all about (whether it is then affirmed or rejected). For most (but not necessarily all) of those who identify themselves as spiritual, relationship to a transcendent order would seem to be what they value as central to their spirituality. For those who distance themselves from spirituality, transcendence may well (perhaps often) be the aspect of spirituality to which they most object.

A rather different argument is brought to bear by Richard Sloan, who fears that the inclusion of spirituality and religion within healthcare will somehow trivialize religion. In his book *Blind Faith: The Unholy Alliance of*

Religion and Medicine, in a chapter entitled 'Trivialising the Transcendent: Be Careful What You Wish For', he writes: 'By implementing the approach of scientific reductionism, the transcendent aspects of the religious experience are diminished if not lost altogether' (Sloan 2006, p. 241).

There is an implication here of the possibility of reducing the idea of transcendence (thus spirituality) to psychological (or other scientific) variables, thus effectively negating its reality other than as a belief in a certain kind of thing (a 'thing' that might be understood not to exist in reality at all). Whether scientific research actually does this, or is even capable of such a thing, is another matter. The possibility of 'trivializing' religion in this way exists, and Sloan therefore argues that it is best kept out of medicine.

Whether the concern is that a transcendent dimension will cause offence to those who deny it, or that it will somehow be degraded for those who value it, the clear implication is that transcendence should be kept out of clinical practice. On the other hand, for those who affirm the place of spirituality in research and clinical practice, it often seems to be transcendence that they are affirming. Transcendence, then, would appear to be at the heart of the debate for both detractors and protagonists. But what is transcendence?

Transcendence in psychological and clinical discourse

We have already seen that Poole refers to 'the transcendent and the supernatural' together – as though these concepts are likely to be related. Koenig et al. also write that 'spirituality is intimately related to the supernatural' (Koenig et al. 2012, p. 46) and defines transcendence in terms of various western or eastern theological traditions (including, importantly, the secular western concept of a 'Higher Power'). However, not all writers on matters of spirituality and health understand transcendence in this way.

Fred Craigie, for example, has suggested that transcendence may in fact, importantly for the psychologist, be concerned with the transcendence of suffering (Craigie 2008). Similarly, in Howden's Spirituality Assessment Scale, transcendence is understood as 'The ability to reach or go beyond the limits of usual experience; the capacity, willingness, or experience of rising above or overcoming body or psychic conditions; or the capacity for achieving wellness or self-healing' (Burkhardt and Nagai-Jacobson 2005, p. 155).

Transcendence in this sense, which I shall refer to as self-transcendence, is about facing pain and suffering, accepting that some things are unchangeable and finding a meaningful way through life that acknowledges these realities. Craigie identifies a variety of clinical approaches to helping patients achieve this kind of transcendence (Craigie 2008, pp. 263–309). These include 'letting go', acceptance, mindfulness, non-attachment, serenity, spiritual surrender, gratitude and forgiveness. Of these approaches, it seems to me, only spiritual surrender more or less requires some kind of understanding of the transcendent as God or a Higher Power. The others all employ a psychological kind of self-transcendence that requires no concept of the supernatural, God or any Higher Power external to the self.

Ellermann and Reed, whose definition of spirituality in terms of self-transcendence was mentioned above, define self-transcendence in terms of 'the person's capacity to expand self-boundaries intrapersonally, interpersonally and transpersonally, to acquire a perspective that exceeds ordinary boundaries and limitations' (Ellermann and Reed 2001).[1] The definition of spirituality that these authors associate with this understanding of self-transcendence clearly refers to a 'higher power', but, again, I don't think it is necessary to infer belief in a higher power from this kind of self-transcendence. It is more about a personal capacity to 'expand self-boundaries', thus a capacity for a certain sort of self-understanding. Self-transcendence certainly might include more than this. It might include some kind of perspective that embraces a transcendent other. However, it does not necessarily do so.

Polly Young-Eisendrath identifies psychotherapy as a kind of 'ordinary transcendence':

> This kind of transcendence provides evidence and insight that being human means being dependent, and that the life space we inhabit is one of interdependence, not independence. It also shows us that self-protectiveness, isolation, and the ubiquitous human desire for omnipotence produce great suffering. (Young-Eisendrath 2000, p. 133)

Ordinary transcendence, again, is a kind of transcendence that does not require reference to a transcendent other in any supernatural or theological sense. It is a form of self-transcendence, a transcendence of self-protectiveness and of the lust for power.

For some clinicians and researchers, then, transcendence is primarily concerned with *self*-transcendence of a kind that reaches out intrapersonally and interpersonally but not necessarily transpersonally. While this kind of self-transcendence clearly has important applications in psychotherapy and counselling, it is more about transcending previous understandings and limitations of the self by expanding them. Each time this occurs, the new understandings, the new limitations, remain a part of the self and do not constitute or refer to any transcendent order external to the self. There cannot be said to have been any movement beyond, or transcendence of, that self that is, in itself, the very agent of the process of self-transcendence. If one does not presuppose a transcendent person or reality, in some sense outside of the self, providing the ability for human beings to transcend their own finite resources, we are really talking here only about *apparent* transcendence or transcendence of previously realized personal resources, but not any fundamental transcendence of human limitations.

---

1 Cf Reed 1991, where self-transcendence is said to refer 'broadly to a characteristic of developmental maturity whereby there is an expansion of self-boundaries and an orientation toward broadened life perspectives and purposes'.

Kenneth Pargament, who defines spirituality as 'a search for the sacred', understands transcendent reality as being at the core of the sacred. Transcendence, he writes, 'speaks to the perception that there is something out of the ordinary in a particular object or experience, something that goes beyond our everyday lives and beyond our usual understanding' (Pargament 2011, p. 39). In this psychological sense, transcendence is concerned with perception, experience or understanding of something that is 'out of the ordinary' or beyond understanding. In this sense, it would appear that transcendence is concerned primarily with human interpretation of human experience. It is about our capacity to identify a thing or experience as being 'extraordinary'. As with self-transcendence, this understanding of transcendence does not require any acceptance of a transcendent reality. Although it might hint at such a reality, or even explicitly refer to it, it is easily understood by a sceptical observer in non-supernatural terms. It is essentially a human capacity to interpret experiences in a certain kind of way. It does make the important step of requiring the conceptualization of a transcendent other (in some supernatural, extraordinary or theological sense) but it does not require a commitment (at least on the part of the impartial observer) to the ontological reality of such a transcendent order. For want of a better term, I will call this 'interpretive transcendence'.

What I am calling interpretive transcendence includes more than just a hermeneutic, perceptual or experiential dimension. Ralph Piedmont, for example, refers to a transcendent perspective that is a motivational domain, constituting a dimension of personality:

> Spiritual Transcendence refers to the capacity of individuals to stand outside of their immediate sense of time and place to view life from a larger, more objective perspective. This transcendent perspective is one in which a person sees a fundamental unity underlying the diverse strivings of nature and finds a bonding with others that cannot be severed, not even by death. (Piedmont 1999, p. 988)

As with Pargament's approach, this is very much about interpretation of experience, but Piedmont describes it more as a 'fundamental capacity of the individual, a source of intrinsic motivation that drives, directs, and selects behaviours' (Piedmont 1999, p. 988). Components of this transcendence include a sense of connectedness, a belief in the unitive nature of life, fulfilment found in encounters with a transcendent reality, tolerance of paradoxes, non-judgementalness, a desire to live in the moment, and gratitude. It thus also shares certain features (e.g. mindfulness and gratitude) with Craigie's approach to self-transcendence. However, it goes beyond this in requiring a perception of or motivation by belief in something beyond the resources of the self.

Interpretive transcendence may or may not be understood in explicitly theological terms as making reference to God (or gods). Where there is not explicit theological language, it is likely that there will at least be a mystical element, relating to the ineffability of the experience (Cook 2004a), but this in itself does not require a theistic stance. Where there is explicit theological language, a degree of ambiguity is often identifiable in relation to any explicitly theological assertions. At least there is often a reluctance to identify unambiguously the transcendent with traditional conceptions of God. For example, Pargament refers to the sacred as encompassing concepts of 'God, the divine, and the transcendent, but it is not limited to notions of higher powers',[2] and later says that 'By defining spirituality as the search for the sacred, we avoid restricting ourselves to narrow or traditional conceptions of God' (Pargament 1999). I think that this kind of ambiguity arises from the perception among many clinicians and researchers that there is a category of experience that patients and research subjects describe which putatively relates to a transcendent reality that lies outside themselves (a reality about which the impartial and scientific clinician or researcher makes no judgement as to whether it really exists or not). The ambiguity arises because it is assumed that subjects who describe this experience in terms of relationship with God, and those who describe it in non-theological terms, are in fact having the same kind of experience. This assumption might well be questionable on scientific, phenomenological and other grounds, but it is a good one to enable a grouping together of experiences that seem to have something ('transcendence') in common. The cost of doing so is the introduction of the ambiguity. Is transcendence about God, or not?

Finally, there must of course be a kind of transcendence that is unambiguously theological. Let's call it theological transcendence. Theological transcendence goes beyond both self-transcendence and interpretive transcendence in requiring a faith commitment. However, whatever position one might hold on this kind of transcendence, a number of things might already seem clear. First, self-transcendence and interpretive transcendence are clinically, psychologically and pragmatically very important. No theological (or a-theological) perspective is likely to undermine or invalidate the relevance of these kinds of transcendence to therapeutic practice or to any understanding of how people cope with adversity (including the particular adversities associated with mental disorder). Whatever one believes about God or any other conception of a transcendent reality, the ways in which people find within themselves resources for self-transcendence, and

---

2 Elsewhere, he writes: 'At the heart of the sacred lies God, divine beings, or a transcendent reality' (my emphasis). It is left unclear, so far as I can see, as to whether a transcendent reality is understood here as an alternative instance of the sacred, contrasted with God, higher powers and divine beings, or a category within which God, higher powers and divine beings are but instances alongside others within a sacred/transcendent category. As noted above, there is also a perceptual, experiential, emphasis to Pargament's understanding of transcendence that puts the focus on the human psychological account of things, rather than on a theological or conceptual account of what it is (if anything) that is actually, objectively, being experienced or perceived.

the extent to which people interpret reality in terms of the transcendent, will remain highly relevant to psychological and clinical understandings of how people cope with and overcome adversity.

At this point, I think that some comment is needed about the 'supernatural'. It is interesting that both Koenig and Poole, writing from opposite and different perspectives on the value of spirituality in healthcare, both associate transcendence with the supernatural. While a certain sort of understanding of the supernatural might well be associated with an interpretive transcendence, I do not think that it has to be. Indeed, there are many who might consider themselves 'spiritual', or who relate to a transcendent reality, who either understand their spirituality or transcendence in very natural terms (Capra 1975; Heelas 2008), or else who do not see the activities of a transcendent (e.g. divine) agency in this world as subverting or contravening the natural order but rather as working within it in some way. The matter of the supernatural, then, is an additional consideration but I do not think that any particular view on the supernatural is necessary to either self-transcendence or interpretive transcendence.[3]

Transcendence and immanence

To some extent the appeal of the term transcendence may lie in the commonality that it represents across diverse faith traditions in a secular age. At the same time (and perhaps for the same reasons), it is a cause of concern to those who do not believe (Hick 1989, p. 6). However, transcendence can be understood in a variety of ways.

In some simple and fundamental sense, transcendence infers a going above or beyond of some kind. Exactly what it is that is exceeded is left unspecified. Implicitly or explicitly, transcendence is usually contrasted and compared with the concept of immanence. It is the immanent order that transcendence goes 'beyond'. Immanence revolves around central themes concerned with remaining within what is immediately present, the natural perceivable order of things. To a large extent, immanence and transcendence are spatial metaphors (cf. Tillich 1955, p. 292), but the fact that they are inherently metaphorical should alert us to the likely difficulty in pinning them down and defining the relationship between them. So, for example, in his *Systematic Theology*, Tillich (1955) expresses the relationship in terms of being. For Tillich, God is understood as 'being itself' or 'the ground of being', but not as 'a being' or even the 'highest being'. Understood in this way, the relationship between immanence and transcendence becomes one of relationship between the finite and the infinite.[4] All beings participate,

---

3 Academic theology also has problems with crude forms of supernaturalism, as for instance in the understanding of miracles (see, e.g., Basinger 2011).

4 I am oversimplifying somewhat, for while Tillich talks of the infinity of being-itself, he also states that 'Being itself is beyond finitude and infinity' (1955, p. 263).

in a finite way, in being-itself while also being transcended by being-itself. God is 'the power of being in everything and above everything' (1955, p. 261), 'God transcends every being and also the totality of being – the world' (p. 263). But Tillich also finds it true to say that 'God is merged into ... finite beings, and their being is his being' (p. 263).

Contrary to the impression that one may gain from the recent debate about spirituality in psychiatry and at risk of appearing to contradict what has already been said above, spirituality is as much concerned with immanence as it is with transcendence. For example, many people today report that their understanding of spirituality is concerned with relationships (Cook 2004) – and these relationships are certainly not always with a transcendent order (or with God). Perhaps some quality of intimate relationships might be considered 'transcendent', but in fact it might also be argued that such human–human relationships are of a very natural, this-worldly, 'immanent' order, and young people especially seem to see their spirituality in immanent rather than transcendent relational terms (Savage et al. 2006, p. 51). Again, art is also seen as a source of spirituality, and while some forms of art (e.g. a still life) are more obviously immanent, and others (e.g. abstract art) more plausibly attempt to represent the transcendent, it is difficult to deny that spirituality is often perceived in very immanent objects.[5] Paul Heelas (2008) suggests that many of the newer strands of spirituality, often referred to as New Age spirituality, are in fact characterized by their immanent focus. While Heelas contrasts this with the transcendent focus of the traditional faiths, traditional spiritualities are also not without their immanent forms, some of which are currently very popular. Thus, mindfulness, deriving from Buddhist practice, has a particular focus on awareness of the present reality. It is, according to Thich Nat Hanh, 'keeping one's consciousness alive to the present reality' (Hanh 2008, p. 11).

However, if spirituality has its immanent, as well as transcendent, side, I would wish to argue that this immanent side is never completely divorced from the transcendent. Arguably, some kind of understanding of transcendence, in dynamic relationship with immanence, is fundamental to the nature of human consciousness which, by virtue of its reflexivity, has a tendency to exceed or transcend its own immanent locus and contents. Thus, for example, James Mackey writes of incarnate, human consciousness that it 'projects beyond the range of reality that is already immanent in and so constitutive of it' (Mackey 2000, p. 115). This kind of projective transcendence, which conceives of possibilities and meanings within, above and beyond perceived reality, is very compatible with psychological understandings of transcendence of the kind considered above. However, this kind of transcendence, 'by which marks on a page are transcended towards meaning', is itself in turn transcended by a 'fuller view of transcendence' within which

---

5 For an interesting essay exploring spirituality in relation to the 'real' and the 'Real', see O'Hear 1992.

'the sign (the marks with the meaning we give them) is transcended towards the reality it represents' (Mackey 2000, p. 257). This 'fuller' transcendence takes us beyond purely psychological forms of transcendence.

John Hick (1989, p. 14) is, I think, talking about 'fuller' kinds of transcendence when he distinguishes between experiences of the transcendent structured by a concept of deity and those that are structured by a concept of the absolute. The former are schematized in such a way as to relate to 'divine *personae*' (Yahweh, Allah, Vishnu, etc.) and the latter in such a way as to relate to 'metaphysical *impersonae*' (Brahman, the Tao, etc.). The former might be considered more strictly theological, whereas the latter (I would suggest) might be considered either philosophical or mystical. However, while this broadly theological level of 'fuller' transcendence is conceptually important, it is still itself a projection of consciousness that is psychologically understandable, based therefore in the immanent order of things and inseparable from this order. Theological transcendence, or fuller transcendence, is a concept imaginable because of the psychological capacity for interpretive transcendence. But interpretive transcendence is firmly located within immanent, psychological, human capacities.

Mircea Eliade employs the term hierophany to 'denote the act of manifestation of the sacred' (1968, pp. 124–5). We noted above that in contemporary psychological usage (e.g. by Pargament or Koenig) there is a close relationship between the sacred and the transcendent. However, for Eliade, the sacred – the 'wholly other' – is a power that is experienced sometimes in very natural ways:

> Beginning from the most elementary hierophany – for example the manifestation of the sacred in any object whatever, say a stone or a tree – and ending in the supreme hierophany, the incarnation of God in Jesus Christ, there is no real break in the continuity. (p. 124)

The sacred, then, is manifest in a continuous spectrum of modalities, ranging from the mundane to the divine, from the completely immanent to the completely transcendent. When Eliade does use the word 'transcendence' specifically (which he mostly seems to prefer here not to do), it is in relation to the Supreme Being, in respect of whom the hierophany becomes a theophany, but this transcendent power is in direct continuity with the power that is experienced in all things.

All of this considered, it seems very difficult to argue that spirituality is only about transcendence. It seems to be at least as much about immanence. But it is also not clear that the categories are as easily separable as they might at first appear. Thus, take for example Polly Young-Eisendrath's reference to psychotherapy as a form of 'ordinary transcendence' (see above). While we can see what she means by use of the term transcendence in the context of psychotherapy, the term is clearly not employed so as to imply anything supernatural or religious. It is, rather, a recognition of transcendence

151

within the immanent order of things. Similarly, the various psychological approaches to self-transcendence, interpretive transcendence and transcendence as motivation are firmly bedded in the immanent order of things.

Connolly has suggested that we might distinguish between 'radical transcendence' and 'mundane transcendence'. Radical transcendence is defined as 'a God who creates, informs, governs, or inspires activity in the mundane world while also exceeding the awareness of its participants' (2010, p. 131).

In contrast, and somewhat more obscurely, mundane transcendence is defined by Connolly as 'any activity outside conscious awareness that crosses into actuality, making a difference to what the latter becomes or interfacing with it in fecund ways, again without being susceptible to full representation' (p. 131).

Connolly clearly understands mundane transcendence as being located in a world of immanence and speaks of 'radical immanence' as advancing 'an image of mundane transcendence' (pp. 132–3). One might say, then, that if immanence and transcendence are at the ends of some kind of spectrum, then there is yet a middle ground within which transcendence is manifest in the ordinary.[6]

While transcendence and immanence have their opposing and contrasting characteristics, it is not the case that theology (at least within the Christian tradition, but probably much more widely) has ever seen them as alternatives, one of which is to be favoured over the other, but rather as a dialectical tension within which neither can be adequately understood without the other. Thus, for example, take James Mackey:

> Transcendence and immanence, in their properly sophisticated senses, turn out to be correlative terms rather than contraries; each calling for the other, rather than replacing each other, as happens when transcendence is taken in the crude sense of separation. (2000, p. 117)

It would seem to be the crude sense of separation of transcendence and immanence that has caused problems in the debate concerning spirituality and psychiatry, rather than the properly sophisticated senses of immanence and transcendence in tension.

We might imagine, then, that some of the present controversies concerning the place of spirituality in psychiatry might be advanced by bringing the

---

6 Although it seems less often to be spoken of, I think that personal and impersonal senses of transcendence may be much more difficult to reconcile than the radical and mundane. Increasing scientific awareness of the enormity of the universe and the discoveries of quantum physics have respectively expanded our awareness of the outer and the inner worlds to which we relate. Both are in a certain sense self-evidently 'transcendent', at least in a mundane sense and in respect to their scale of size and power, but they are not necessarily evidence of any personal, intelligent or self-aware transcendent reality. It is less easy to think of 'middle of the spectrum' forms of transcendence between the personal and impersonal than it is between the radical and mundane.

immanent dimension of spirituality back into the conversation. If psychiatry represents, in some sense, an immanent frame of reference within which mental disorder and well-being have been understood, and if spirituality has been seen as a transcendent frame of reference within which meaning and well-being might be found, then perhaps there is a way of relating these frames of reference in a creative tension, or at least of finding middle ground between them.

A secular age

An important account of the dynamics between transcendence and immanence in our secular age has been provided by Charles Taylor. The implications of Taylor's account of secularity for the practice of psychiatry are just beginning to be assessed (Crossley 2012; Cook 2012), but there is reason to think that it has much relevance to the present debate about the place of spirituality in psychiatry (King and Leavey 2010; Cook 2010).

In the world today, transcendence is associated both with diverse emerging new forms of spirituality and with traditional religious faith. In either case, according to Charles Taylor, it is something to which secularity seems to be deeply opposed (2007). For Taylor, in the context of a secular age 'in which the eclipse of all goals beyond human flourishing become conceivable' (p. 19), religion is definable in terms of transcendence.[7] Transcendence in turn is to be understood in three dimensions (p. 20). First, it is an agency or power or God of faith, a good higher than or beyond human flourishing. Second, however, and intimately related to this, is a possibility of human transformation, a higher good attainable by human beings only through participation in God's power and love. Third, this transformation opens the possibility of life transcending the natural scope of life between birth and death in this world.

In contrast, for Taylor's secular age, immanence confines itself to the limits of possible knowledge. The immanent frame of our present secular age is constituted by a natural, this-worldly order of scientific, social, technological, epistemological and other 'structures'. Among these are certain 'closed world structures' (CWS) that restrict our grasp of things. Appearing obvious, neutral, objective and natural, they are often more or less invisible and unrecognized for what they are. However, they are also deeply value laden and, in particular, are closed to transcendence. Taylor believes that the immanent frame of our present secular age is associated with a 'malaise of immanence' characterized by fragility of meaning, loss of solemnity in life transitions and a sense of flatness and ordinariness about everyday life. In this context, he describes a 'nova' phenomenon (or immanent counter-enlightenment) of an explosion of new ways of apprehending transcendence

---

7 We should note, however, that there are non-religious forms of transcendence, and that religion is not necessarily associated with transcendence (Casanova 2010).

within our secular age. These include both a return to ancient faith trad-itions and also new, more subjective and individual, forms of spirituality.[8]

Taylor's account, I believe, goes a long way towards accounting for the controversies around spirituality in the mental healthcare arena. Spiritu-ality – when introduced into a secular context such as that of healthcare – breaks the rule of the immanent frame that transcendence should not be included in public discourse on important issues. Moreover, it challenges the CWS, which are central to that immanent frame, and thus provokes a strong reaction from within the immanent frame. At the same time, that immanent frame, as represented by psychiatry, contributes to the malaise of immanence, a malaise to which the 'nova phenomenon' with all its various options for transcendence is itself a reaction. One might almost say that psychiatry, to the extent that it has resorted to the immanent frame as its primary reference point, has in fact provided exactly the kind of context within which one might have expected transcendence to be sought. It is a part of the malaise to which transcendence is seen as a solution, a solution that it more or less invites.

Taylor's analysis is conducted at a social level, but psychological research is increasingly providing an evidence base to suggest that the transcendent (or the sacred, or spirituality) provides many people with important coping resources in times of illness or adversity, including mental ill health (Parga-ment 2011). Now that users of mental health services are taking advantage of opportunities to voice their need for such resources, and many more mental health professionals also are seeing attention to spirituality as being an important aspect of their vocation to meet those needs, the scene for the present controversies about spirituality and psychiatry is set.

Immanence, transcendence and psychiatry

Psychiatry, as a scientific discipline, largely finds its identification with the immanent frame of reference described by Taylor. It does this most espe-cially when it focuses on neuroscience, on pharmacological treatments and on forms of psychotherapy that fundamentally exclude transcendence. However, it does have its moments of 'ordinary transcendence', for example in certain forms of psychotherapy, as described by Polly Young-Eisendrath. It has also been open to some forms of spirituality such as mindfulness – now incorporated in official guidelines for relapse prevention of depres-sion (National Institute for Health and Clinical Excellence 2009) – perhaps precisely because they are recognized as being of a more immanent (or mun-danely transcendent) nature.

---

8 Taylor also acknowledges that there are certain kinds of 'immanent transcendence', wherein there is not understood as being any life beyond death, but where, paradoxically, there is yet 'life beyond life' (2007, pp. 374, 726)

Given a more sophisticated notion of the relationship between immanence and transcendence and given the present state of affairs in our secular
age that Taylor describes, I would suggest that there are potential problems
when either immanence or transcendence is exaggerated at the expense of
the other. Thus the present problems are with an exaggeration of immanence: transcendence is trivialized or denied, and spirituality becomes a
utilitarian phenomenon that is either completely excluded or else put to the
service of improved health and well-being rather than to any transcendent
aim (Shuman and Meador 2003). Meanings associated with spirituality in
this context are fragile, this-worldly phenomena and many ordinary people
find themselves looking for something more.

While it is not our present primary problem, I can also envisage an
imbalance within which transcendence is exaggerated at the expense of immanence. In this situation, we might find spirituality devoid of content. No
longer anchored in any particular historical tradition (perhaps because it is
emphasized as a common feature of different traditions in which it becomes
overemphasized in reaction to the immanent frame, or perhaps because
it adopts an anti-intellectualism), this kind of transcendence might resort
to supernatural explanations that completely deny the place of science or
of immanent explanations for things. Such an overexaggeration of transcendence might find itself completely divorced from present this-worldly
realities. Tendencies in this direction might be found in certain healing
practices (both traditional and New Age) that reject conventional medical
treatments and emphasize the need for faith (even 'blind' faith).

But neither of these situations, in which immanence or transcendence
are respectively exaggerated, truly represents the nature of traditional
understandings of spirituality. It may therefore be the case that recent controversies concerning the place of spirituality in psychiatry are based on a
misunderstanding of the true nature of spirituality (as opposed to religion).
Or they may simply be about the use of the word 'spirituality'. Perhaps if we
spoke only of such things as relationship, meaning, value and self-awareness
there would be less controversy? Yet this again would be a triumph of the
CWS in keeping transcendence out of the conversation, and, if Taylor is
right, the malaise of immanence would seem to require some kind of more
explicitly transcendent therapy.

Ironically, spirituality, theology and psychiatry share common concerns
with immanent subjective human experience, and perhaps it is because of
this common ground that they have come into conflict with each other.
Belief, or non-belief, in the transcendent is associated with important ethical, psychological and professional concerns in clinical practice. Can one
really understand why an alcohol-dependent patient fails to make progress
with relapse prevention therapy, for example, unless one has understood
her reasons for wishing to stop (or not to stop) drinking? Very often, in
my experience, these reasons are concerned with the most important things
in life – often given very non-religious names and often explained in very

non-spiritual terms. They are, nonetheless, deeply spiritual concerns and sometimes (often if the patient is involved in Alcoholics Anonymous) given a transcendent reference under the name of a 'Higher Power', if not a more explicit name for God.

Spiritual practices are found in immanent as well as transcendent forms, and so it is difficult to know why there should really be any objection to their use in practice – as has already happened with guidelines for the use of mindfulness in the treatment of depression. A patient-centred model of treatment would identify the most relevant spiritual language (usually that employed initially by the patient) and the most relevant spiritual practices for the person at hand. However, in reality, immanence and transcendence are always closely correlated, and it might be argued that such a process is more about avoiding offence, more about avoiding controversial challenges to CWS, than it is about avoiding transcendence. To those inclined to inter-pret reality in terms of a transcendent order, it will in any case be difficult to have an adequate clinical conversation about meaning without employing the language of transcendence.

In fact, the language of transcendence (especially in its ordinary or mun-dane forms) does provide some common ground within which clinical and scientific conversations can take place. It does not require participants in the conversation to take a confessional stance, either asserting or denying their belief in God or in any particular faith tradition. It is accessible to psycho-logical interpretations (self-transcendence and interpretive transcendence), which also do not require that any particular theological or philosophical position is adopted by either or both of the conversation partners. Thus, it creates the possibility of meaningful dialogue, with integrity, between a clinician and a patient. It also allows the possibility of scientific research, within the immanent frame of reference, to be undertaken in relation to the part that beliefs in the transcendent play in helping (or hindering) people in their recovery from mental disorders.

This does not mean that the word 'transcendence' has to be used by clin-icians, for clearly many patients will not understand this or else will not find it conducive. However, it does provide a relatively neutral category within which conversations about God, a Higher Power, a natural spirit, energy or force can be placed. Because the concept of transcendence does not require theological interpretation, I do not see why it cannot be employed with integrity by the atheist psychiatrist. Because it is amenable to theological interpretation, it provides space within which the Christian, Muslim, Hindu or other religious person can conduct their conversation meaningfully.

If the account of things that I have sketched out here, based on Taylor's understanding of our secular age, has validity, it is to be expected that an immanent frame will continue to reject reference to the transcendent and that exaggerations of emphasis on the transcendent will continue to emerge in response. A better hope for resolution of this state of affairs is thus to pursue a more sophisticated (theological) discourse that recognizes the true nature of the relationship between immanence and transcendence and that refuses to be polarized or drawn into defence of the crude use of terms. This is not a merely academic point. It has implications, for good or ill, for the way in which mental health service users in the future find themselves able (or unable) to discuss the things that matter most deeply to them with those who care for them.

Conclusions

Transcendence emerges, I would suggest, as a central concept both for protagonists and antagonists within the debate concerning the proper place of spirituality in psychiatry. If we accept and apply Taylor's model of an immanent frame of reference, with its CWS opposed to transcendence, as applicable to psychiatry, then this is not surprising. Transcendence is both the source of offence to those who accept and prefer the immanent frame of reference, and it is the appropriate remedy for those who (consciously or unconsciously) find themselves suffering from the malaise of immanence. However, transcendence, understood in its properly more sophisticated sense as inseparable from immanence, also provides a language that can potentially bridge the gap and enable both scientific research and clinical engagement to proceed and also facilitate a less polarized conversation.

References

Basinger, D. (2011), 'What is a miracle?', in G. H. Twelftree (ed.), *The Cambridge Companion to Miracles*, Cambridge: Cambridge University Press, pp. 19–35.

Burkhardt, M. A. and Nagai-Jacobson, M. G. (2005), 'Spirituality and health', in B. M. Dossey, L. Keegan and C. E. Guzzetta (eds), *Holistic Nursing: A Handbook for Practice*, 4th edn, Sudbury: Jones & Bartlett, pp. 137–72.

Capra, F. (1975), *The Tao of Physics*, Glasgow: Fontana.

Casanova, J. (2010), 'A secular age: dawn or twilight?', in M. Warner, J. Vanantwerpen, and C. Calhoun (eds), *Varieties of Secularism in a Secular Age*, Cambridge MA: Harvard University Press, pp. 265–81.

Connolly, W. E. (2010), 'Belief, spirituality, and time', in M. Warner, J. Vanantwerpen and C. Calhoun (eds), *Varieties of Secularism in a Secular Age*, Cambridge MA: Harvard University Press, pp. 126–44.

Cook, C. C. H. (2004a), 'Psychiatry and mysticism', *Mental Health, Religion and Culture* 7:2, pp. 149–63.

Cook, C. C. H. (2004b), 'Addiction and spirituality', *Addiction* 99:5, pp. 539–51.

Cook, C. C. H. (2009), 'Substance misuse', in C. C. H. Cook, A. Powell and A. Sims (eds), *Spirituality and Psychiatry*, London: Royal College of Psychiatrists Press, pp. 139–68.

Cook, C. C. H. (2010), 'Spirituality, secularity and religion in psychiatric practice', *The Psychiatrist* 34:5, pp. 193–5.

Cook, C. C. H. (2011), The Philokalia *and the Inner Life: On Passions and Prayer*, Cambridge: James Clarke.

Cook, C. C. H. (2012), 'Self-belief: holistic psychiatry in a secular age. Commentary on … holistic psychiatry without the whole self', *The Psychiatrist* 36:3, pp. 101–3.

Craigie, F. C. (2008), *Positive Spirituality in Health Care*, Minneapolis MN: Mill City.

Crossley, D. R. (2012), 'Holistic psychiatry without the whole self', *The Psychiatrist* 36:3, pp. 97–100.

Dein, S., Cook, C. C. H. and Koenig, H. (2012), 'Religion, spirituality, and mental health', *Journal of Nervous and Mental Diseases* 200:10, pp. 852–5.

Eliade, M. (1968), *Myths, Dreams and Mysteries*, London: Fontana.

Ellermann, C. R. and Reed, P. G. (2001), 'Self-transcendence and depression in middle-age adults', *Western Journal of Nursing Research* 23:7, pp. 698–713.

Flanagan, K. and Jupp, P. C. (eds) (2007), *A Sociology of Spirituality*, Aldershot: Ashgate.

Goddard, N. C. (1995), '"Spirituality as integrative energy": A philosophical analysis as requisite precursor to holistic nursing practice', *Journal of Advanced Nursing* 22:4, pp. 808–15.

Hanh, T. N. (2008), *The Miracle of Mindfulness*, London: Rider.

Heelas, P. (2008), *Spiritualities of Life*, Oxford: Blackwell.

Hick, J. (1989), *An Interpretation of Religion: Human Responses to the Transcendent*, Basingstoke: Macmilllan.

Jones, C., Wainwright, G. and Yarnold, E. (1986), *The Study of Spirituality*, London: SPCK.

King, M. and Leavey, G. (2010), 'Spirituality and religion in psychiatric practice: why all the fuss?', *The Psychiatrist* 34:5, pp. 190–3.

Koenig, H. G., King, D. E. and Carson, V. B. (2012), *Handbook of Religion and Health*, New York: Oxford University Press.

Mackey, J. P. (2000), *The Critique of Theological Reason*, Cambridge: Cambridge University Press.

National Institute for Health and Clinical Excellence (2009), *Depression: The Treatment and Management of Depression in Adults*, London: National Institute for Health and Clinical Excellence.

O'Hear, A. (1992), 'The real or the Real? Chardin or Rothko?', in M. McGhee (ed.), *Philosophy, Religion and the Spiritual Life*, Cambridge: Cambridge University Press, pp. 47–58.

Pargament, K. I. (1999), 'The psychology of religion *and* spirituality? Yes and no', *International Journal for the Psychology of Religion* 9:1, pp. 3–16.

Pargament, K. I. (2011), *Spiritually Integrated Psychotherapy*, New York: Guilford.

Piedmont, R. L. (1999), 'Does spirituality represent the sixth factor of personality? Spiritual transcendence and the five-factor model', *Journal of Personality* 67:6, pp. 985–1013.

Poole, R., Higgo, R., Strong, G., Kennedy, G., Ruben, S., Barnes, R., Lepping, P. and Mitchell, P. (2008), 'Religion, psychiatry and professional boundaries', *Psychiatric Bulletin* 32:9, pp. 356–7.

Principe, W. (1983), 'Toward defining spirituality', *Studies in Religion* 12:2, pp. 127–41.

Reed, P. G. (1991), 'Toward a nursing theory of self-transcendence: deductive reformulation using developmental theories', *Advances in Nursing Science* 13:4, pp. 64–77.

Roof, W. C. (1999), *Spiritual Marketplace: Baby Boomers and the Remaking of American Religion*, Princeton NJ: Princeton University Press.

Savage, S., Collins-Mayo, S., Mayo, B. and Cray, G. (2006), *Making Sense of Generation Y: The World of 15–25-Year-Olds*, London: Church House Publishing.

Sheldrake, P. (2010), 'Spirituality and healthcare', *Practical Theology* 3:3, pp. 367–79.

Shuman, J. J. and Meador, K. G. (2003), *Heal Thyself: Spirituality, Medicine, and the Distortion of Christianity*, Oxford: Oxford University Press.

Sloan, R. P. (2006), *Blind Faith: The Unholy Alliance of Religion and Medicine*, New York: St Martin's Press.

Taylor, C. (2007), *A Secular Age*, Cambridge: Belknap.

Tillich, P. (1955), *Systematic Theology*, vol. 1, London: Nisbet.

Young-Eisdendrath, P. (2000), 'Psychotherapy as ordinary transcendence: the unspeakable and the unspoken', in P. Young-Eisendrath and M. E. Miller (eds), *The Psychology of Mature Spirituality*, London: Routledge, pp. 133–44.

Zinnbauer, B. J., Pargament, K. I., Cole, B., Rye, M. S., Butter, E. M., Belavich, T. G., Hipp, K. M., Scott, A. B. and Kadar, J. L. (1997), 'Religion and spirituality: unfuzzying the fuzzy', *Journal for the Scientific Study of Religion* 36:4, pp. 549–64.

9

Thriving through Myth

DOUGLAS J. DAVIES

Summary

Narratives help us flourish as individuals within families, churches and other communities as shared accounts of life's meaning that enhance our sense of well-being. While many take such narratives, whether religious, scientific, political or literary in form, entirely for granted, others question their authority and critically ponder their unique truthfulness in the light of the diversity of narratives evident in other cultures. Some may come to think of their world-explanations less as revealed truths and more as ideas of human origin, prompting personal reappraisal of life perspective in the process. Here such narratives are loosely viewed anthropologically and sociologically as 'myths', accounts that enshrine core cultural values and beliefs and prompt appropriate emotions and moods. Myth is not intended to be a negative word, nor as the opposite to 'truth'. Such myths frequently stand as life-framing and identity-enhancing narratives, encountered and appropriated through ritual, ceremony and a whole spectrum of social events. They also have the capacity to help deplete a sense of identity if aligned with a person's withdrawal from a cultural group and its beliefs. Whether enhancing, depleting or transforming the manner in which narratives are myth-like, they still speak powerfully to our sense of identity and purpose in life.

Background

It is now more than half a century since French anthropologist Claude Lévi-Strauss discussed the power of ritualized narratives, invoking in the process W. B. Cannon's early work on how social forces helped instigate Voodoo deaths. His point was to show how a myth remains potent through its many versions 'as long as it is felt as such' (Lévi-Strauss 1968, p. 217). In theoretical terms, Lévi-Strauss's engagement with the power of psychosomatic domains, through which people may be described as coming to 'live in' and benefit from their myths, can be taken further through the concept of what I have termed the moral-somatic relationship existing between individual and society (Davies 2011, pp. 68–94). In this context, 'moral' refers to the 'social', with society being understood as a moral community.[1] To view society in this way is to conceive of the social world as a dynamic resource available to increase the vitality of its individual members. This, in turn, throws a spotlight upon key institutions of a society and their role in either fostering or harming the identity of their members. In negative terms, we can observe contexts in which agents responsible for human well-being betray the trust vested in them to cause suffering involving a sense of harm framed by a sense of injustice. Following such malevolence people often speak of it as making them sick. 'It made me sick', 'it makes you sick', these are the negative expressions indicative of the moral-somatic relationship. Here feeling-states interplay with a knowledge of how things ought to be. Similarly, when people speak of justice not simply being done but needing to be 'seen to be done', we also hear a direct expression of the deeply social nature of human beings, of our nature as highly self-conscious social animals. Injustice makes people sick when the policing or judicial systems are seen to fail or be corrupt. Similarly, abuse of trust by some priests who abuse, not least sexually abuse, their people brings its own form of crisis that undermines a person's sense of identity and of the way things should be. So, too, when doctors kill rather than heal their patients, they invert our view of the world. Because all of these cases involve social institutions that exist to foster human well-being, malpractice is felt all the more strongly.

To be a member of society is to be socialized into one's group and its life-framing narrative and to gain a sense of identity by engaging with those charged with sustaining it. Furthermore, to participate in the events rooted in that narrative is to benefit from an intensification of that sense of identity and to be filled with hope and the sense of the possibility of many things. This is the power known by the initiate and often seen in the religious convert. It is also embodied in core community or religious leaders, not least in those we often describe as possessing charismatic qualities or holding key offices. By contrast, we may speak of identity depletion when abuse or other forms of harm are done to a person in and through their social supports. This approach to individual identity and its social network not only takes seriously the *Bio-Cultural Approaches to the Emotions*, as one book title has it, but of the bio-cultural approach to life at large (Hinton 1999). It is on that larger canvass that I see a bio-cultural generation of meaning not only driving the human capacity to survive but also to flourish. If early forms of hominid communication aided co-operative forms of social action of positive adaptive significance, then our communicative development over time into song, music, oral and later into written narrative has taken human flourishing further still.

---

1 Here 'moral community' reflects Durkheim's notion of society (1915, pp. 45, 47, 210).

Moral/social meaning-making

So it is that societies, their subgroups, religious traditions, professions, occupations, sports and artistic streams all entertain story-form narratives that handle cultural ideas and provide an environment within which human beings may thrive. What is more, these contexts usually favour and manage patterns of emotions that pervade narrative-ideas, often transforming them into moral–religious values that energize a sense of identity and aid human flourishing, for human beings are not simply cognitive meaning-making agents but also moral-meaning-making agents. Cognitive meaning, if separated out, might produce a degree of intellectual satisfaction, even passing into what William James spoke of as an 'ontological emotion', a 'moment of energetic living' in which a questioning over the nature of reality gives way to an engagement with wonder (James 1956, p. 74). Yet for many, I imagine, key moments of engagement come less in the train of intensive philosophizing than in social contexts where a moral meaningfulness offers an end in itself; an end that, paradoxically, also generates that life orientation to the future signalled by the idea of hope. Inherent in this perspective is a model of society as a field of power, full participation in which intensifies human thriving and distance from which depletes it. It also involves individuals who embody that power in distinctive ways and are able to communicate it to the wider population. For most people, the complex yet general life-framing narratives evident in society at large are regularly complemented by family-based narratives. In the British context, this means that broad social ideas of national identity involving economic, healthcare, educational and sporting/leisure activities play out within family-focused narratives of related issues. What we might call family myths themselves help foster and maintain identity within wider social myths.

One of the best examples of a mythological and ritual world developed on this basis is furnished by Mormonism. Indeed, there are few better examples within the history of Christian culture than that provided by the life-framing narratives of the Latter-day Saints. It begins in a pre-mortal council in heaven, when plans are laid for the future salvation of humanity once it has become disobedient to God (Davies 2000). But even in that discussion, disobedience and self-opinionated pride emerge in the heart of Lucifer, who becomes the fallen Satan. The narrative continues with the formation of the earth and of human life upon it as mortal bodies furnish homes for pre-existing spirits. The story tells of migrant groups from the Middle East, the Holy Land, establishing cultures in America, of how Jesus appears in America after his resurrection, of how worldwide Christian disobedience engenders a lapsed world and of how Jesus and his Father restore the ways of salvation through the teenage prophet Joseph Smith through visionary appearances. These stories, taken by some Mormons to be accurate accounts of historical events but by non-Mormon scholars as examples of myths, pass into actual history through Joseph's life, through founding converts migrating to and within the USA, through their establishing a culture zone in Utah and through their missionary engagement across the world. For a long time, and still to this day, the identification of what might have actually taken place and what is imagined experience compete for priority in Mormon thought. But what is unmistakable is the way the values associated with these stories, real or imagined, have become lodged in family life, church life and in rituals that take place in temples, with the great Salt Lake City Temple being the best known case.

Here, in Mormonism, we are faced with facticity, with the way narratives lead to architecture and to patterns of ritual behaviour that forge identity and create environments for thriving. The very fact of sacred buildings makes concrete what otherwise is a story told, a story that sometimes has roots in imaginative narratives and sometimes in more evidence-based history but that, in the place and events that occur in it, mixes into a sensed reality that feeds individual and community identity. Examples fill the world from Salt Lake City and other temples, the Vatican and cathedrals galore, Mecca and worldwide mosques, Amritsar's Golden Temple and gurdwaras of the Sikh diaspora, not to mention Jerusalem as contested sacred space. In all such contexts, we face very persuasive geographical/architectural support for myths through the allure of meaning inherent in sacred places and in sacred places experienced today in emotional ways.

On a still wider front, human meaning-making has generated not only ideological explanations of our environment, of how the world came to be, but also of what lies ahead in stories of alternative environments, occupancy of which is, albeit, related to moral behaviour. We may gain the ancestral realm, or heaven or paradise if we are good and if proper rites take place: if not, there may be trouble ahead. Something about the nature of human life has, at the same time, acknowledged the fact that socially created rules are often broken, and in terms of that societies, and especially what we often call the religious aspects of society, have developed the idea of deliverance from trouble. So it is that we often speak of world religions as salvation religions: salvation being a concept that maximizes moral meaning in a world of responsible agents but not without accommodating and transforming human failure. Here human emotions, be they, for example, guilt, fear, mercy or love, are all invoked, often alongside ideas of supernatural agents or processes controlling human morality, and often leading to ideas of an afterlife.

Death and beyond

Death constitutes a key constraint in the meaning-engendering power of myth. It often appears as a frustration to a flourishing identity, with many arguing that death and loss offer a basic challenge to human hope and to the task of living. However, the psychological emotions of grief that challenge identity have not been left alone, for here most major world religions have come into their own as one fundamental form of human cultural adaptation to the fact of grief and the potential loss of hope (Davies 1997). Ideas of an afterlife, with their myths and surrounding doctrines, provide their own form of meaning-making, with a strong emphasis upon morality. Whether or not we are cognitively hard-wired to engage in reciprocity and altruism, cultures invariably set standards of moral rules.

There are, for example, millions of Muslims in the world who say that once a person has died and been placed in a grave, sometimes designed in such a way that there is free space above the corpse, two angels come to interrogate the dead as to their belief and to give some indication of whether they are destined for a heavenly paradise or for punishment, whether they will go to the paradise garden or to the fire (Rustomji 2009). Whichever is the case they are believed to experience the process of being dead as a painful one as their soul is withdrawn from their body by the angel of death. That soul has to be drawn out from each blood vessel in an excruciating manner, especially if the body does not want to give up its spirit. The sides of the grave, especially for the wicked, are thought to press in on the corpse, crushing its ribs. All in all, death is a terror and it makes great sense that some might, for example, wish to die the death of a martyr, for martyrs in the cause of God are largely free from such torments. The recitation of such grave torments plays its own role in helping to form a moral conscience in many.

Christianity's own history and current spectrum of afterlife beliefs includes its own version of afterlife purging and a moral horizon scanned by the ever-watchful divine eye, with recording angels keeping a record of good and evil deeds. In both the Islamic and Christian contexts, many have brought ideas of merit and prayer and other rites that help generate merit for the dead to ease their afterlife existence. Though many contemporary Christians are much more doubtful of such an afterlife geography and scenarios of punishment, some such ideas still remain, with notions of post-mortal purgation and cleansing prior to the divine vision having their contemporary protagonists. Yet others are committed to beliefs in a post-mortem sleep until the last day and its resurrection transformation. Some believers are, however, embarrassed by these stories, and distance themselves from them or reinterpret them in more culturally acceptable forms. Still, many ordinary Christians operate on clusters of ideas often comprised of apparently disconnected items of belief. One of my postgraduates (Armstrong 2011) is currently exploring this for active Christians, including some who think that while resurrection is important for Jesus it is not so for their own post-mortem future. They think of their own destiny more in terms of an immortal soul going on after death and less in terms of a personal resurrection. Their easy acceptance of such a 'soul discourse' is much disliked by many Protestant, resurrection-focused theologians working at a more technical level of debate.

Myth failure

To thrive through faith is one thing, to come to find that it fails is another. Here I refer to some of our current research on the Sea of Faith group, mostly people born and bred in mainstream Christian churches, often having accepted a straightforward Christian mythical narrative of God, Jesus, sin and salvation, and who then, for various reasons, give up belief in such a self-existent deity to hold that all religious ideas are humanly generated, and to think in a 'non-realist' way about God (Davies and Northam-Jones 2012). Here we encounter an interesting phenomenon in which the charisma of one theologian, Don Cupitt of Cambridge, has allowed these people to remain, largely, as very active churchgoers who now operate on such an explicitly non-realist view of God and religion and who also explicitly see myths as human stories that help people to make sense of the world and to flourish thereby. Here we encounter a most interesting example of a higher-order form of self-identity: a kind of initiation from having been born, born again and born yet again to an explicit myth-form of thought. This succession of insight may not apply to many, and may not apply to those who, say, are born again into a mythical world only for it to lose its power over them. One element of the Sea of Faith movement lies in what amounts to a ritual of reflection and expression of doubt and loss of one world-view and the adoption of another, but within a group of like-minded and like-experienced people. In our study of this group, none of its participants now believed in life after death, though many remained quite active churchgoers. They had simply changed in their understanding of the content and nature of life-narratives, and decided to retain the myth-making and ritual-enactment aspects of religion. Inherent in this example is the question of feeling or sensing the truth of things. These individuals retain a sense of flourishing in life through an intellectual excitement over understanding the nature of doctrine as story, and of rite as something that may contribute to human experience, but on a different interpretive base from that held earlier in their life.

Christmas

But let me now explore a different zone of life-narrative in British society, one that is full of complexity over the emotional triggers of social identity and yet links with issues of well-being; that is, Christmas. With December each year, many of us enter more deeply into a period of domestic and social activity for which consumerist sources will already have prepared us. We will give little or no theoretical thought to the decoration of our streets, shops and then our homes. Greetings cards will be sent to mark family, friendship and other alliances, with presents being bought and, in due course, given and received. Children will be told stories about a man responsible for these presents and his wonderful journey through the skies and across the world with his magical reindeer. He knows if we are good or bad and may give or withhold presents accordingly. Young parents who, only some ten or fifteen years earlier learned, sometimes to their dismay, that this is 'only a story', now tell that same story to their children. Here I take one clear case, that of the northern British town of Middlesbrough. Here, today and in recent years, many families take their little children to watch Father Christmas arrive in his sleigh, pulled by real reindeer. He emerges from the impressive civic hall and proceeds through the streets that are filled with music provided by the local radio station and with a happy presence of the police. The little ones look in excitement-pervaded wonder at the real man and the real reindeers and 'see' Father Christmas. Here we encounter a magnificent collusion of many parties to tell the tale focused on Father Christmas. Civic authorities, the media, the police who keep order in genial fashion, the shopkeepers and their decorations, as well as families and schools and a mix of generations together work the magic of Christmas. The Middlesbrough streets present a moving tableau, a paradigmatic scene, of Christmas.

For many, this scene interplays with another as schools and churches mount nativity plays and carol services whose *dramatis personae* are those of Mary, Joseph, wise-men, angels and shepherds and with domestic animals replacing the reindeer, all framing the baby Jesus. Here a complex interplay of images, motifs and narratives allows participants optional levels of reflective access to ideas of an incarnation of the divine son, the second person of an eternally existent holy Trinity, a virgin birth, social marginalization, refugee status and also of salvation, that divine goodwill towards human plight. Some contexts may also provide bridging scenes between Father Christmas and the baby Jesus, in tales of St Nicholas, not least by deploying the medium of the gift set amid a cluster of values concerning family, care, concern, compassion, love, poverty, need or abandonment. The emphasis lies upon familiar emotions of group unity, peace and good will to all people. Here I will not delve into how these motifs of inclusion may also foster a sense of social exclusion for those not in 'happy families', nor how non-Christian groups or secular bodies take issue with the Christian symbolism and ritual; my point is that many of us will come to live within a distinctive symbolic world for a specified period of time. It is a period where emotions pervade ideas to produce values. But what of those few priests who sometimes make newspaper headlines with their concern that perhaps children will confuse the Father Christmas and the 'real' Jesus message of this shared period of ritualized time? Nearly every year some keen curate tells young schoolchildren that Father Christmas is not real. He does so to make the point that the Jesus story is 'real', something that reminds me of Hocart's comment that a ritual myth 'flourishes most where there is no professional priesthood, because there it remains in contact with reality'. Indeed, he described 'an all-grasping priesthood' as 'that bugbear of scholars' (Hocart 1973, p. 25). For what is interesting about Christmas is the way the two ritual scenes of Father Christmas and Baby Jesus are controlled, whether by ordinary lay folk, whether churched or non-churched, or by clergy. For my purposes in this chapter, I can see very little difference between the two narratives in the sense that they each create a world of emotional significance, much edited, much socially created, and ever changing with time.

Locating interpretation

What can these examples teach us about mythical narrative and our 'living in' them and, in particular, about the nature of 'suspending doubt' as we do so? We need very little instruction in the need to suspend doubt about the reality of Father Christmas given that he is a symbol of the pragmatic reality of social attitudes of relationship, care and gift-giving among kin, friends, colleagues and clientele. He symbolizes the nature of the gift underlying human social life. Christmas is the myth of social reciprocity, ritually intensified in the family. It is even one means of parenting, albeit for a brief period.

We might, in a slightly similar way, describe the fascinating mythical world of family, domesticity, home and hope, created, for example, in the material world of IKEA, a kind of realm reminiscent of Plato's ideal world where we can see and move about in 'perfect' environments presented to our senses. In symbolic ways, the three-dimensional space of house and objects, becomes animated by the fourth dimension of human presence, appreciation and desire, all can then be selected in flat-pack form and taken away to be reconstructed in one's own home environment. Media adverts add shopping sales to such contexts of desire with the deep family symbol of the sofa often presented as the sought-for object around and upon which ideal lives may be realized. Indeed, such sales follow Christmas in a grand immediacy of ritualized homes-and-families. Martin Hansson, UK manager of IKEA, introduces the most recent catalogue with the idea of 'happiness', an emotion to be found 'in the little things' present to our sight and sound and tactile senses. Indeed, the store expresses IKEA's 'restless pursuit of a happier home', it is their 'obsession', and their catalogue 'is full of thousands of products meant to do just that'. In other words, domesticity has its life-narrative partly written in and through the furnishing of a home. And a visit to the store, the purchase of objects and their home installation will help create that domesticity (Miller 2008). To live in these myths is to be energized and to be caused to thrive.

Science

In the pursuit of thriving through myth, I now want to move from the kitchen or sitting room to the laboratory, or at least I want to talk about religion and science as meaning-making processes. Here that part of social science often called the sociology of knowledge is useful to see how the 'driving force' of emotion motivates scientific work and allows us to see that scientific ideas carry persuasion within the life-world of scientists, including laboratories, the scientific method, journals and conferences. These are the arenas of meaning, rite and identity-generation for those so involved. However, it is practically impossible to isolate only the theories and expect non-scientifically involved people to be persuaded by them. The same can be said of priests or theologians and their life-world immersion in texts, rites and a tradition that affords identity. At the heart of all successful myths and doctrines lies an attractive story that is not only relatively easy to understand but also one with which it is easy to identify. This is one reason why scientific paradigms are problematic, for while they carry much empirical 'truth' about how the world works, they seldom take narrative forms and it is not easy to identify with them.

What is more, scientific ideas are not easily embodied or ritually practised by many ordinary people: there is no Eucharist of Evolution, no Friday Prayers of Electro-magnetism or a Sabbath for Genetics. The few individuals who are well known, Charles Darwin and Stephen Hawking, say, are largely known for aspects of their own life-stories. While Darwin's scientific ideas can possess a story-form to them, they lack an ultimate persuasion because of a lack of moral meaning. A person needs a degree of immersion in science and scientific methods to begin to be attracted to the 'beauty' or challenge of evolutionary processes: they are not self-evidentially meaningful. Here again, Hocart was wise to note in his 1939 essay that while 'scientific work is the very type of intellectual activity; yet it is accompanied and sustained by emotion' (1973, p. 52).

How and why: category errors

It is this notion of the life-world, of the dynamics in which we live and have our being, that underlies any grasp of the power of myths as a world in which to live. To argue, for example, that science explains the 'how' of life while religion explains the 'why' is, it seems to me, to presuppose that 'how' questions and 'why' questions are different, and that they should be complementary. I imagine that to a scientist like Stephen Hawking the 'how' question has already become so fully identified with the 'why' question that 'why' no longer carries significance. For some Christians, however, I imagine that the 'how' question has become largely irrelevant when compared with the 'why' answers of propositional belief.

Still, this chapter is not concerned with that issue of classification as such, but with the nature of the life-world and its own persuasive power. Rather than dwell on the idea of the life-world and its phenomenologist authors, let me simply invoke William James's emphasis on the way custom and familiarity 'banish uncertainty from the future' so that 'the mere familiarity with things is able to produce a feeling of their rationality' (1956, p. 77). This very link between thought and feeling was raised to the level of definition in the 1960s by Clifford Geertz, when his cultural definition of religion described religion as 'a system of symbols which acts to establish powerful, pervasive, and long-lasting moods and motivations ... by formulating conceptions of a general order of existence' and by 'clothing those conceptions with such an aura of factuality that these moods and motivations seem uniquely realistic' (1966).

The latter aspect of Geertz's definition is guaranteed to trouble a sizeable minority of theology undergraduates year in and year out, for they tend to dislike his reference to an 'aura of factuality' and this pinpointing of beliefs as ideas sensed as being uniquely realistic. Their dislike lies in their awareness that these are descriptions of their own outlook: indeed, many of us dislike being described to ourselves. There is something disarming about seeing one's condition described and, in that process, apparently relativized, for if my religion and belief appears uniquely realistic to me and if someone else also has a similar sense of unique realism, then one of us must be wrong: or so it seems to some. Yet as the study of emotions asserts itself in many academic disciplines, Geertz's emphasis upon long-lasting moods, on the aura of factuality and on the sense of a unique reality attending upon beliefs is of particular importance for the way we inhabit our thought-worlds and relate to their legitimating narratives. And this is the point about the power of myths, whether they take the Indian forms of cosmic transmigration, karma, moksha, nirvana and cessation of human desire, or the Jewish, Christian and Islamic form of divine revelation, the nature myths of origin and ancestors in many local cultures, or even the myth-like accounts of social revolution in Communism. And of those with an affinity for it, the same persuasive power may be found in narratives of scientific discovery and its heroic actors.

To those bred in them, familiar with the rites that intensify their accompanying values and emotions, such narratives seem so true. And if a person or a movement argues, as many do, that an experience of conversion brings one from darkness to light, from one level of understanding to quite another, then the idea and sense of 'truthfulness' acquires even more power. Indeed, one characteristic feature of religious worlds lies in this sense of revivification aligned with religious insight. The expression 'to be born again' typifies this sense of life intensification in a shift from survival to flourishing. From a theological perspective, worship offers one such context for the process of self-transcendence. In the Christian scheme and in terms of morality, worship takes the devotee beyond the transgressive self into a morally renewed self through contact with the divine transcendent who is the very source of moral purity. But, of course, cultures differ, their narratives differ, and the idioms through which the agents of divine otherness are described and the motifs that portray morality may all appear quite diverse. The boundaries of a culture perpetuate these characterizations.

Everything makes sense as long as we share the same cultural idioms, motifs and the grammar of discourse that is appropriate to them. If we begin to get the grammar wrong, problems emerge. It is perfectly good for me to confess that Jesus is the incarnate Son of God but not that I am a new incarnation of the divine son. What is a Christian priest to make of the young man who comes to church and speaks to him quietly afterwards to say that he is Jesus who has returned? If either the young man's or the priest's symbolic speech bears certain impediments, then one or the other is likely to be identified as mad. In other words, the cultural range of meaningful expression possesses an appropriate range of normality and abnormality. In strictly theological terms, these are issues of orthodoxy and heresy, with liberal bands between; in strictly medical terms I suppose these are issues of sanity and madness, doubtless with appropriate bands between. Pressing the point, orthodoxy does seem to relate to sanity as heresy does to madness. Even Jesus was described by some as mad when he spoke of himself as the good shepherd owning the power not only to lay down his life for his sheep but also the power or right to take his life up again (John 10.17–20).

Cultural intensification

Returning to a group's ritual events, we find that in them the narrative elements and the values they enshrine become intensified whereas doctrinal and philosophical reflection tend to take matters into a variety of meta-levels of explanation. It is here that we encounter the issue of normality. Many cultural contexts with which we are familiar embed some core values in stories and events that are widely shared, as with Christmas, which brings images of human families and divine families into coalescence. The baby Jesus is at once an image of all human babies and of the unique incarnate Son of God. Carol services, themselves symbolized in the worldwide broadcasting of the King's College carol service, provide one base for this mythical construct, as do domestic Christmas mornings. The shared singing of Christmas carols, too, creates a shared universe of meaning in which the most remarkable things are said about a being coming from heaven to earth through a virgin birth, and so on. In and during such ritual events these assertions often assume a sense of truth. Here the role of music as the medium for words that are the medium for doctrine is vital in fostering emotions that help frame the whole event as authentic. To sing is to assent profoundly: singing makes it so. Participation in carol services, nativity plays and Christmas shopping draws individuals into the core ideas and, just as importantly, evokes within them shared cultural emotion. Sociologists have, long ago, spoken of the sense of transcendence of self and of an integrated communality that emerges through such ritual. Cultural intensification and self-transcendence belong together.

Myth and spirituality

Christian creeds often function as part of liturgical life, especially in sacramentally driven Christian traditions. In many other traditions, too, doctrinal formulae become utterances of power: when God is pronounced great in Islam or the ultimate one proclaimed as pure in Sikhism, doctrine pervades an emotion of collective submission and collective strength and vice versa. In the Indian tradition, to engage in the annual rites of, for example, *Durga Puja* is to sense something of the battle between good and evil, and to enter into a sense of the deities coming to visit and going away again as models of the deities are submerged in a river as the sun sets. Here we approximate to the end of the Christian Eucharist when, confession, absolution, consecration and participation completed, believers are charged to go in peace to love and serve the Lord.

Such participation and its attendant insight have long since constituted that formation and intensification of identity recognized as the tradition's spirituality. The formation of a self, character or *habitus* emerges from such participation in the core moral-meaning-making processes of a cultural world, always acknowledging that such a world may focus on a partner or spouse, a family, a leisure and friendship network or a work-based grouping (see Davies 2002, pp. 40, 181, 205). The degree to which a person participates in one or more of these is the degree to which they are likely to experience a meaningful existence, thrive and flourish or, by contrast, if they are frustrated or betrayed in their relationships, be diminished. Nicole Toulis described how Jamaican women who had attained a certain level of flourishing or 'sense of presence' in their homeland lost some of it when migrating to Britain. Deploying De Martino's notion of 'presence', she spoke of a crisis of presence, a lack of being in control of one's life. She showed, too, how a Christian Pentecostal life-narrative of the battle between good and evil, God and Satan, helped reconfigure this crisis and restore a new form of 'presence' (Toulis 1997).

Distance from a community's core values and emotions is often discussed in terms of marginalization, alienation and potential anomie. We might even speak of people as culture-rich or culture-poor depending upon the intensity of their participation within their own appropriate groups. Many of the key professions in our society – medicine, the law, education, the churches – are centres of cultural power that feed core ideas with emotion to generate prime values. But somewhat similar processes underlie family life, leisure and sporting circles and so on. The degree to which these circles cohere is, I would argue, the degree to which sanity prevails. Mental health is, in this context, one aspect of participation in meaningful systems.

Religious ritual

What we loosely call religious institutions, along with social events in which core values are announced, appropriated and practised, have long furnished arenas for such participation. Theoretically speaking, it is now a long time since that remarkable theologian-anthropologist of the later nineteenth century, William Robertson Smith, described sacrificial ritual, for example, as fostering a people's 'joyous confidence in their God', a notion reflected in Emile Durkheim's affirmation of the 'confidence, joy and enthusiasm' engendered by ritual (Robertson Smith 1894, p. 255; Durkheim 1915, p. 389). Robertson Smith inspired Durkheim and the sociology of religion just as he touched Sigmund Freud's own mythical storytelling of primal hordes, dominant fathers and jealous sons – itself a myth that inspired generations of psychoanalysts. Smith and Durkheim certainly helped interpret such collective human activity – ritual if you wish – as a time that intensifies group belonging and engenders a feeling of transcendence. This sense of transcendence, of being 'taken out of oneself' is basic for ideas of thriving, and narratives of meaningfulness set the stage for it. But other arenas of operation ought not to be ignored when it comes to human well-being across its mental, physical and socially interactive domains. One such arena in Great Britain is that of the National Health Service.

National Health Service

Human thriving seems to depend as much upon factors that aid survival in an intellectual/moral environment as upon nourishment and shelter for survival in our physical environment. In the broad scheme of things, of course, people change, times change, internal chemical systems and mental systems all change. Small-scale traditional societies also change as they expand, experience contact, and have their beliefs shift in focus. As secularization impacts upon certain societies, the task of moral-meaning provision opens up to other than religious institutions, not least to educational and health systems. Indeed, the national coalition spearheaded by the National Council for Palliative Care and entitled Dying Matters, whose brief is to foster talking about death and bringing it into popular discourse, has recently set up a Meaning, Faith and Belief group, comprised of representatives of religious and secular bodies. Through the National Health Service, as the major arm of the welfare state, despite or alongside the long-established role of chaplains, we are currently witnessing a rise of interest in the notion of a generalized spirituality as one element among other elements of social and medical care. Indeed, we are witnessing an interesting moment of a clash of cultures, one reflected in uncertainty over language and appropriate personnel. Some dislike the word spirituality because it smacks of traditional religion, may imply mystical supernaturalism and signals the chaplains' domain. Others see it as an essentially secular word for care of the whole person and their life-concerns. One theoretical question implicit in this scenario of conceptual and linguistic change is whether, and if so how, the challenge of sustaining life-meaning can be provided by non-ecclesial institutions through agents capable of embodying such meanings and fostering them in others, especially those in contexts of anxiety and life-crisis.

Cultural wisdom and folly

In short, some people believe things that to others are meaningless and, depending upon the impact of ideas of toleration and understanding that I may possess, I might regard some views of other people as quaint, curious or plain stupid. Historical studies show, for example, that some cultures once adopted the practice of killing living dependants of a famous man when that man died. Joerg Fisch has documented this quite extensively in the phenomenon of what he calls 'following into death'. We are somewhat familiar with this in the Indian notion of widow-cremation or suttee but, for example, Fisch documents the following into death of hundreds of 'wives, concubines, slaves, servants, members of the court' in ancient China. But, then, from about the second century BC, changes led to opposition towards the practice, which resulted in the replacement of human beings by manufactured figures (Fisch 2006, p. 461). Probably none of us here would accept an idea of the afterlife that required so much supportive company provided through a form of sacrifice and corporate interment: it is not a mythical world of our choice. My point here is that many are happy with their own narrative landscape but can regard other landscapes as totally alien. It is here that we can see fairly clearly the kinship between myth and doctrine. Indeed, I can see no ultimate distinction between them as explanatory schemes of moral meaning-making, except that doctrines tend to have been more extensively subject to critical/philosophical refinement. This brings me to the question of intimacy and distance with our own mythologies as far as spirituality and mental health are concerned.

There are many, I suppose, whose sense of well-being is sustained by a belief in a deity and a deity-approved moral order. Worship, prayer and ritual acts allow for participation in the narratives in such a way that they appear entirely true. They are sensed as true and lived as true: 'In thee, O Lord, I put my trust', and similar utterance-texts in Judaeo-Christianity, or Buddhism, where a devotee takes refuge in the Buddha, the Dharma and the Sangha, all express an emotion of dependence and of what some would see as an engagement with 'the truth'. Just what it is to sense something as true and to love 'the truth' is, itself, an immense issue lying beyond the scope of this chapter. But it is an important issue for much religion. It underlies, for example, those religious people who wish to differentiate between nominal believers and 'true' believers. This is the domain of emotion, of preferred, shaped and managed emotion. But in our critically self-conscious worlds, such embedded pleasure is also a luxury. We now know much about the way religions develop and how myths and doctrines grow. For some this is a deeply problematic situation; they would see it as the basic process of secularization. Ideas are human, myths are human, theologies are human, much as Feuerbach argued in the eighteenth century and many others before and after. So, too, in eastern thought where, for millennia, some have spoken of the illusionariness of things. This raises the proper question of the spirituality of illusion or of reductionism, an important question for human well-being in our contemporary world.

Concluding comments

In this chapter, I have used 'myth' as a form of shorthand for emotion-pervaded, meaning-making narrative texts serving to explain the way things are and to foster a sense of identity. I have not entered into definitions and theories of myth in any technical fashion. In one sense this is irresponsible of me, but time – an often recurring mythological motif – is ever passing, and I want to try and see the forest of human meaning while not getting lost in the naming of trees. Though some might see particular irresponsibility in equating religious doctrines with myths, I see no essential problem here, since philosophically and historically framed doctrines constantly dwell upon and derive material from biblical narrative stories of deity and divine agents and frequently transform them into liturgy. The Christian creeds typify a participation in such doctrinal storytelling.

Here, in conclusion, I speculate on kinds of responses some people might make to my depicting religious ideas in this way. One is strongly fundamentalist and affirms against all-comers ideas from the past. Whether in Christianity, Islam or many other contexts, reformers seek to purify decayed traditions and restore a pure religion. Such processes are usually doomed to failure for they always interpret the past through the constraints of the present. Another approach is one of cynical inactivity, probably involving withdrawal from active community life, while yet another involves a commitment to engage with the acknowledged mythical schemes of a group or culture in the knowledge that this is precisely what human life is like. It is like telling the Father Christmas story to infant family members, perhaps within years of only coming to learn its story-like nature oneself. Here we witness the double cultural process of 'seeing' and 'seeing through'. One outcome of this is a changed sense of human obligation as a meaning-making animal in a cosmos whose 'meaning' belongs to a middle range and not an ultimate range of significance. There are wider issues that could be explored here, including the degree to which some narratives are self-evidently mythical – fantastic stories embodying cultural values – while other narratives that might seem very mythical to outsiders are regarded as 'true' and not 'myths' at all by insider members of a religious community or culture. This has obvious applications to those who see the creation narratives in Genesis as myths enshrining cultural or theological 'truths' while others see them as historical fact; so too with the resurrection narratives of Jesus. Within western cultural contexts this kind of argument is conducted in terms of 'historical' proof and diverse interpretation of scientific data. Somewhat similar discussions of 'truthfulness', factuality or verifiability have also been extended by some to ideas such as that of psychoanalysis: is it a mythical construct or something more deeply constrained by verifiable material (Lévi-Strauss 1968, pp. 181–4)?

Getting the range 'right' becomes an epistemological challenge, something that becomes evident for some folk when they are bereaved. Indeed, many have the experience of slippage on this range when they experience bereavement, when life may seem to lose its meaning, its colour vanishes and that quality of human existence called hope, vitality, energy or the like becomes depleted and with it also the sense of identity. But such identity depletion, while for a few may become chronic, is for most a passing period of time after which hope is restored and life progresses. The human animal ever lives between the poles of hope and despair, of meaning and senselessness, with everyday life fostering a middle range of meaning that suffices for most purposes most of the time. The goal of spirituality, in its move of alliance with mental health, lies in a committed sense of engagement with cultural intensification that fosters a person's sense of social worth and individual identity. This entire chapter could, of course, have been pursued more in terms of an emotional progress from the joy of meaning, through the anxiety of uncertainty and the pain of grasping the scope of meaning and chaos, to the gravitas of commitment to living through society as a cultural animal.

Whatever is the case, we are left with issues of cultural wisdom and cultural folly and the way thinking people emerge as they see life through accepted beliefs, then come to see through them, questioning their validity, and then perhaps move to a different standpoint of understanding. The question of thriving through myth known to be myth will then arise as its own challenge to moral-meaning-making. One solution to this standpoint is that of self-commitment to an explicitly provisional narrative of life's meaning. In etymological terms, 'thrive' apparently derives from an old Norse verb – to grasp or grasp for oneself. It is reminiscent of Colin Turnbull's study *The Mountain People*, an account of an Ethiopian famine in which the prime value, he said, had become to possess food for oneself. This is a symbolic opposite to one prime biblical text describing the nature of Christ and seeking to outline the basis for Christian ethics where, in Philippians (2.6), Jesus Christ is described as 'finding himself in the form of God' and, in that sense of self-awareness, did not regard that status as something to be grasped, seized or plundered but, rather, adopted the form of a servant who self-humbles in an obedience to death by crucifixion. In this complex contradiction of opposites, the biblical author calls believers not to 'seek their own' but to care for each other. In other words, the ethics of sacrificial relations is advocated.

I highlight this element at the close of this chapter because it is obvious that some degree of insight into the relativity of human meaning systems, including that of Philippians, leaves the intellectual in an odd position. Unlike the many who dwell within accepted stories, be they deep or shallow stories, he sees stories for what they are: potential homes of meaning that, echoing William James again, saps the home-dweller of his curiosity over a potentially dangerous world. One kind of existential response to this is, quite naturally, that of despair, nihilism and even self-destruction. Another response lies in an acknowledgement of the real relativity of meaning systems and even of the potential senselessness of being a meaning-making system faced by such a variety of less than ultimate materials. For those who 'find themselves' in the form of human beings there arises the option of a kind of self-sacrifice to or into a relative scheme of things, whether home-grown or foreign, or of an abandonment of meaningful ideas at all. Here Hutch's study, *The Meaning of Lives*, offers one example of a response to waking up to the potential meaninglessness of things. He offers what he calls 'the formation of saintliness as a process of ongoing human sacrifice' enacted through what he calls the two 'laws of the natural body' (Hutch 1997, pp. 87–90), one being the turnover or succession of generations and the other the 'biological/gender complementarity' (1997, p. 119). His location of meaning lies less in a high-level or meta-narrative of cosmic origination of destiny and more in a limited, middle or low range level of expectation, that is, the embodied sense of being connected to others through the past and into the future. Here human identity in community generates a sense of well-being even if it sacrifices some sense of 'ultimate truth' in the process, or, to put it another way, the sense of ultimate truth lies in its proximate realization.

References

Armstrong, M. R. (2011), 'Lay Christian views of life after death: a qualitative study and theological appraisal of the "ordinary eschatology" of some Congregational Christians'. Durham University PhD.

Davies, D. J. (1997), *Death, Ritual and Belief: The Rhetoric of Funerary Rites*, London: Cassell.

Davies, D. J. (2000), *The Mormon Culture of Salvation*, Aldershot: Ashgate.

Davies, D. J. (2002), *Anthropology and Theology*, Oxford: Berg.

Davies, D. J. (2011), *Emotion, Identity, and Religion: Hope, Reciprocity, and Otherness*, Oxford: Oxford University Press.

Davies, D. and Northam-Jones, D. (2012), 'The Sea of Faith: exemplifying transformed retention', in E. Arweck and M. Guest (eds), *Religion and Knowledge: Sociological Perspectives*, Aldershot: Ashgate.

Durkheim, E. (1915), *The Elementary Forms of the Religious Life*, London: George Allen & Unwin.

Fisch, J. ([2005] 2006), *Burning Women: A Global History of Widow-Sacrifice from Ancient Times to the Present*, trans. Rekha Rajan, London and New York: Seagull Books.

Geertz, C. (1966), 'Religion as a cultural system', in M. Banton (ed.), *Anthropological Approaches to the Study of Religion*, London: Tavistock.

Hinton, A. L. (ed.) (1999), *Biocultural Approaches to the Emotions*, Cambridge: Cambridge University Press.

Hocart, A. M. ([1952] 1973), *The Life-Giving Myth and Other Essays*, London: Tavistock.

Hutch, R. A. (1997), *The Meaning of Lives: Biography, Autobiography and the Spiritual Quest*, London and Washington: Cassell.

James, W. ([1879] 1956), 'The sentiment of rationality', in *The Will to Believe: And Other Essays in Popular Philosophy*, New York: Dover Publications, pp. 63–110.

Lévi-Strauss, C. (1968), *Structural Anthropology*, London: Allen Lane.

Miller, D. (2008), *The Comfort of Things*, Cambridge: Polity Press.

Robertson Smith, W. (1894), *The Religion of The Semites*, London: A. & C. Black.

Rustomji, N. (2009), *The Garden and the Fire: Heaven and Hell in Islamic Culture*, New York: Columbia University Press.

Toulis, N. R. (1997), *Believing Identity: Pentecostalism and the Mediation of Jamaican Ethnicity and Gender in England*, Oxford: Berg.

Turnbull, C. (1987), *The Mountain People*, New York: Touchstone.

Spirituality, Self-Discovery and Moral Change

JOHN COTTINGHAM

Summary

Most contemporary analytic philosophy of religion tends to focus on epistemological questions about the grounds or justification for religious belief and on analysing the precise cognitive content of claims about God. But an examination of what religion means for those who practise it shows that is has far less to do with abstract intellectual questions and far more to do with the individual search for integrity and moral growth. There is thus far more convergence between religious and psychotherapeutic goals than is often supposed. This chapter explores several important aspects of this convergence and also suggests an implicit lesson for philosophy about the inadequacy of purely theoretical attempts to understand the human predicament; reflecting on the disciplines of psychological and spiritual praxis may help us to see the way towards achieving a more abundant and integrated life.

Introduction: an unexpected convergence

Our current academic culture is fragmented: specialists do their own thing and rarely find time to talk to other specialists, even those in quite closely adjacent disciplines. So philosophers, mental health experts and theologians all pursue their separate agendas, often using esoteric jargon that would tend to block communication, even if dialogue were to be attempted.[1] Yet if we look beyond the compartmentalized structures of the modern university, the goals of these different disciplines are by no means as far apart as might at first seem. Philosophy, at least as traditionally conceived, saw one of its main objectives as that of discerning how humans can live a harmonious and fulfilled life – how they can achieve a 'good flow of life', as the ancient

---

1 An honourable and very welcome exception was afforded by the conference at which the original version of this paper was presented, on the theme of 'Spirituality, Theology and Mental Health', St John's College, Durham University, September 2010.

Stoics put it.² And that obviously has at least some connection with what modern mental health practitioners take themselves to be concerned with. The goal is to address the problems of a divided or disturbed or disharmonious mental life – to avoid what the Epicureans called *taraxia*, disturbance.³ And one does not have to buy into every aspect of the psychoanalytical approach to mental health to accept that a key factor in the disturbed life, perhaps its very essence, is lack of *integration* – something that happens when the parts of the psyche are split off, or working against each other, instead of meshing harmoniously.

This brings us right back to philosophy; for the harmonious meshing of the different parts of the psyche has, from Plato onwards, been seen as the key to a happy and fulfilled life.⁴ And if we now look across to the domains of theology and spirituality, we find something remarkably similar. The Judaeo-Christian tradition places great importance on a unified or integrated life. In one of the Psalms (86) we find the prayer 'Give me, O LORD, an undivided heart', a petition for a psychological and ethical unity.⁵ The Gospels speak of the importance of finding one's *true self*. Even gaining the whole world is not enough to compensate for the loss of oneself (*heautos*), says a famous passage in Luke 9.25. A few chapters later in the same Gospel, we find the story of the Prodigal Son, who goes into exile to squander his inheritance, but one day wakes up and 'comes to himself' (*eis heauton elthôn*) (Luke 15.17). As the Dominican writer Timothy Radcliffe has luminously put it, the Prodigal's decision to go back to his home and family is really the same as rediscovering his true self, 'since his exile from his family is an exile from his true identity as son and brother. He can only find himself again with them' (Radcliffe 2008, p. 20).⁶

So from very different directions, philosophical, psychotherapeutic and theological, we seem to converge on the importance of a unified, integrated self, the self I am meant to be, the self that expresses all that is best and most

---

2 The phrase 'a good flow of life' (*eurhoia biou*), coined by Zeno, the founder of Stoicism, is preserved in the compilation of the anthologist Stobaeus (early fifth century CE); see Long and Sedley 1987, no. 63A and B.

3 For the Epicurean notion of *ataraxia* (freedom from disturbance), see Epicurus, *Letter to Menoeceus* [*c.* 290 BCE] 127–32 (translated in Long and Sedley 1987, p. 124); the notion is discussed in detail in Julia Annas 1994, pp. 238ff. For the Stoic ideal of tranquillity (*summum bonum animi concordia*), see Seneca, *De Vita Beata* [*c.* 58 CE], VIII, 6 (compare also Letters, 92.3, quoted in Long and Sedley, 63F). For a general discussion of these matters, see Cottingham 1998, ch. 2.

4 Plato, *Republic* [475 BCE], Bk. IV.

5 Psalm 86 [85].11. In Hebrew the Psalmist prays to God *yahed levavi*, literally 'unite my heart!' (the imperative verb *yahed* comes from the root *ehad*, meaning one). For more on the importance of integrity, see Cottingham 2010.

6 The idea of a true self or soul (as opposed to the 'conditioned self') is also present in Islamic spirituality, as explained in Sabnum Dharamsi's illuminating paper presented to the conference referred to at footnote 1, above.

distinctive about me – and the idea that the goal of my life should be to eradicate the inner sources of conflict and disturbance, and to grow into that unified self. In this chapter, I want to explore some important aspects of this convergence between the seemingly distinct domains of philosophy, psychotherapy and spirituality. I will begin by looking at religion, which has come under particularly heavy attack from a number of secularist critics over the past few years, and will suggest that many of the current critiques of religion are curiously off-target, because they tend to construe religious allegiance as a set of theoretical doctrines or hypotheses, rather than focusing on the all-important role of spirituality and actual religious praxis. After exploring what precisely this dimension of spirituality and praxis consists of, I shall then argue that the notion of the *primacy of praxis over theory* is equally applicable and equally illuminating in the psychotherapeutic domain. Finally, I shall attempt to see what lessons philosophers might learn from all this, about how philosophy might emerge from its specialized academic ghetto and recover its traditional role of enabling us to understand ourselves and how we can achieve a fulfilled and integrated life.

Religion: theory and praxis

One of the striking features of our current intellectual culture is the rise of atheist militancy, exemplified in the sustained onslaught against religion mounted by Richard Dawkins, Christopher Hitchens and the other 'undergraduate atheists', as they have aptly been dubbed. The pejorative label (coined by the Princeton philosopher Mark Johnston (2009, p. 38)) draws attention to something that has been widely remarked in the writings of Dawkins and company, namely a certain hastiness and lack of depth. No doubt many of the intellectual difficulties they find in theism are serious ones; and no doubt much of the history of religion is the sad catalogue of oppression or worse that they allege; but the impartial observer is led to wonder whether the balance sheet can really be as negative as they suggest. For whatever one's final intellectual assessment of theism, it seems to take a kind of emotional or spiritual deafness to be utterly unmoved by the moral resonance of the Judaeo-Christian-Islamic legacy that informs so much of western culture – a resonance that is manifest in literature, liturgy, music and art, in common myths and inherited rites of passage, in notions of the sacred, and in the power of certain redemptive moral ideals that call us to transcend our ordinary mundane existence.

Of course no tradition is sacrosanct, and we might decide to abandon all this and embrace the more neutral, detached and impersonal structures of modern liberal secularism. But if we do make the change – as many western intellectuals would claim to have done already – we should be aware of what we are giving up. The long heritage of spirituality just referred to is something whose significance cannot lightly be dismissed – or at least, its dismissal is not cost free. Moreover, it is something whose value seems at least partly independent of the metaphysical claims of theism as a supposed explanation for the origins of the universe. There is, in short, much more to religion than the truth or otherwise of the 'God hypothesis', as Dawkins insists on calling it.

Indeed, one might go further, and wonder if religion really consists of intellectual theories or explanatory hypotheses in the first place. I have argued elsewhere that it is a mistake to construe religious adherence as *primarily* a cognitive matter – a matter of assenting to certain propositions, or being satisfied of the truth of certain doctrines; instead, religious allegiance, it seems to me, is principally a matter of orienting one's life towards certain values. To be sure, the distinction implied here is not a completely neat dichotomy: practical and moral orientation may go hand in hand with certain doctrinal beliefs, and, conversely, adopting certain doctrines may have implications for how one lives. Nevertheless, there is a broad general distinction that is clear enough for our purposes (a distinction that goes back a long way in philosophy) between the practical or action-guiding and the theoretical or abstract domains of human understanding. Religious allegiance, I would suggest, is not primarily a matter of intellectual assent to certain explanatory hypotheses about the nature or origins of the cosmos or the acceptance of certain metaphysical claims about ultimate reality, but involves above all (to borrow some much misunderstood notions of Wittgenstein) a 'passionate commitment', which is inextricably bound up with a certain 'form of life'.[7] The collective evidence of Scripture, which is a rich source for our grasp of what is involved in religious allegiance, is pretty clear on this point: the divine call is chiefly heard as a moral and practical as opposed to a theoretical or purely cognitive one. The reality that the patriarchs and prophets of the Hebrew Bible and the key protagonists of the New Testament are made aware of is one that calls them to change their lives, to follow a certain path of righteousness, to hear the cry of the oppressed, to love one another, to forgive those who have wronged them, and so on through a long catalogue of luminous moral insights that form the living core of the Judaeo-Christian tradition.[8]

Let us give the name *spirituality* to all the moral and practical components of religious observance that are left when one brackets off the doctrinal elements – in short, pretty much everything a religious adherent does, *qua* religious adherent, when they are not standing up reciting the Creed, or

---

7 For a conspectus of the many passages where Wittgenstein discusses the importance of activity and 'forms of life', see Glock 1996, pp. 124–9. For the notion of 'passionate commitment', see Wittgenstein 1998 [1947], p. 73. For some of the misunderstandings of these texts, in particular the tendency to interpret Wittgenstein's view of religion as entirely non-cognitivist, see Cottingham 2009b, pp. 203–27.

8 Similar calls, for compassion and self-purification, for example, are found in the Islamic Scriptures.

engaged in theological analysis of the contents of that creed.[9] Ignatius of Loyola, in the sixteenth century, spoke of 'spiritual exercises', which is a convenient label for the various religious practices most religious adherents engage in from time to time and which are undertaken in a more systematic and formal way in the kind of extended retreat that Ignatius had in mind. This general category includes prayer, fasting, meditation, *lectio divina* (the attentive reading of Scripture), participating in communal worship, group activities such as singing psalms, individual self-examination and confession and moments of prayer or reflective silence at key moments of the day (for example before eating or before retiring).

The first point to be made about such activities is that they are not exclusively intellectual. They may well have an intellectual component, but they are not characteristically directed towards the analysis of propositions or the evaluation of doctrines. Spiritual exercises are typically *polyvalent* – they operate on many different levels, emotional, physical, aesthetic, moral, pre-rational, subliminal, introspective, collaborative, to name but a few categories in a very heterogeneous list. The singing of psalms, to take one key example that is at the centre of the divine office in Benedictine spirituality and many subsequent monastic traditions, comprises the recitation of words learned by heart over a long period of weekly, monthly and yearly repetition. It entails a *formalized structure* of praxis – regulated patterns of observance assigned to set hours throughout each day. There is a *physical* component,[10] prescribed movements of sitting and standing, in which the whole community participates, collectively as well as individually. It involves *music*, not just as an optional extra, but essentially and integrally: there is a plainsong chant, again carefully regulated, with an antiphonal structure and other laid-down forms, for example the crucial two beats of silence at the colon or pause that occurs in the middle of each verse.

It is pointless to ask if the experience of one who takes part in the divine office is an intellectual one or an emotional one or a religious one or a moral one, an aesthetic or musical one: these sorts of questions are beside the point, since *all* these elements are involved, and not just involved as separate elements, but interfused in a total act of devotion. (Music, we may note in passing, is a part of praxis that can be thought of as a kind of icon or image of the whole; for of all the arts it is the one that most integrates all the aspects of the person – physical activity (of lungs and vocal chords, mouth, shoulders, diaphragm and bodily posture), emotional expression and response, sensory appreciation, intellectual grasp and, in the examples found in the finest music, more complex kinds of moral elevation and self-transcendence.

To return to the singing of psalms, as far as the cognitive or intellectual aspect goes there is of course a precise semantic content to the sentences

---

9 What follows in this section draws on my 'Theism and spirituality', in Taliaferro, Harrison and Goetz 2012.

10 Compare Mark Wynn's chapter in the present volume.

that are chanted; but these sentences are typically not, or not very often, assertions about the truth of certain religious doctrines; they are cries of remorse, desperate pleas for help, shouts of praise, songs of thanksgiving, expressions of hope and trust and so on. And their point is that they should work holistically, gradually transforming and perfecting the lives of those who participate; not just changing their intellectual outlook, but irradiating the very quality of their lived experience.

I hope that this very crude and brief sketch of the typical features of a spiritual exercise will serve to make the central point I wish to bring out about the primacy of praxis. *One can to a large extent understand spirituality while bracketing off the doctrinal content.* Notice that bracketing off is not the same as deleting. I am not claiming (as some of the non-cognitivist philosophers of religion of the latter twentieth century used to do) that religious observance is non-doxastic – that it does not involve anything propositional or truth-directed whatsoever. For it is hard to deny that certain truth-claims are *presupposed* in the kinds of activity just mentioned; at the very least (to take an obvious point), the prayer and praise and thanksgiving expressed in a typical psalm presupposes the existence of a God, who is being thanked and praised and prayed to. But it would be a mistake to suppose that the praxis requires or depends for its authenticity on our being able to unpack the precise meaning of these presupposed truth-claims, let alone on our being in a position to provide evidence that supports the claims. As centuries of theological debate have shown, the very idea of God as conceived in the three great Abrahamic faiths, a creative power that transcends the natural world, is sufficiently outside the realm of ordinary human discourse as to generate a host of philosophical problems about the precise meaning of assertions about the deity, not to mention the question of their epistemic warrant. But this does not negate the validity of the praxis.

Why not? The answer is a very simple one, as can be seen, once more, in our part-for-whole analogy, the case of music. Music would be a valid human activity if there were no musicologists and no valid metaphysical account of what music was about. One can go further: even if that which is expressed in a great work of music is utterly ineffable – that is, even if no cognitive or intellectual analysis were available that could pretend to capture what is expressed – we would still know with absolute certainty that such music was among the most valuable and important enterprises that humans can undertake. In a certain sense (if you will forgive my putting the matter somewhat hyperbolically), the very ineffability of that which is expressed in music is the stamp of its transcendent value. Of course (as we know only too well from the dubious domain of 'New Age spirituality', which includes everything from massage oils to magic crystals), mystery and ineffability can be used as a cloak for all sorts of questionable activities for which their practitioners cannot offer any articulate justification. But here one may invoke the maxim 'by their fruits ye shall know them'. The evaluation of spiritual praxis is not a logical free-for-all, shrouded in the obfuscating mists of ineffability; it can be tested, at least in part, by reference to the moral and psychological difference it makes in the lives of the practitioners.

The psycho-ethical dynamics of spiritual praxis

What is too often ignored by abrasive critics of religion such as Dawkins is the difference that authentic religious spirituality makes to the moral quality of a life. Not all religion, to be sure, is authentic. Mark Johnston, in his fascinating recent study *Saving God*, has described the phenomenon of what he calls 'spiritual materialism': this involves retaining our ordinary selfish desires (for security, comfort, success, etc.) and trying to get them satisfied by manipulating supposed supernatural forces. The debased form of religion known as idolatry is similar, placating the gods to get what we want. Authentic spirituality, by contrast, has it as its task (according to Johnston) to address the 'large-scale structural defects in human life' – arbitrary suffering, ageing, the vulnerability of ourselves and our loved ones to time and chance and, ultimately, death. The religious or redeemed life, Johnston argues, is one where we are morally purified in such as way as to be reconciled to these large-scale defects (Johnston 2009, pp. 14ff.).[11]

How might this work? A purely academic or intellectual approach might suppose that it must work on a doctrinal level: the religious believer is one who subscribes to certain doctrines like the afterlife, which reconcile him to the fear of death; or she subscribes to the idea that the right kind of prayer will produce divine interventions, to cure illnesses or avert dangers and difficulties. I do not deny that the religious adherent may believe in life after death, or in miracles. But there is always a danger that such beliefs will be the catalyst for the growth of superstitious, idolatrous, manipulative and inauthentic forms of religious observance. And taking my cue from Johnston (though I would question many other aspects of his approach), I suggest that authentic spirituality puts far less emphasis on miraculous divine intervention, or next-world eschatology than the critics of religion often imagine (Cottingham 2010b).

Consider a life informed by spiritual praxis of the kind we were sketching earlier. I am aware that the contrasts I am about to draw are necessarily somewhat crude and simplistic, but I hope they may nevertheless convey something of the moral and psychological dynamic of such a life, in contrast to what I shall, for convenience, label the 'secular life'.

On waking up in the morning, the secularist simply gets out of bed, washes and dresses, and starts the day's business. The spiritual practitioner, by contrast, though of course also doing these things, sets aside an assigned

---

11 Compare Paul Moser's comment that 'If a person sincerely holds that we have no fatal problems, that person may benefit from consultation with a psychiatrist', Moser 2008, p. 9.

time near the start of each day to collect the thoughts. This will be a time of silence and meditation. It will be a time to reflect with gratitude on the gift of life and the blessing of another day. It will be a time to recall the mistakes of the previous day, and summon the strength to improve. It will be a time of focused contemplation on the tasks to be done this day and of awareness of the need for grace in performing and accomplishing those tasks. It will be a time of recalling the needs of others, both of loved ones and in the wider world.

All this may sound rather pious and precious, but it need not be a matter of prolonged and elaborate devotions, but simply a comparatively short time of *focused and morally oriented reflection.* Now it may well be that there is no logical impossibility in the secularist finding such a time for focused reflection each morning; but we are concerned not with logical possibil-ities, but with realistic probabilities, and I suggest that honest self-reflection reveals that the chances of such an assigned time being set aside within the life-framework of the average contemporary secularist are, as a matter of empirical fact, close to zero. Add to this that the praxis just described will, in the traditions we have been referring to, not be just a free-floating indi-vidual decision that could peter out at any time, but will take the shape of a formalized structure, where the reflections and silences are interspersed with prescribed readings of Scripture and recitation of psalms and so on. In short, there will be a *vehicle* for the spiritual activity – one that has been developed and refined through long centuries of tradition and continued practice, and that is designed and structured with the aim of nurturing the integration of the self and furthering the slow process of coming to greater self-awareness and moral maturity. What is more, the same kinds of difference we have been outlining between a secular and a religious structure of life will be exemplified throughout each day, for example in the habit of saying grace before meals, or in meditative reflection before retiring last thing at night. The relevant structures will also be available in moments of special stress and difficulty such as arise in the major crises of every life and even, to some smaller extent, on a quotidian basis. And they will be reinforced at a com-munal level, by weekly rhythms of Sunday or Sabbath observance and by the organized patterns of collective worship that mark the regular seasons of the liturgical year, not to mention the more momentous turning points of an individual's life in the community, such as birth, marriage and death.

My purpose in outlining these more or less familiar structures is not to offer some kind of propaganda for the religious life, still less to criticize the secular way of living that tries to make do without such structures (a decision that over the long term could well call for great courage and deter-mination). The point rather is to bring out how the structures of spirituality are integrally bound up with certain psychological and moral goals, not too dissimilar from what the Stoics had in mind by a 'good flow of life'. By their rhythmical and repeated character they are productive of internal focus and attentive self-awareness; they foster psychic integration and tranquillity of mind; they are geared to the achieving of a progressive and deepening moral sensibility. No doubt the picture I have presented is a somewhat idealized one, representing an optimal outcome rather than a statistically typical portrait of any given actual religious adherent (who of course may often diverge radically from the ideal). But the point remains that the religious framework we are considering cannot be evaluated simply as a set of credal beliefs, divorced from the patterns of moral and spiritual praxis that give it life and meaning.

Psychotherapy and integration

Let me now move from the domain of spiritual praxis to the seemingly very different domain of psychotherapy. I have already noted, in my opening remarks, that these two apparently very distinct spheres do in fact share some degree of overlap: both in different ways have the goal of psychological and moral integrity within their sights. Admittedly this will not apply to the psychotherapeutic case if we are simply considering those somewhat manipulative cognitive and behavioural techniques that are aimed solely at the alleviation of surface symptoms of psychological disorder (and that, because they offer quick and measurable results, are often favoured by public funding bodies); but it will certainly be true of the various mainstream psychoanalytic approaches of Freud, Jung, Klein and their successors, all of which are concerned with enriching the subjects' self-awareness, and enabling them to live more responsible and morally mature lives in relation to themselves and others.

But the parallels between the psychoanalytic and the spiritual domains are not exhausted by this common moral purpose. Two further similarities may be noted. First, the ultimate object posited in each domain is what may be called *anomalous*. In the psychoanalytic case, the object is the Unconscious, while in the religious case it is God; and the anomaly lies in the fact that neither object can be brought entirely within the arena of ordinary human understanding. The unconscious is, by its nature, that which is opaque to conscious apprehension – a fact that led early philosophical critics of Freud to declare with supercilious condescension that the very idea of the unconscious mind was a contradiction in terms, since what could not be brought within the domain of mental awareness could not, by definition, count as a mental phenomenon. Yet in truth the fact that the unconscious is anomalous, outside the framework of ordinary mentation, need not be a fatal objection to positing it; for what cannot be fully encompassed may nonetheless be something we can reach towards. The 'shadowy presentations' of the unconscious mind, as Jung termed them,[12] while remaining beneath

---

12 The psychoanalytic aim is to observe the shadowy presentations – whether in the form of images or of feelings – that are spontaneously evolved in the psyche and appear, without his bidding, to the man who looks within. In this way, we find once more what

the threshold of what is consciously registered, can nevertheless leave their traces in the forgotten memories of childhood or the weird and only partly recoverable deliverances of dreams; and they can make sense, as Freud so brilliantly showed, of a whole range of similar phenomena, thereby illuminating and transforming aspects of our affective life that would otherwise be wholly baffling.

There is a close analogy here with what the religious adherent holds with regard to God – the elusive and mysterious source of being who, as Augustine declared, can never be brought fully within the grasp of the human mind. This resistance to being mentally encompassed is in the very nature of the divine: *si comprehendis, non est Deus*, wrote Augustine – if you grasp him, he is not God (*Sermones* (392–430), 52, vi, 16 and 117, iii, 5). For the very fact of our encompassing him, bringing him entirely within the horizon of our human understanding, would be the best evidence that what was so grasped was not God but a mere idol of our own construction. Hence, to use the striking image of René Descartes, God is like the mountain that we can never comprehend or grasp, never put our arms round, but that we can nevertheless touch; we can somehow reach towards him in our thought (Descartes, Letter to Mersenne of 27 May 1630). This anomalous aspect, which applies both to God and to the unconscious – their resistance to the encompassing grasp of human inquiry – is only an obstacle to their acceptance for those who make the mistake of equating the limits our conscious apprehension with the limits of reality.

A critic may object here that if we are to allow into our ontology objects beyond the ordinary grasp of human consciousness, there must at least be some evidential basis for doing so – some data that provides an epistemic warrant for positing their existence. Yet here we run up against our second parallel between the two domains under discussion. The believer in the unconscious mind, like the believer in God, will indeed take his or her beliefs to be supported by the character of their own experience; but crucially, *this is not the kind of evidence that a detached impartial observer will be in a position to access or evaluate*. In the religious case, I am here following a fairly standard theological line developed by Pascal and others: God is *Deus absconditus*, the hidden God, whom we glimpse by traces or intimations that are given only to those in a suitable state of grace – only, as Pascal put it, to those who earnestly seek him (Pascal 1962, no. 427).[13] Similarly, the psychoanalytic approach does not (or at least should not, in my opinion) claim to provide evidence for the unconscious that is of the

---

we have repressed or forgotten. Painful though it may be, this is itself a gain – for what is inferior or even worthless belongs to me as my shadow, and gives me substance and mass. How can I be substantial if I fail to cast a shadow? I must have a dark side if I am to be whole; and inasmuch as I become conscious of my own shadow, I also remember that I am a human being like any other (Jung 1933).

13 For a discussion of Pascal's position, see Cottingham 2005.

kind a detached scientific observer can measure; if the unconscious could be reached through the gathering of neutrally available data, then, as Freud observed, it might be a simple matter to 'cure' the patient simply by providing him with the relevant information about the forgotten parts of his childhood that are distorting his present psychic equilibrium. Yet in reality, the traces of the unconscious can only be disclosed as a result of the hard process of dialogue with the therapist, the serious work of dissecting the dreams and other psychological debris that are painfully recovered as the analysis proceeds. In short, both in the religious case and in the psychotherapeutic case we are not dealing with 'neutral' data, but data that are made manifest only through a process of *commitment*, a long and difficult journey of psychological growth and moral change.

These then are two striking parallels between the psychoanalytic and the religious domains: both are concerned with an anomalous object, which can never be brought fully within the bounds of conscious apprehension; and both have to rely on evidence that is not available neutrally and impersonally, like scientific evidence, but only in response to moral and psychological change in the subject.

To these two parallels, let me now add a third, related one, which links up with one of my main themes, the primacy of praxis. The primacy of praxis does not mean that praxis is everything. Like religion, psychoanalysis has, to be sure, a theoretical or doctrinal component; and just as we find in the religious case, that component can be the subject of fierce intellectual controversies and convoluted debates (the precise structure and dynamics of the unconscious mind calling forth almost as much furious factionalism as one finds in the long history of denominational schisms and heresies in the Church). But exactly as I argued in the case of spirituality, so in the psychoanalytic case, *one can to a large extent understand the process while bracketing off the theoretical and doctrinal content.* Psychoanalytic theorists may debate the precise role of the pleasure principle, or the depressive position, just as theologians will continue to thrash out the niceties of the Monophysite versus Nestorian views of the incarnation. But the healing work of psychotherapy, like the salvific work of religious devotion, depends not on intellectual wrestling with metaphysical doctrines (which in any case, let us remember, concern what cannot ultimately be brought within the grasp of complete human cognition), but rather in the *psycho-ethical dynamics of the praxis,* which the subject commits herself to, week by week, as she embarks on the path of guided reflection and self-discovery.

There are no shortcuts here; no clever intellectual moves that can bypass the moral and spiritual process that each subject must undergo. I have already given a sketch of how this might work out in the religious case, drawing on some of the traditional structures of spiritual praxis. In the psychotherapeutic case, the kind of practical process involved has been well documented by Freud and his successors. Typically, it involves a long and hard process of guided dialogue with the past; repeated discussion of episodes from childhood that have not been thought about for years if at all; the agonizingly slow revival of half-forgotten memories; the accumulating analysis of dreams; the difficult process of breaking down resistance in the consulting room, the evasions, rationalizations, the sullen silences, the emotional catharsis of angry outbursts, unexpected tears, reluctant confrontations ... and so on.[14] The precise details are less important than the underlying ethical structure: a gradual surrender of autonomy and self-sufficiency; an acceptance of vulnerability; the slow realization that we did not shape the conditions of our lives, and consequently often need help to recover our true selves. The underlying nature of the process involved must remain partly opaque, and no amount of intellectual theorizing will capture it completely. For although real hidden entities and processes are surely at work, what must occur in order for the required healing and self-understanding to take place is the requisite effort on the part of the subject, a willingness to relinquish the narcissistic fantasy of self-sufficiency, and the humility to accept the need for change. The framework that makes sense of it all, in the therapeutic as in the spiritual case, is inescapably a practical and a moral one; and it is one that must be activated on the level of each individual psyche or soul.

Concluding reflections

Let me draw to a close, very briefly, by reflecting on some of the results that have emerged so far. In tracing a close convergence between the structure and methods of psychoanalytic and spiritual praxis, I may seem to some readers to have glossed over fundamental differences. For surely the spiritual life is not *merely* about mental health and equilibrium; and conversely, the psychotherapeutic process can be and very often is undergone without any commitment to, perhaps even with a downright hostility to, the religious framework. That is of course true; and I have been drawing parallels, not arguing for complete assimilation. Nevertheless, I hope it is by now clear that the two different domains are informed by a *common teleology*: they address the task of how best to live a good and fulfilling life given our weak and conflicted natures, and the short time at our disposal to seek wholeness or integration.

Freud famously observed that it was his aim to eliminate neurotic misery, and that he would be content if he could leave people with no more than ordinary human misery.[15] Taking our cue from this, let us imagine a subject who has undergone a successful course of psychotherapy, who has man-

---

14 For a more specific description of the kind of process involved, see Cottingham 1998, ch. 4, §7.

15 Freud's self-proclaimed aim was to 'turn hysterical misery into ordinary human unhappiness'. See the opening of his 'Studies in Hysteria' ('Die Studien über Hysterie', with J. Breuer, 1896), in Freud 1985, vol. 2.

aged to integrate the split off portions of the psyche and achieved the kind of equilibrium that enables them to set about the ordinary decisions of life unencumbered by distortions and false projections – in short, someone who is equipped to love and to work (the two activities that Freud considered to be the principal ingredients of a healthy and fulfilling human life). What more might be needed to achieve that ancient philosophical goal, *eudaimonia* or happiness, or, in the Stoic phrase we began with, a 'good flow of life'?

The question immediately answers itself: a great deal of 'ordinary human misery' will still threaten the attainment of long-term happiness. Even the most fortunate individual will inevitably be subject, sooner or later, to those 'large-scale structural defects in human life' we referred to earlier – arbitrary suffering, ageing, the vulnerability of ourselves and our loved ones to time and chance and, ultimately, death. Human happiness is, by its very nature, precarious, subject to what Martha Nussbaum has aptly called the *fragility of goodness* (1986). How may one live with grace and courage in such a world?

A glib answer would be to invoke the consolations of religion – divine protection and, ultimately, an afterlife where all will be redeemed. But without denying those possibilities (philosophy alone is surely not in a position to pronounce on them one way or another), I have already suggested earlier that authentic spirituality should not be thought of as trying to manipulate supernatural forces so as to obtain special protection or privilege or some guarantee that all will be made to turn out well. Instead, the aim of spiritual praxis is moral purification, a growth towards moral maturity, informed by a steadily increasing knowledge and love of the good.

What does this amount to? At a meta-ethical level, it implies the existence of absolute *objective values and demands* by which human life must be lived, whether we like it or not independently of our contingent desires and subjective inclinations. In my view, this leads us directly to a religious metaphysic, to an eternal divine source of value and goodness, since the required strong objectivity and normative power cannot be secured in any other way. But that is a complex argument, which I have made elsewhere and which there is no space to recapitulate here (see further Cottingham 2009a). I want to close instead by focusing on the psycho-ethical dynamics of an individual life that is guided by such a conception of the good. And this brings us back to the concept of integrity.

In the parallel psychoanalytic case, what the patient learns, if all goes well, is to confront the therapist without evasion, or projection; to allow oneself to be seen, exactly as one is, without concealment, without trying to manipulate or extort a response, simply as a human being among others, weak and dependent, yet for all that, deserving of respect and equality. Integrity, in short, implies the ability to stand before the wise and compassionate and discerning gaze of the other, the other who cares, but not in a needy or demanding way, who knows one's failings and weaknesses, and yet who is prepared to offer support in the continued endeavour to trust and to grow. I hope this says enough to convey the authentic power of the psychoanalytic framework, at its best.

But what happens when, in Carl Jung's phrase, the 'chains of the consulting room are finally severed' (1933, p. 62) and the individual goes out into the world? Jung himself envisaged an ongoing post-therapeutic process of independent self-discovery and self-education, where the therapist is no longer needed, but psychotherapy 'transcends itself and now advances to fill that void which hitherto has marked the psychic insufficiency of Western culture' (pp. 61–2). Yet unlike Freud, who considered the religious impulse to be infantile, Jung had the insight to see that the Promised Land for such continued moral growth could *not* be just the dry terrain of rational, scientific self-sufficiency; for the complexities of the human psyche generate a need for far richer modes of awareness. Religious imagery and symbolism, in Jung's view, could perform a vital function here, in facilitating that integration of conscious and unconscious elements of the self that is a precondition for wholeness.[16] The struggle for what he called 'individuation', in Jung's eyes, requires just those modes of thought and expression that the religious archetypes provide. And from here it is a short step to acknowledging the importance of the archetypal figure of the compassionate Other, before whom one must present oneself in wholeness of being, without concealment or manipulation or dissembling. In brief, holding one's life up to the presence of God becomes part of the psycho-ethical framework for the growth of the morally mature individual in his or her entirety. What we have here is a kind of *cosmic or theological analogue of the consulting room*, a permanent presence to support and cherish the individual's continued wholeness of being.

Is this just an imaginary being, or a metaphor, or is there a real divine presence behind the symbol? Jung himself refused to pronounce on this, and although our current scientifically oriented culture is obsessed with the need for yes or no answers, neither science nor philosophical reason alone (here I would agree with Kant) can settle the question of whether or not there is such a transcendent divine reality. Yet what remains true is that having faith that one's life is presented in its entirety to such a being can be a powerful vehicle for continued moral growth and integration. There are no guarantees here, since spirituality, like any humanly mediated enterprise, can go wrong, can degenerate. But at its best, spiritual praxis is a way of living better, under the benign influence of images that have the power to transform our lives and morally enrich them. And from this, in conclusion,

---

16 From *Aion* (1951), in Jung 1966–67 vol. 9:2, p. 183. In similar vein, Jung observes that 'the living and perceptible archetype … has been projected onto the man Jesus, and … has historically manifested itself in him'; *Psychology and Religion* (1938), in Jung 1966–67, vol. 11, p. 95. These and other significant passages are quoted in Michael Palmer (1977), pp. 121, 135, who summarizes Jung's thought as asserting that 'what the individual identifies in Christ … is the archetype expressing his own need for wholeness and unity' (p. 135).

we can perhaps learn something of the benefits and the limits of philosophy. For if philosophy on its own cannot secure happiness (that would be an arrogant fantasy of controlling reason), it can at least enable us to see the inadequacy of purely theoretical attempts to understand the human predicament, and help us to glimpse how the disciplines of psychological and spiritual praxis might point us towards a more abundant and integrated life.

References

Annas, J. (1994), *The Philosophy of Happiness*, New York: Oxford University Press.

Cottingham, J. (1998), *Philosophy and the Good Life*, Cambridge: Cambridge University Press.

Cottingham, J. (2005), *The Spiritual Dimension*, Cambridge: Cambridge University Press.

Cottingham, J. (2009a), *Why Believe?*, London: Continuum.

Cottingham, J. (2009b), 'The lessons of life: Wittgenstein, religion and analytic philosophy', in H.-J. Glock and J. Hyman (eds), *Wittgenstein and Analytic Philosophy: Essays for P. M. S. Hacker*, Oxford: Oxford University Press.

Cottingham, J. (2010a), 'Integrity and fragmentation', *Journal of Applied Philosophy* 27:1, pp. 2–14.

Cottingham, J. (2010b), 'Spirituality, religion and the naturalist challenge', *Standpoint*, September issue.

Freud, S. (1985), *The Penguin Freud Library*, London: Penguin Books.

Glock, H.-J. (1996), *A Wittgenstein Dictionary*, Oxford: Blackwell.

Johnston, M. (2009), *Saving God: Religion after Idolatry*, Princeton: Princeton University Press.

Jung, C. (1933), *Modern Man in Search of a Soul*, London: Routledge.

Jung, C. (1966–67), *Collected Works*, rev. edn, London: Routledge, vol. 9:2.

Long, A. A. and Sedley, D. N. (eds) (1987), *The Hellenistic Philosophers*, Cambridge: Cambridge University Press.

Moser, P. (2008), *The Elusive God*, Cambridge: Cambridge University Press.

Nussbaum, M. (1986), *The Fragility of Goodness*, Cambridge: Cambridge University Press.

Pascal, B. (1962 [c. 1660]), *Pensées*, ed. L. Lafuma, Paris: Seuil.

Palmer, M. (1977), *Freud and Jung on Religion*, London: Routledge.

Radcliffe, T. (2008), *Why Go to Church?: The Drama of the Eucharist*, London: Continuum.

Taliaferro, C., Harrison, V. and Goetz, S. (eds) (2012), *The Routledge Companion to Theism*, London: Routledge.

Wittgenstein, L. (1998 [1947]), *Culture and Value*, Oxford: Blackwell.

'My God, my God, why have you forsaken me?'

Between Consolation and Desolation

SIMON D. PODMORE

Summary

Christ's crucified cry of abandonment 'My God, my God, why have you forsaken me?' symbolizes one of the darkest and most ineffable moments in the meeting (perhaps even the 'synthesis') of the human and the divine – an abyssal moment in which human and divine suffering meet, and in which absence (*desolation*) reaches out to presence (*consolation*). Exploring the meaning, and meaninglessness, of this cry with reference to treatments in western mystical and theological literature, I consider how this cry might be read as a psycho-palliative allegory for experiences of the ostensible absence of God: that is, as an image of the dark night of *desolation* in which the soul cries out, in *protest* as well as in *despair* and *longing*, for the *consolation* of God's presence. Ultimately, this chapter questions whether imagery of the God-forsaken God might serve contemporary pastoral theology and psychotherapy as a source of palliative consolation in which *despair itself* is validated or whether appeal to this ineffably and irreducibly *christological* image rather serves as a *mystification* in which theology ultimately seeks to gloss, veil or prematurely sublimate the personal problem of *human* suffering.

> From noon on, darkness came over the whole land until three in the afternoon. And about three o'clock Jesus cried with a loud voice, 'Eli, Eli, lema sabachthani?' that is, 'My God, my God, why have you forsaken me?' (Matt. 27.45–46, NRSV)

Introduction: madness, melancholia and the God-forsaken God

Michel Foucault (1989, pp. 74–7) poses an agonistic reminder that, while its history encompasses attitudes of confinement as well as compassion,

Christianity nurtures in its heart a moment of irreducible 'madness' – polarized according to modern rationalism as unintegrated 'unreason'. Pastoral concern with mental health should therefore occupy a privileged position within Christianity, partly in reflection of Jesus' own ministry towards the sick, but also, perhaps more scandalously, because Christianity itself holds, in tension, a moment of divine madness at its cruciform centre: namely the madness of the cross, the scandal of the incarnation, the unreason of God become human, which Søren Kierkegaard (1813–55) identifies as the irreducible *paradox*, the *offence to reason* of the incarnation. In Foucault's vision of the incarnation, Christ takes upon himself 'the very stigmata of fallen nature ... and of madness' (1989, p. 76). Christ's madness thus serves to *sanctify* blasphemous madness, as well as the profanity of death itself – the sanctification of non-being within being. Foucault's description still resonates as a challenge to Christianity: 'because it was one of the forms of the Passion – the ultimate form, in a sense, before death – madness would now become, for those who suffered it, an object of respect and compassion' (p. 76). The spirit of madness (*Ruach Shoteh*) is sometimes acknowledged within Jewish tradition as sharing a potential affinity with the spirit of prophecy (Cooper 1997, p. 66), and a 'divine madness' is also valorized within Greek thought (e.g. Plato's *Phaedrus*). Yet while such divine gifts of genius are ecstatic in nature, 'madness' in Christ also becomes 'the lowest point of humanity to which God has submitted in His incarnation, thereby showing that there was nothing in man that could not be redeemed and saved' (Foucault 1989, p. 76). In the madness of the cross, however, it is *abasement* rather than inspiration that is made manifest – the abyss of despair itself is recognized, shared and made sacred. In this most degraded form, therefore, it is not the effusive ecstatic spirit of *mania* or frenzy, but the gloomy spirit of *melancholia* (depression), even *desperatio* (despair), that is sanctified.

Nowhere is such holy 'madness' more mystifying, more absurdly *de profundis* in its *melancholia*, than in the cry of the God-forsaken God: Jesus' cry of dereliction from the cross, 'My God, my God, why have you forsaken me?' (Matt. 27.46; Mark 15.34; an Aramaic form of Ps. 22.1). 'Jesus forsaken is the image of darkness, melancholy, conflict', as Lubich articulates; 'the image of all that is indefinable, strange, because he is a God who cries for help! He is non-sense' (2003, p. 90).[1] This cry of abandonment echoes as a lacuna and *aporia* within the crucifixion scene – an expression of the madness of the death of God itself.[2] In struggling to make the consoling divine

---

1 For Lubich this inscrutable image is also recognizable through our own experiences. While it is possible to see madness in Jesus, it is also possible to discern Jesus in madness: 'we can see him also in every brother and sister who suffers ... Jesus forsaken is peace for the restless, a home for the evicted, and reunion for the outcast' (2003, p. 90). Council suggests that Psalm 22 symptomatically 'offers a clear and concise picture of the anguish of depression' (1982, pp. 59–60).

2 Boulton submits that the psalms of lamentation bear fertile comparison with

light of reason transfigure such ineffable desolation, mystics, theologians and philosophers have resorted to speaking – perhaps maddeningly – of *an abyss within God-in-Godself*. Such efforts to speak of this darkness are confronted by a paradox that problematizes Foucault's own engagement with the *History of Madness*. That which Jacques Derrida (1930–2004) calls 'the greatest merit, but also the infeasibility of the book' (1997, p. 33) is the attempt to speak '[o]f madness itself ... letting madness speak for itself' (p. 33) without submitting madness to the heteronomy of reason.

Leaving aside Foucault's critical reading of psychiatry's attempt to subordinate madness to rational objectivity (which is also moderated by his critique of the romanticization of madness), I wish to acknowledge an important comparable folly in this present essay: the desire to derive meaning (theological and psychotherapeutic, or psycho-palliative[3]) from an essentially unfathomable *mysterium*. How can *meaning* be derived from a cry of *meaninglessness*, a cry that perhaps is haunted by the shadow of madness, of possibility and impossibility (Jinkins and Reid 1997, pp. 33–4)? Before the God-forsaken God must we, as God appears to have done, finally fall silent? And might such a silence become the means for honouring irreducible mystery? Or does silence merely serve to *mystify*, to mute the cry of protest? Does silence surrender to the abyss of despair? Or can silence itself become a protest against suffering, a form of struggling with God (Podmore 2012)? Mindful of such difficulties, I attempt to speak of the ineffable God-forsaken cry as evoking a compassionate ('with-suffering') palliative human space – even a breathing space, a pause – *between* consolation and desolation.[4] The crucifixion scene is shrouded in a darkness that covers the land between the sixth and the ninth hour (Mark 15.33; Matt. 27.45; Luke 23.44). At the ninth hour, the darkness departs – at the same moment that Jesus cries out in God-forsakenness. Light returns at the darkest moment of divine abandonment. Minear contends, 'The cry triggered the return of light ... that this light itself provided another component in God's answer to the Messiah's *why*' (1995, p. 73). Yet might the juxtaposition also suggest that

---

Nietzsche's assertion – even 'lament' – 'in the mouth of a madman' that 'God is dead' (Boulton 2002, p. 62 n. 7).

3 The term 'psycho-palliative' is also used by Smith (1995, pp. 209–17) to refer to an approach that is non-judgemental, non-evaluative, emphasizing care for the other in recognizing their religion, philosophy and spirituality, and considering enlightenment with reference to spiritual journey. A psycho-palliative approach is one that seeks to 'care for the client without trying to "change" or cure the client' (Smith and Olsen 1993, p. 7).

4 The terms *consolation* and *desolation* are perhaps most famously employed in Ignatian spirituality to designate interior feelings inspired by good and evil spirits respectively. See Ignatius of Loyola's (1491–1556) rules for the discernment of spirits in his *Spiritual Exercises* 313–36. In this essay, I consider these terms more broadly, as appealed to in, for example, German Dominican as well as Spanish Carmelite literature. In general, the Latin *consolatio* denotes a state of (divine) comfort or solace; while *desolatio* is traditionally viewed as its theological opposite: abandonment, forsakenness, aloneness – even with reference to the feeling that God is not merely absent but being actively hostile to the soul.

both light and shade can co-exist, generating meaning and meaninglessness in the twilight of light bleeding into darkness, a perennial struggle between hope and despair?

'Eli, Eli, lema sabachthani?': Speculative metaphysics and the problem of suffering

Jesus' cry of dereliction, as recorded in Aramaic – the Hebraic vernacular – issues forth in a 'powerful' or 'great' (*megalē*) voice at the ninth hour.[5] While these haunting words are the only words that Jesus proclaims from the cross in the Gospels of Matthew and Mark, they are conspicuously absent in the later Gospels of Luke (which does note the darkening of the sun) and John, which, as if all too conscious of their scandal, replace the God-forsaken cry with words of consolation and encouragement (Marshall 2009, p. 246). In reciting this opening line of Psalm 22, Jesus can be regarded as invoking the entirety of the psalm, passing *through* despair to its final avowal of *hope* (even a hope against hope). Jesus thereby establishes a connection between the divine and the human by invocation of liturgical lament (Mays 1985, p. 323).[6] For the reader, however, there is discernible difficulty integrating this desolate moment into the life of Jesus. Such an impossible image threatens to deliver even the believer over to melancholy, even to God-forsaken despair over salvation itself.[7] Perhaps hermeneutics can sever this Gordian knot; or metaphysics deliver us from the gravity of this abyss. If the cry *'Eli'* refers to 'my power' rather than 'My God', then it expresses Jesus' powerlessness but not – *surely not* – his *God-forsakenness*.[8] Perhaps the notion of 'forsaking'[9] is better understood as 'abandonment', or even 'leaving', in the sense that God 'leaves' Jesus at the moment of suffering – since surely divinity itself does not suffer with humanity? Perhaps *only the Son* suffers; but *not the Father*?

Yet accepting that God *does* suffer in this moment, many interpreters have sought to further expiate this dark saying of the God-forsaken God by appealing to the finally optimistic conclusion of Psalm 22 (e.g. Trudinger 1974). In spite of such apparent consolation, however, Boulton poignantly

---

5 'Great (*megalē*) voices were those that penetrated the normal barrier between heaven and earth ... the power of Jesus' cry [stemmed] from its immediate access to God' (Minear 1995, p. 74).

6 Rowan Williams also attests to the 'unity of the divine and human voice' in Christ's cry (2004, p. 18).

7 The contemporary effects of reading this passage on mental 'well-being' are also explored in van Beest and Williams (2011, pp. 379–86). See also Richard Beck's empirical study (2006, pp. 43–52).

8 On the translation of the Aramaic sentence and its relation to the Hebrew of Psalm 22, see Buckler 1938, pp. 378–91.

9 Being forsaken by God is a vital fear throughout the law and the prophets (Minear 1995, p. 68).

observes that the conclusion of the psalm is itself ambivalent: ending with the *vow* to praise, 'an eschatological form of speech ... both present and absent, "already" and "not yet"' (2002, p. 70). The vow to praise, therefore, 'is spoken from the desolation of lament ... [it] is neither merely doxology nor merely its absence – rather, it is both doxology and its absence' (p. 71). Furthermore, as Marshall has contended, the final praise of the psalm does not mitigate the idea that Jesus has passed through God-forsakenness itself. What is more, the notion that the cry signifies the psalm's hopeful conclusion is 'a suggestion for which the texts of Matthew and Mark themselves offer no support, and which seems at odds with the desolate scenes they depict' (2009, pp. 246–7).

If the presence of a genuine divine lament over the ostensible absence of God *is* accepted then a dark metaphysical mystery appears to open up before us: 'If God himself is abandoned by God ... then the abyss of hell seems to open up in God himself' (Marshall 2009, p. 247). What sense can reason make of such unreason? Among the most influential and re-capitulated modern attempts to fathom this unfathomable abyss in God is G. W. F. Hegel's (1770–1831) attempt to inscribe the *death of God* within a philosophical metanarrative of God's kenotic (self-emptying) self-becoming. In Hegel's speculative philosophy, this abyssal moment constitutes a decisive point in the evolution of 'Spirit' (*Geist*) coming to consciousness-of-itself in-and-through-history. And yet, as Hegel himself acknowledges, the trinitarian mystery of the crucifixion also betrays an abyssal moment of contact between the death of God and the despair and melancholy of human subjectivity. Hegel refers at this moment to 'the Unhappy Consciousness', manifest when the self suffers 'the conscious loss of itself and the alienation of its knowledge about itself', and expresses its anguish in the 'hard saying that "God is dead"' (1997, pp. 454–5). Hegel elsewhere names this as an 'infinite grief', which exists historically as the God-forsaken 'feeling that "God Himself is dead," upon which the religion of more recent times rests' (1977, p. 190). For Hegel, however, this hard saying also signifies God's superseding ('sublation' – *Aufhebung*: analogous to *sublimation*; for Hegel to sublate is to lift up, to negate, *and also* to preserve in a higher form) of the self-alienation posited in the abyss between Father and Son. As Spirit (*Geist*), God comes back to Godself in universal self-consciousness (1997, p. 470f.).

Yet while Hegel might lure philosophy far from the cross and into the Mind of God, other more avowedly theological readings have sought to centralize metaphysical meaning within the paradox of the incarnation itself. Appealing to Gregory of Nazianzus' (330–89) dictum, 'The unassumed remains unhealed', Jinkins and Reid suggest that Jesus' cry of dereliction signifies that the experience of God-forsakenness is 'drawn into the inner life of God through Jesus Christ' (1997, p. 33). By experiencing in Christ 'the Godforsakenness that it is impossible for God to suffer', God transubstantiates, or sublimates, desolation into consolation: 'God breaks the boundaries

of possibility ... takes into God's innerlife the Godforsakenness we experience' (p. 47). And yet while such a metaphysical account of the immanent
Trinity may appear to promise consolation it might also raise similar concerns to Hegel's position. From an apophatic[10] perspective, how is it that
one can acquire *knowledge* of this inner life of Godhead? Does it not give
undue credence to the metaphysical excesses of onto-theology?[11] I do not
here make any *absolute* claims as to the unknowability of such things, or
the im/possibility of revelation (in itself a potentially un-apophatic claim);
but I do suggest that it does not necessarily follow that such a metaphysical
insight can translate across an infinite qualitative abyss and perform consoling metanoia in the human heart. The most demanding sublimation is to
understand why and how the thought that God suffers God-forsakenness
actually heals one from (Jinkins and Reid 1997, p. 33), or even sanctifies
one in, one's own suffering. Might such a consolation – of gnosis used to
sublimate visceral human anguish – prove offensive, even destructive, for
those in desolation?

The Godforsaken image

Theology should not project – and thereby exile – the cry of God-forsakenness into the transcendent and essentially unknowable life of God-in-
Godself. The image is harrowing because it announces a mystery that also
speaks to – by invoking the language of – inescapably human experiences
of estrangement, experiences that are not simply negated nor sublimated
by being taken up into the life of God. The human lament of the psalmist
has not been sublimated into the Trinity – that is, not stolen like a sacred
fire of anguish – but rather reflected back to us by and in the image of
Christ. Christ thus symbolizes the presence of an absence: crucified as the
God-forsaken God; God becomes God's other – experiencing the abyss of
non-being, dis-integration, even madness, on the cross (Jinkins and Reid
1997, p. 38). Nonetheless, Christ also hangs alone as an ineffable spectacle
of suffering. And at the same moment, he also reflects human sufferings
as an unfathomable image for the unimaginable abyss between the human
and the divine. Yet emerging within this symbolism there is also another
relatively neglected sense of God-forsakenness: the God-forsakenness that
renders the notion that one has already forsaken God as an absurdity.[12]

---

10 *Apophatic* denotes a form of negative theology that acknowledges the limits of
language, the value of negation, and the Wholly Otherness of God. It approaches God
through a *via negativa*: the desire to contemplate God that leads to a state of unknowing,
recognizing our inability to comprehend intellectually the essence of God-in-Godself. For
a concise critical overview, see Milem 2007.

11 'The term "onto-theology" was first used by Kant in reference to the metaphysical
deduction of God's existence with no appeal to experience' (Rubenstein 2003, p. 389).

12 By referring to the absurdity of suffering I offer a counter-point to attempts to
derive meaning (whether existential, consolatory, teleological or transcendent) from the

Namely, the innocent suffering in which the 'consolation' that one suffers *as guilty* becomes an offensive desolation. Such is the absurd suffering of Job, the abyss of the *Shoah*, the gratuitous and meaningless personal suffering in which one might cry out in 'Promethean' (Blank 1953, p. 1) moral objection, 'My God, my God, why have you forsaken me?' At this moment, theodicy (the attempt to justify the ways of God) appears as nothing but metaphysical absurdity – it is reduced to ashes, exposed as a mystification of the problem of suffering.

At this death of theodicy, however, a psycho-palliative rather than onto-theological question of personal God-forsakenness might also be recognized in Jesus' cry of dereliction. In her treatment of melancholy and depression, *Black Sun* (1987/1989), Julia Kristeva explores the imaginative relationship between human and divine suffering with reference to Hans Holbein the Younger's (1497–1543) haunting painting, *The Body of the Dead Christ in the Tomb* (1522), which in Dostoevsky's *The Idiot* becomes an image for the death of God: 'that picture! Why, some people may lose their faith by looking at that picture!' (Dostoevsky 1955, p. 236). The melancholy image thus suggests the triumph of death and despair over resurrection and hope. The open mouth of the dead Christ evokes the last breath, the final evacuation of life-giving spirit, echoing the cry of God-forsakenness – which according to Vermes signifies Jesus' despair over his messianic failure (2004, pp. 193–4).

Kristeva relates such 'hopeless grief' over the death of God to the lost object of melancholia: 'of Christ forsaken by the Father ("My God, my god, why have you deserted me?") and without the promise of resurrection' (1989, p. 113). It is resonant with the polyvalence of the cry of dereliction that both Dostoevsky and Kristeva read Holbein's *Dead Christ* in a negative sense. For Holbein himself, the absolute deadness of this broken body is one side of a dialectic that points, impossibly, to the hope of resurrection – echoed in Holbein's more optimistic 1524 depiction of the post-resurrection Jesus, *Noli me tangere* (Podmore 2011). For the artist, the ultimate intention is faith in the midst of despair, of consolation overcoming desolation. Yet in contemplating the experience of being unable to get beyond the desolation of the image, Kristeva also discovers empathic meaning in this potentially nihilistic vision. While 'Christ's dereliction is here at its worst: forsaken by the Father, he is apart from all of us' (1989, p. 113), the image itself also

existence of suffering. In the face of human suffering, the suggestion that every experience has meaning from the divine perspective can seem absurd, even offensive to our sense of human innocence and even divine goodness. By affirming the absurdity of suffering, one can acknowledge the apparent meaninglessness of much human suffering, thus, in a sense, fortifying our sense of defiance against the injustice of evil. This is not to deny that one may discover meaning in suffering but that much human experience of suffering appears to defy any normative consolation of suffering as the outworking of an unknowable divine plan. Even Jesus' disciples despaired before the absurd image of their crucified saviour.

suggests a moment of profound contact between divine and human suffering: it offers 'that hell' of depression or paroxysmal clinical melancholia 'with an imaginary elaboration; it provides the subject with an echo of its unbearable moments when meaning was lost, when the meaning of life was lost' (p. 133).

However, while psychoanalysis contemplates the imagery with reference to personal suffering, theology wishes also to speak of God – or, more appropriately, of *the relationship between the divine and the human*. Theologically speaking, the impossible image of the God-forsaken God cannot itself be sublimated into the mere echo of the human subject's own personal melancholy. The meaning of the *mysterium tremendum*, even *horrendum*, of the God-forsaken God is not ultimately reducible – even as 'an imaginary elaboration' – to human experience if there is, as Kierkegaard asserts in defiance of Hegelian speculation, an 'infinite qualitative difference' between the human and the divine, even between the suffering of God in Christ and our own human suffering. In his penetrating discourse on 'The Gospel of Sufferings', Kierkegaard wonders whether the notion that only Christ has suffered in true innocence means that only Christ can protest, in truth, against God by saying 'My God, my God, why have you abandoned me?' Yet in response to Kierkegaard I suggest that it is possible to hold in tension the thoughts that the God-forsaken cry of Christ is metaphysically ineffable and also at the same time spiritually and psychologically consolatory: that the unimaginable can have palliative appeal for the imagination and yet remain essentially and apophatically beyond imagination. The image brings metaphysics to desolation; but offers to the psyche an im/possibility of consolation along with this desolation. With reference to the contemplation of the image of Jesus' God-forsakenness within western Christian spirituality I therefore seek to at least partially enlighten a dark pathway *between* desolation and consolation – a between interpreted as an unresolved and unsublimated dialectic between both that does not seek to finally negate either at the expense of the other.

De Profundis: God-forsakenness and mystical theology

The extent and depth of devotional and theological attention dedicated to the cry of God-forsakenness is visceral testament to the *mysterium tremendum et fascinans* evoked by this numinous image. Even in spite of understandable reticence to contemplate the God-forsaken God, a comprehensive survey of treatments of this theme in western Christian theology alone could constitute an immense study.[13] With this caveat in mind, I focus on just four figures drawn from Protestant and Catholic traditions: Johann Tauler, Johann Arndt, John of the Cross and Teresa of Avila. Lubich observes that

---

13 For a useful, though not comprehensive, overview of trinitarian interpretations of this cry, see Jinkins and Reid 1997.

the forsaken cry of Christ is relatively neglected after the apostolic age, revived only centuries later in mystical theology (2003, p. 89). In medieval mysticism, the cry is often contemplated as a reflection of the soul's suffering – thereby in this sense completing a circular move of excursion and return. From the human (psalmist) to the divine (Trinity) and back to the human (mystic). But does this hermeneutical movement imply that the cry returns to the human via a process of *apophatic mystification*: that is, taken from the human lips of the psalmist, transfigured in Christ and sublimated into the Godhead, from where it is reflected back to humanity, only now transcendent and ineffably Wholly Other?

In the aspiration for the soul's union with Christ in medieval Catholic, and latterly Lutheran, German mystical literature, 'forsaking' itself is contemplated as a *via negationis* (or a *via remotionis* – from *removeo*: 'to remove, withdraw, take away, move back') of the human will in imitation of Christ (*imitatio Christi*). Forsaking comes to mean to forsake all that is not of God in the self-remoting act of resignation (*Gelassenheit*; letting be; releasement; remotion as kenosis). Such *Gelassenheit* is a *via negationis* passing through the dreadful *tentatio* (temptation) known in German devotional tradition as spiritual struggle (*Anfechtung*: *fecht* – fight; as Jacob struggled with God at Peni'el in Gen. 32). The Dominican Johann Tauler (*c.* 1300–61) contemplates Christ as the consolatory prototype for this death-to-self: 'Christ died a physical death that He might show us the way to die a spiritual death' (1910, p. 243). In the grief of Christ's God-forsakenness Tauler discovers 'Joy, that with this cry of desolation He should comfort all sorrowful men' (1910, p. 619). In another sermon Tauler also counsels, 'May you also utter those words with Christ crucified. Our Saviour's head as He hung dying was without support, and in His desolate abandonment, His love gave forth those words' (p. 703). Through spiritual death, the soul discovers an intimate union with God such that 'whosoever totally dies to self … is wholly made alive in God and without any separation' (p. 244). In dying to self, hidden under its opposite (*absconditus sub contrario*), 'Life has its hiding place in death … consolation has its hiding place in desolation' (p. 246). Here, in a move characteristic of the cathartic *via* from spiritual struggle (*Anfechtung*) to letting-be (*Gelassenheit*), the mortified will follows the tearful kenosis of Christ in Gethsemane who says 'not as I will, but as Thou wilt' (p. 247).

The Dominican mystical tradition's contemplation of *Anfechtung* is later revived in the *True Christianity* of the Lutheran Johann Arndt (1555–1621). While Arndt suggests that 'The most considerable temptation [*Anfechtung*] and obstruction in prayer seems to be when God withdraws the grace of a fervent and lively devotion', nonetheless, the prayer that 'climbs up to the throne of grace in affliction, temptation [*Anfechtung*], spiritual dryness, and brokenness of soul, is still more pleasing in [God's] sight' than a prayer born of consolatory presence (1917, p. 238). In this sense, Arndt offers the brooding consolation that such 'trials [*Anfechtungen*] are not to be looked upon as tokens of God's anger, but rather of his infinite *mercy*, since he is hereby fitting us to be partakers with them who have through many temptations entered into glory'. What is more, 'Nor, lastly, did the Son of God himself, escape severe trials [*Anfechtungen*], when his holy body trembled, and his soul was exceeding sorrowful (Matt. 26:38), and he cried out, "My God, my God, why hast thou forsaken me?"' (1979, p. 357). In the desolate cry of God-forsakenness, Arndt thus discovers an intimate moment of contact between Christ and the soul: there is consolation because God remains present in Christ even in the dark hour of apparent forsakenness; furthermore, if Christ himself endured such suffering, surely the sinful cannot expect to be exempted:

> He complains that he was forsaken of God, though He was continually present with him, and preserved him under all his trouble ... Yet God had so withdrawn his consolations from him, that his *human nature* was left desolate and comfortless. (p. 350)

The search for divine reassurance in the anxiety of God-forsakenness resonates throughout the treasury of Christian literature and is expressed with comparable passionate ardour in Spanish Carmelite tradition. In parallel to Arndt, John of the Cross (1542–91) writes of the 'dark night' by which God purges the soul in preparation for the union of love. In his *Ascent of Mount Carmel*, John describes how before dawn breaks upon this dark night, 'God will lead the soul by a most lofty path of dark contemplation and aridity, wherein it seems to be lost' and the soul will be tempted by the thought that it is forsaken by God (1962, p. 62). At such moments of *desolatio*, the soul should turn to the image of Christ as a source of *consolatio*, precisely because Jesus himself was deprived of all consolation. As Arndt speaks of the desolation of Christ's 'human nature', John also appears to understand 'the lower part of [Jesus'] nature' as forsaken by the Father, annihilated in death, without the Father's protection (who seems to absent himself at this moment of suffering). At this moment, he (or his 'lower human nature'?) pays the price of human sin, reuniting humanity with God:

> [I]t is certain that, at the moment of His death, He was likewise annihilated in His soul, and was deprived of any relief and consolation, since His Father left Him in the most intense aridity, according to the lower part of His nature. Wherefore He had perforce to cry out, saying: 'My God! My God! Why hast Thou forsaken Me?' ... And thus He wrought herein the greatest work that He had ever wrought ... the reconciliation and union of mankind, through grace, with God (p. 109).

In *The Dark Night of the Soul*, John further elaborates this notion of the dark night that – as in Jesus' crucifixion – precedes the soul's union with the love of God. John describes the purgative dark night of spiritual mortification as a 'sepulchre of dark death', the darkest moment of *desolatio*, which is nonetheless – *via negativa* – the form of God's spiritual assaults, preparing the soul through 'purgative contemplation' of its God-forsakenness for the spiritual resurrection in which it is made divine. Here John appeals to the empathic words of the psalms, while also acknowledging that such suffering ultimately 'transcends all description' (1959, pp. 51–2).

Comparable treatments of *desolatio* and *consolatio* are also invoked within the writings of John of the Cross's senior fellow reformer and founder of the Discalced Carmelites, Teresa of Avila (1515–82). As with Tauler, Arndt and John, Teresa's sense of desolate God-forsakenness is initially an intensification of *aridity*: the sense of *acedia* (the noonday devil, or sloth) and remoteness from prayer's divine object of love. As Teresa explores in *The Interior Castle or The Mansion*, dryness and boredom may infect prayer life, in contrast to the moments of blissful union the soul has otherwise known. At this point, God seems absent or remote to the point of *indifference* towards creation. When such a feeling of nothingness intensifies into the thought that not only is God distant, but God has actively forsaken you, the *consolatio* of spiritual union with God is not only absent (as in aridity), it is negated by its very opposite: *desolatio* (analogous to the God-forsaken extremis of *Anfechtung* in German devotional literature). Yet even as with ephemeral moments of consolatory union, the experience of God-forsakenness is itself transient and ultimately purgative: it is intended to bring the soul to a state of abandoning itself completely to the embrace of divine love, resigning the self to the will of God (Teresa 1921, p. 49). In this dark night, desolation negates consolation, and is in turn sublimated – *via negationis* – into the higher consolation of mystical union of the soul abandoning itself to divine love.

The dark night of suffering: protest and innocence

Such mystical/devotional literature shares the higher consolation of the soul's union with Christ – an aspiration which ostensibly suggests that the infinite qualitative difference between the human and the divine is not the final word; that the relationship between the suffering of Jesus and the soul is not only imaginary or symbolic but can also possess deep ontological, even unitary, meaning. Within this literature, however, the crisis of God-forsakenness becomes a dialectical and purgative *via negativa* ultimately traceable in origin to the primal question of one's having already *forsaken God*: that is, rooted in the anxiety of sin-consciousness and the temptation to believe that one is justly damned – *forsaken by God*. By becoming God-forsaken, Christ enters into forsakenness on our behalf, taking human sin upon himself and overcoming the abyss in himself. Because of this, the dark nights of *desolatio* and *Anfechtung* (spiritual struggle) are understood with reference to a *via negativa* that brings the soul, through the *mortificatio* of

SPIRITUALITY, THEOLOGY AND MENTAL HEALTH

the self-will (released in *Gelassenheit*: letting-be), to the union of *consolatio* in divine love.

In respect to the abyss of sin, however, Kierkegaard suggests that there still remains an inexorable 'infinite qualitative difference' between Christ's experience of God-forsakenness and our own. In honour of this absolute difference, Kierkegaard expresses suspicion towards mystical talk of union between soul and Christ, preferring instead to focus upon *following* or *imitating* Jesus rather than seeking union with him. For Kierkegaard, Christ's cry of 'My God, my God, why have you forsaken me?' signifies 'freedom's ultimate spiritual trial [*Anfægtelse* – the Danish cognate for *Anfechtung*: spiritual struggle]' (1967–78, 4:4611). Since unlike that of the psalmist, Jesus' cry signifies an *Anfechtung* undergone voluntarily by God for the sake of human salvation, it is 'the last spiritual trial [*Anfægtelse*]' (1967–78, 4:4699), which is also the last moment before the blessedness of being with God in eternity. Only Christ has truly suffered, on our behalf, the abyss's moment of death. While Christ's suffering is human, Kierkegaard therefore reminds us that 'it is also superhuman, and there is an eternal chasmic abyss between his suffering and the human being's' (1993, p. 281). Only Christ has suffered the abyss – in pure innocence – and therefore only he can truly, unfathomably, cry 'My God, my God, why have you forsaken me?' By contrast, the thief crucified by Christ's side, who endures the same punishment but who suffers as one who is guilty, cannot legitimately say this since 'it is not God who has abandoned him but it is he who has abandoned God' (1993, p. 280).

From this Kierkegaardian perspective, ecstatic union between the soul and Christ could be suspected of a desire to mystify the absolute difference of sin. In light of this difference, one might wonder whether only Christ has the right, as the only innocent individual, to justly pose the question of God-forsakenness? In drawing this veil of infinite qualitative difference (a veil that perhaps has been torn apart at this very moment of crucifixion: Matt. 27.51), the cry of God-forsakenness is seemingly snatched from our lips and replaced with the guilt of having forsaken God: a guilt that is identified in and thus prohibits the dreadful question that doubts the love or existence of God. The movement to relate all human suffering to the notion that 'in relation to God a person always suffers as guilty' (Kierkegaard 1993, p. 269) or that one is always in the wrong before God (p. 272), signifies a potential lacuna in the interpretation of the cry of God-forsakenness. It is an evasion of what is perhaps more scandalous than the image of the God-forsaken God: the image of a God-human who cries out against God in protest at the experience of divine absence in the throes of absurd human suffering. In this cry, Jesus as the revealed Face of God cries out to the hidden Face of God in the vernacular of human despair. While mystical consolations of union with Christ may prematurely sublimate the abyss between the self and God, it could also be claimed that this Kierkegaardian displacement of the theodicy question via an emphasis upon human guilt and sinfulness constitutes a regrettable sin of omission – perhaps even a flagrant mystification of another kind.

Such a critique does not, however, seek to transcend Kierkegaard's infinite qualitative difference. Kierkegaard himself avows that it is not his intention 'to confuse the concepts, to deprive the, humanly speaking, innocent sufferer of the comfort that he, humanly speaking, is suffering as innocent' (1993, p. 282). Kierkegaard seeks paradoxical joy in the thought that *before God one is always in the wrong* in so far as it suggests that such an acknowledgement can save the consoling thought that 'God is love' from the abyss of doubt, despair and desolation (Podmore 2005). Here Kierkegaard moves between a sense of 'innocence' from the apophatic perspective of the 'infinite qualitative difference', and 'innocence' 'humanly speaking'. In light of this distinction, therefore, what might Jesus' cry of dereliction say to the problem of suffering encountered otherwise than the *via negativa* of sin, salvation and self-mortification? In other words, humanly speaking, can the innocent suffering of Christ speak to 'innocent' human suffering? Does this cry 'speak humanly' other than in the discourse of guilt, of being in the wrong before God, and to the possibility of crying out against God in protest and despair as well as longing and hope?

Jesus cries divinely, as God calling unto God, by which he conveys a divine *mysterium* that, according to the apophatic infinite qualitative difference, surpasses even the speculative human understanding. Yet Jesus is also speaking humanly. In the shadows of a 'God-forsaken epoch',[14] which Kierkegaard did not live to witness, the personal connotations of this cry continue to be transfigured – even deformed. In response to the God-forsaking cries of modern atheism, Jürgen Moltmann suggests, 'The only way past protest atheism is through a theology of the cross which understands God as the suffering God in the suffering of Christ and which cries out with the godforsaken God, "My God, why have you forsaken me?"' (1974, p. 227).[15] With this cry resonating in the background, Moltmann appeals to a harrowing passage from Elie Wiesel's account of the Holocaust, *Night*:

> The SS hanged two Jewish men and a youth in front of the whole camp. The men died quickly, but the death throes of the youth lasted for half an hour. 'Where is God? Where is He?' someone asked behind me. As the

---

14 According to Kerr, 'a form of life from which God has withdrawn, in which God gives himself now only in ways which either run counter to the traditions and customs of the particular form of life in question or anyway in ways which are more or less unrelated to them' (1965, pp. 670–1).

15 Moltmann recounts how, as a prisoner of war, reading the psalms of lament 'gave expression to my own despair and intensified my search for God. I then read Mark's Gospel, and when I came to Jesus' death cry – "My God, my God, why have you forsaken me?" – I knew that in my God-forsakenness Jesus had found me' (2005, pp. 148–9). See also Moltmann 1997.

youth still hung in torment in the noose after a long time, I heard the man call again, 'Where is God now?' And I heard a voice in myself answer: 'Where is he? He is here. He is hanging there on the gallows ...' (Moltmann 1974, pp. 273–4)

According to Moltmann's reading, this response represents the definitive 'Christian answer to the question of this torment' (p. 274). Moltmann presents God as somewhat analogous to Whitehead's Process philosophy: 'the great companion – the fellow sufferer who understands' (Whitehead 1969, p. 413). Yet whereas Dostoevsky's and Kristeva's desolate readings defy Holbein's consolation of hope, Moltmann's consolatory reading of this passage appears to defy the desolation that Wiesel's scene depicts. However, this consolation remains tragically unconvincing. It is not sufficiently evident how a christological imagining of God's death on the gallows at Auschwitz attests to a consolatory, let alone redemptive, sense of solidarity and empathy between human and divine suffering. The answer that God is hanging on the gallows seems to speak also of absolute desolation: the death of God which, as Rubenstein's more abyssal Holocaust theology observes, is announced with a cry of agony rather than kenotic joy (1996, p. 264).

Today the cry now lingers in the absence of absolute or universal answers to such questions. The divine providence that consoled medieval mysticism has long vanished. As Wiesel himself stated, 'what is called the literature of the Holocaust does not exist, cannot exist. It is a contradiction in terms, as is the philosophy, the theology, the psychology of the Holocaust. Auschwitz negates all systems, opposes all doctrines' (1977, p. 405). Elsewhere Moltmann himself later concedes that 'the experiences of Auschwitz and Hiroshima raise questions for which no answers are endurable, because the questions are fundamentally protests' (1985, p. 91). If the God-forsaken God has any consolatory force, humanly speaking, it is not necessarily, I suggest, as a 'Christian answer to the question of this torment'. Rather it is in solidarity with the one who asks, 'Where is God now?' This question – rather than its absolute answer or consolation – is thus more akin to Jesus' sacredly profane cry of desolation against God.[16]

In conclusion: the crucified 'Why?' – between desolation and consolation

God-forsakenness in itself is not necessarily made holy, sacred, sanctified, redeemed – or even yet consoled. The abyss is not sublimated by the image. However, there may still remain theological and psycho-palliative senses

16 In the shadows '[a]fter Auschwitz', Metz profoundly questions Christian theology's resort to trinitarian speculation in response to the theodicy question – that is, 'to see human suffering sublated [*aufgehoben*] in God God's self, in the inner-trinitarian history of God' (1994, pp. 619–20).

in which the question of God-forsakenness itself is made at once holy and yet unholy, sacred and profane, meaningful and meaningless in the maddening possibility of the cry of a God-forsaken God who hangs, cruciform, between consolation and desolation. The psalmist's 'Why?' of lament is not, as Boulton insightfully proposes, suspended 'between Yes and No', but rather incorporates both simultaneously. The cry of 'Why?' entails both a 'No to God' in 'lament' that also struggles with the 'Yes to God's promise' of 'praise' (Boulton 2002, pp. 61–2). In saying a 'No of indictment' to God, the psalmist 'echoes God's No of desertion' thereby 'forsaking the God who has first forsaken the psalmist' (p. 63). Boulton thereby pertinently points to a forsaking of God that responds to an ostensibly prior forsaking of the innocent by God. It is not a matter of being forsaken by a God whom we have already forsaken in our guilt, but rather a protest against the experience of the absence of God in the absurdity of suffering.

While Psalm 22 in its entirety expresses forsaking and forsakenness reconciled in an im/possible future hope, I suggest that Jesus' cry from the cross, while perhaps evoking the whole of the psalm, might also be read as a despair that, humanly speaking, does not yet reach out to the distant shores of eschatological hope. Is it possible, therefore, to contemplate an image of a cruciform God dying in despair? Would this mean necessarily inferring messianic failure, as Vermes does? Or might the *possibility* that Jesus experienced a *moment* of utter despair potentially give 'powerful voice' to those who suffer in silence?

Absolute despair, by rejecting all expressions of meaning and hope, suffocates the self in an abyss of silence. Kierkegaard thus ultimately counsels against becoming 'silent in despair' in the forlorn belief that one's suffering is 'suprahuman and no one could understand it' (1995, p. 121). While there is an infinite qualitative abyss between Christ's suffering and ours, the cry of God-forsakenness is nonetheless 'consoling to those who imitate [Christ]' and who are on the brink of losing themselves in the thought that God has abandoned them. At this moment, 'life truly seems to be infinite despair. [One] is lost for this life.' Yet 'This, you see, is why the prototype consoles by showing that this, too, belongs' (Kierkegaard 1967–78, 4:3903). *Despair belongs* – even infinite despair. Unsublimated. *As yet* unconsoled. *As yet* perhaps unconsolable.

Humanly speaking, the cry of God-forsakenness may offer the *possibility* of a pastoral, even psycho-palliative, moment of consolation – an assertion, even an imagination, of the presence of God in the depths of human suffering, of a God who takes up the words of a human psalmist and speaks them directly *to God, as God* and *as human*. Yet the cry also speaks to a human experience of the absence of God that deserves more than the sublimating theological consolations.[17] Christ speaks for us; but also for God *against*

---

17 Similarly Anderson suggests that a consoling, even mediating, pastoral presence should not necessarily negate the difficult experience of divine absence: 'The words of the Psalmist and the cry of dereliction from the Cross are frequently heard in hospital

God. Jesus sanctifies the blasphemous cry against God by preserving it in innocence. Before this cry, God is silent. In sanctifying the cry as struggle with God – rather than the suffering itself – God protests against God, suggesting the profanity of God and the sanctity of the human. The image is not only a mystical catharsis for despair. It is a cry of despair that, crucified between consolation and desolation, nevertheless struggles after a God who does not condemn it for its doubt. In the abyss opened up by this cry might there yet arise the im/possibility of a consolation that accompanies, without denying, the silence of desolation?

References

Anderson, H. (1984), 'Incarnation and pastoral care', *Pastoral Psychology* 32:4, pp. 239–50.

Arndt, J. (1917), *True Christianity*, trans. A. W. Boehm, Philadelphia PA: General Council Publication House.

Arndt, J. (1979), *True Christianity*, trans. P. Erb, New York/Ramsey/Toronto: Paulist Press.

Beck, R. (2006), 'Communion and complaint: attachment, object-relations and triangular love perspectives on relationship with God', *Journal of Psychology and Theology* 34:1, pp. 43–52.

Blank, S. H. (1953), 'Men against God: the promethean element in biblical prayer', *Journal of Biblical Literature* 72:1, pp. 1–13.

Boulton, M. (2002), 'Forsaking God: a theological argument for Christian lamentation', *Scottish Journal of Theology* 55:1, pp. 58–78.

Buckler, F. W. (1938), 'Eli, Eli, Lama Sabachthani', *The American Journal of Semitic Languages and Literatures* 55:4, pp. 378–91.

Cooper, H. (1997), 'The cracked crucible: Judaism and mental health', in D. Bhugra (ed.), *Psychiatry and Religion: Context, Consensus and Controversies*, London and New York: Routledge.

Council, R. J. (1982), 'Out of the depths: pastoral care to the severely depressed', *Pastoral Psychology* 31:1, pp. 58–64.

Derrida, J. (1997), 'Cogito and the history of madness', trans. A. Bass, *Writing and Difference*, London: Routledge, pp. 31–63.

Dostoevsky, F. (1955), *The Idiot*, trans. D. Magashack, New York: Viking Penguin.

Foucault, M. (1989), *Madness and Civilization: A History of Insanity in the Age of Reason*, trans. R. Howard, London and New York: Routledge.

Hegel, G. W. F. (1977), *Faith and Knowledge*, trans. W. Cerf and H. S. Harris, Albany NY: State University of New York Press.

Hegel, G. W. F. (1997), *Phenomenology of Spirit*, trans. A. V. Miller, Oxford: Oxford University Press.

John of the Cross (1959), *Dark Night of the Soul*, trans. E. A. Peers, New York: Image Books.

---

corridors and from people whose anguished cry pleads for a sign of God's presence ... The assurance of presence prematurely given may short-circuit the painful but positive process of discovering the depths of human autonomy in the face of God's absence' (1984, pp. 242–3).

John of the Cross (1962), *Ascent of Mount Carmel*, trans. E. A. Peers, New York: Image Books.

Jinkins, M. and Reid, S. B. (1997), 'God's forsakenness: the cry of dereliction as an utterance within the Trinity', *Horizons in Biblical Theology* 19:1, pp. 33–57.

Kerr, F. (1965), 'Theology in a Godforsaken epoch', *New Blackfriars* 46:543, pp. 665–72.

Kierkegaard, S. (1967–78), *Journals and Papers*, 7 vols, trans. and ed. H. V. Hong and E. H. Hong, Bloomington IN and London: Indiana University Press.

Kierkegaard, S. (1993), *Upbuilding Discourses in Various Spirits*, trans. and ed. H. V. Hong and E. H. Hong, Princeton NJ: Princeton University Press.

Kierkegaard, S. (1995), *Without Authority*, trans. and ed. H. V. Hong and E. H. Hong, Princeton NJ: Princeton University Press.

Kristeva, J. (1989), *Black Sun: Depression and Melancholia (Soleil Noir: Dépression et mélancolie, 1987)*, trans. L. S. Roudiez, New York: Columbia University Press.

Lubich, C. (2003), 'Unity and Jesus crucified and forsaken: foundation of a spirituality of communion', *The Ecumenical Review* 55:1, pp. 87–95.

Marshall, B. D. (2009), 'The dereliction of Christ and the impassibility of God', in J. F. Keating and T. J. White (eds), *Divine Impassibility and the Mystery of Human Suffering*, Grand Rapids MI and Cambridge: Eerdmans, pp. 246–98.

Mays, J. L. (1985), 'Prayer and Christology: Psalm 22 as perspective on the passion', *Theology Today* 42:3, pp. 322–31.

Metz, J. B. (1994), 'Suffering unto God', trans. J. M. Ashley, *Critical Inquiry* 20:4, Symposium on 'God', pp. 611–22.

Milem, B. (2007), 'Four theories of negative theology', *Heythrop Journal* 48:2, pp. 187–204.

Minear, P. S. (1995), 'The Messiah forsaken … Why?', *Horizons in Biblical Theology* 17:1, pp. 62–83.

Moltmann, J. (1974), *The Crucified God: The Cross of Christ as the Foundation and Criticism of Christian Theology*, trans. R. A. Wilson and J. Bowden, London: SCM Press.

Moltmann, J. (1985), *God in Creation: An Ecological Doctrine of Creation*, trans. M. Kohl, London: SCM Press.

Moltmann, J. (1997), 'Wrestling with God', trans. M. Kohl, in *The Source of Life: The Holy Spirit and the Theology of Life*, Minneapolis MN: Fortress Press, pp. 1–9.

Moltmann, J. (2005), 'The blessing of hope: the theology of hope and the full gospel of life', *Journal of Pentecostal Theology* 13:2, pp. 147–56.

Podmore, S. D. (2005), 'The dark night of suffering and the darkness of God: God-forsakenness or forsaking God in The Gospel of Sufferings', in R. Perkins (ed.), *International Kierkegaard Commentary. Vol. 15: Upbuilding Discourses in Various Spirits*, Macon GA: Mercer University Press, pp. 229–56.

Podmore, S. D. (2011), 'Lazarus and the sickness unto death: an allegory of despair', *Religion and the Arts* 15:4, pp. 486–519.

Podmore, S. D. (2012), 'The sacrifice of silence: *Fear & Trembling* and the Secret of Faith', *International Journal of Systematic Theology* 14:1, pp. 70–90.

Rubenstein, R. L. (1996), *After Auschwitz: History, Theology, and Contemporary Judaism*, Baltimore MD and London: Johns Hopkins University Press.

Rubenstein, M.-J. (2003), 'Unknow thyself: apophaticism, deconstruction, and theology after ontotheology', *Modern Theology* 19:3, pp. 387–417.

Smith, D. C. (1995), 'Psycho-palliation and the enlightened counselor', *Counseling and Values*, 39:3, pp. 209–17.

Smith, D. C. and Olsen, P. (1993), 'The right to choose death', *The American Journal of Hospice and Palliative Care* 10:5, pp. 7–9.

Tauler, J. (1910), *The Sermons and Conferences of John Tauler*, trans. W. Elliott, Washington DC: Apostolic Mission House.

Teresa of Avila (1921), *The Interior Castle or The Mansions*, trans. the Benedictines of Stanbrook, London: Thomas Baker.

Trudinger, L. P. (1974), '"Eli, Eli, Lama Sabachthani?" A cry of dereliction? Or victory?', *Journal of the Evangelical Theological Society* 17:4, pp. 235–8.

van Beest, I. and Williams, K. D. (2011), '"Why hast thou forsaken me?" The effect of thinking about being ostracized by God on well-being and social behavior', *Social Psychological and Personality Science* 2:4, pp. 379–86.

Vermes, G. (2004), *The Authentic Gospel of Jesus*, London: Penguin.

Wiesel, E. (1977), 'Art and Culture after the Holocaust', in E. Fleischner (ed.), *Auschwitz: Beginning of a New Era? Reflections on the Holocaust*, New York: KTAV Publishing House.

Whitehead, A. N. (1969), *Process and Reality: An Essay in Cosmology*, New York: The Free Press.

Williams, R. (2004), 'Augustine and the Psalms', *Interpretation* 58:17, pp. 17–22.

Conclusions and Reflections

CHRISTOPHER C. H. COOK

In the Introduction, it was proposed that spirituality, theology and mental health are all intimately related and that theology has a particular part to play, within the context of a broad interdisciplinary endeavour, in enriching our understanding of mental health and mental disorder. To what extent and in what ways may we now see the various chapters of the present volume as having realized this potential? In order to seek some answers to this question, I will now consider just some of the themes that seem to me to run through this book.

The themes that I have chosen are: boundaries, evil, immanence and transcendence, and narrative. Necessarily, my selection of these themes is subjective, but I think that they are all important in the field of mental health.

Boundaries

In Chapter 1, I outline briefly the ascendance of spirituality within the field of mental health, both in practice and research, and also some of the controversies that have been associated with this. In particular, boundary issues emerge as an important concern; boundaries between different domains of expertise, boundaries between secular and religious domains, and boundaries between personal and professional values. These boundaries and others are an identifiable theme running throughout Part 1 of the book. Sometimes (as in the controversies outlined in Chapter 1) it is the need to respect and define boundaries that comes to the fore. The inappropriate crossing of significant professional boundaries has been a fear that has driven much of the concern about the integration of spirituality into clinical practice. But, in this book, we also see a creative crossing of disciplinary boundaries that enriches our thinking about mental health and mental disorder and gives us scope for new ways of conceiving clinical and pastoral practice.

Patricia Casey, in Chapter 2, challenges the assumption (perhaps more common in clinical than theological circles) that spirituality and religion are the same construct, but also draws attention to the way in which spirituality can become confounded with mood states and psychological variables. The boundary between these constructs is, I think, reflective of the professional boundaries that are sometimes drawn between spirituality, now a concern of psychologists and mental health professionals, and religion, a concern of chaplains, clergy and religious communities. However, her analysis of the difficulty of drawing a boundary between spirituality and psychology also alerts us to the way in which spirituality is something of a hinterland between religion and psychology, overlapping in important ways with each domain. Any serious attempt to understand the nature of spirituality (or religion) necessarily takes us also into the affective, cognitive and behavioural concerns that are the province of psychology.

In Chapter 3 Colin Jay, a mental health chaplain, draws attention to some of the difficulties in identifying, assessing and responding to spiritual needs. In particular, he argues that spiritual care is more about a quality of relationship that affirms a person and their values than it is about particular interventions or activities. He further argues that clarity of professional boundaries is important as a framework within which this quality of relationships can be developed. But clarity of such boundaries does not preclude the 'Ubuntu', the interdependent understanding of self within community, upon which he draws for a vision of richer and more deeply valued relationships.

Alexandra Pârvan, in Chapter 4, drawing on the thinking of Augustine of Hippo, demonstrates that the practical work of psychotherapy engages directly with the concerns of philosophy and theology and that this has relevance for how we construe, discuss and manage the nature of evil in clinical practice. Whether we agree, or not, with her particular conclusions, she makes it difficult, I think, for us to continue with any illusion that psychotherapeutic work can be separated by any professional boundaries from the domains of philosophy or religion. Philosophical and religious assumptions are implicit, even if they are not explicitly identified, in clinical practice. Making them visible enables and facilitates our thinking about better ways of managing them.

Chris MacKenna, an Anglican priest and psychotherapist, in Chapter 5, offers a depth-psychological perspective on demon possession and deliverance ministry that breaks down some of the boundaries between a biblical world-view and the world-views of contemporary pastoral and clinical practice. Psychology (here represented by the depth psychologies of Freud and Jung) now necessarily engages across the divides of history, culture and practice with narratives of demon possession, which importantly opens up new possibilities for conversation and mutual understanding. This chapter is a contrast with Pârvan's, but also complements it. In deliverance ministry very explicit and unambiguous narratives of evil are in a sense opposite to those of the kinds of psychotherapy that Pârvan is primarily discussing, and yet they carry the same risk of conferring an ontological understanding that is not helpful. MacKenna provides us with a way of negotiating between the contemporary psychological narratives and the contemporary interpretations of ancient scriptural narratives that all too easily confer such ontologies. We are left with an impression of a very different kind of therapy that Pârvan and MacKenna are engaged in, but in both cases a dialogue of psychology with theology offers a richer and more promising way forward.

In all of these chapters, then, boundaries make an appearance of some kind, even if (as in Pârvan's chapter) they are not explicitly mentioned. Clarity of boundaries, important for research and for professional practice, is in contrast with the crossing and blurring of boundaries that seem to enrich interdisciplinary engagement and offer new ways of thinking about possibilities for therapeutic practice.

Evil

Chapters 4 to 6 of this book are all concerned with the problem of evil. All are psychologically realistic about the potential power that negative forms of spirituality can adversely exert, but they presume and imply different therapeutic approaches – as noted above in respect of the chapters by Pârvan and MacKenna.

In Chapter 6, Loren Stuckenbruck's in-depth consideration of the biblical material relating to the demonic gives a perspective to the Gospel accounts of Jesus' ministry that is significantly richer and more complex than many more superficial readings would allow. Stuckenbruck's account of the ontology of the biblical narratives is in contrast to Pârvan's (Augustinian) assertion of the non-existence of evil but, like Pârvan, he also draws attention to the need to reconcile this with the very different ontology of contemporary psychological narratives. While acknowledging the important differences between the biblical/Jewish world-view and the contemporary mental health context, he shows that there are important points of contact, notably the understanding of evil as 'relocated', rather than destroyed in the process of therapy/exorcism.

In clinical practice, belief in the demonic is all too easily dismissed, either as a part of a delusional system or else as culturally determined. Pârvan draws attention to the problems that arise when therapy does not allow a legitimate language of discourse concerning the nature of evil. Perhaps we do have to be realistic, in our pluralistic and secular society, about the lack of any shared framework within which to discuss such things. However, this surely means that clinicians need to be better at learning the language of discourse about evil used by their patients and at working respectfully and thoughtfully with it.

Immanence and transcendence

In Chapter 8, I consider the concept of transcendence and the appearances that it has made in the psychological and clinical literature, as contrasted with its use in theology and in the work of Charles Taylor. Theologically, at least in the Christian tradition, transcendence is only adequately understood as inseparable from the concept of immanence. The immanent frame that Taylor describes is biased against transcendence, and it is transcendence that is usually associated with spirituality, but in fact there are a variety of spiritualities that emphasize the immanent rather than the transcendent in their practices and in other ways. I think that the dynamic that Mark Wynn describes in Chapter 7 is understandable in such immanent terms, while also clearly involving a psychological transcendence that does not allow it to be completely confined within the immanent frame.

For Wynn, there is an intimate relationship between internal emotional well-being and religious orientation and perceptions of the outer world. What we believe affects the way in which we perceive the world around, and, in a state of emotional well-being, there is a correlation or match between these internal and external perceptions of things. While this is a very different account of things from Stuckenbruck's or Pârvan's, and deals with very different material, we are again drawn into reflecting on the relationships between inner worlds of emotion, belief and perception and the outer world within which we live. Here, however, Wynn encourages us to think much more about this outer world in its literal physical sense, as we perceive it in immanent terms, rather than in terms of its cultural, religious and psychological narratives.

Each of the chapters of this book might be viewed as offering both immanent and transcendent narratives that interweave and either inform or challenge each other, and it is therefore to the theme of narrative that I now wish to turn.

Narratives

The myths, or narratives, that form the focus of Douglas Davies's attention in Chapter 9 provide a framework within which many (perhaps all) of the other chapters of the book can helpfully be understood. Thus, for example, we have already considered the very different (but each in their own way very effective) narratives of evil analysed by Pârvan, MacKenna and Stuckenbruck. I have suggested that Wynn's chapter, as well as my own, are concerned with narratives of transcendence and immanence, narratives that are concerned with the accounts that we construct to make sense of our affects, perceptions, thoughts and behaviours. Narratives make connections between the immanent and transcendent realms.

John Cottingham, in Chapter 10, considers the ways in which spiritual praxis and psychotherapy both help us to live better lives. Not that either should be completely assimilated into the other, or that there are no points of tension between them, but rather that they share much common ground. In a sense, with a more philosophical slant, this takes us back to Patricia Casey's awareness of the readiness with which spirituality assumes psychological language. However, it also reminds us that the narratives by which we live, be they primarily spiritual, religious or psychological, are not just affective and cognitive constructions – they are reinforced, expressed and made visible in praxis. And these practices, Cottingham and others might give us cause to believe, are an important part of what brings about healing and instils well-being.

In Chapter 11, Simon Podmore provides a christological perspective on desolation and experiences of the absence of God. Whether Christ's cry of dereliction from the cross offers something 'between' consolation and desolation, or whether it draws attention to the paradox that experiences of consolation (in Ignatian terms) are not always comfortable, it is another point in this book in which immanent and transcendent narratives share the same space. While the language of immanence and transcendence used in my own chapter has utility in pluralistic conversation, in Christian terms it might be seen as a thinly veiled Christology. In the incarnation of the Logos, the immanent and the transcendent co-inhere. Podmore makes his Christology more explicit, and explores the question of the extent to which it provides an adequate account of how the consoling presence of God might be encountered in the most God-forsaken moments in human experience. Here, the Christian narrative is brought into a critical engagement with the atheistic experience, albeit primarily considered within the context of faith. This is not a comfortable place, but it is one with deep relevance to those who struggle with experiences of mental disorder that seem to challenge, and render more fragile, the Christian narrative within which they have sought to live.

Davies assumes, I think rightly, that narratives are usually good for human well-being, but they do also have the potential (in the wrong circumstances) to be 'identity depleting'. Interestingly, narrative has also been a recent concern of medicine, including psychiatry (Roberts and Holmes 1998; Greenhalgh and Hurwitz 1999), although the emphasis has been more on the individual story and less on the collective ('mythical') meaning-making with which Davies is concerned. Theological, philosophical, psychological, anthropological and personal narratives of mental health and mental disorder share a capacity to confer meaning, provide hope of transformation and make points of contact between the immanent and transcendent realms. Each has its own strengths and weaknesses to this end, and together, it seems to me, they provide a richer narrative than any one of them can do in isolation.

Theology as interdisciplinary engagement

The picture that is painted here makes a good case, I think, for proposing that theology does well in engagement with other disciplines. Anchoring theological narratives in the reality of mental health practice, controversies and research makes them more robust, informative and realistic than they might be if theologians went away on their own to consider a biblical account of mental well-being (interesting though that could be) or construct a spirituality of mental health based only upon traditional texts. This interdisciplinary engagement might be called 'practical' or 'contextual' theology, thus setting it apart from such disciplines as biblical studies or systematic theology, but I do not think that this kind of distancing is helpful. It suggests that there is something that (some) theologians do that is quite apart from the concerns of the immanent order, and in fact all theology is engaged with this order of things in some way or another. It might much better be understood as Williams's 'communicative' style of theology, referred to in the Introduction, but in fact there has been evidence in the chapters of this book of all three of Williams's styles of theology. Williams himself suggests that these styles move in a kind of cycle, and cautions us against imagining that 'whole theologies really fall under one or the other style' (2000, p. xv).

Thus, for example, the scriptural demonologies referred to by MacKenna, and explored in depth by Stuckenbruck, can be (and are) interpreted today as literal narratives. Such interpretations do not seek any reconciliation with contemporary psychological accounts and, at least for some people, they appear to be accepted unquestioningly and are even reassuring. This is a version of Williams's celebratory style of theology. For others, however, psychological interpretations may render the biblical narrative more fragile, more seemingly discrepant from the accounts of contemporary science, and thus the narrative becomes a source of anxiety rather than reassurance, life-depleting rather than life-enhancing. But the interdisciplinary engagements that MacKenna, Stuckenbruck, Pârvan, Davies and others offer here suggest that such anxiety, such depletion, is in fact unnecessary and avoidable. Scriptural narratives, when understood in the light of critical scholarship, in a more communicative style of theology, prove to have been more sophisticated, more relevant, more flexible and more purposeful in their original cultural and historical contexts than more rigid contemporary interpretations now allow them to be. Indeed, studies of the demonologies of the desert fathers, later adopted and elaborated on by the Orthodox tradition, might suggest that (at least in some Christian traditions) there has always been a psychological dimension to such narratives, which need not be in any conflict with the theological dimension (Cook 2011).

It is also important to note Stuckenbruck's qualifications with regard to the possible links between the Gospel accounts of Jesus' exorcisms, and the present situation of those diagnosed with mental disorder. The former might be the closest biblical analogy for the latter, but it is a complex one, and subject to significant discontinuities. I think that this is where Podmore's attention to the passion narrative offers a helpful alternative perspective. Here is a narrative that can be seen to have relevance to all who feel God-forsaken, who experience the desolating absence of God rather than his consoling presence. As an example of Williams's critical style of theology, it is a risky enterprise, because it can take us in different directions, some of which might seem hostile to faith, but I think that any theology that lacks the courage to explore such places is always likely to fail to do justice to the challenges that mental health (and life) presents.

There is surely scope for fruitful reflection on the many other scriptural narratives that might have been explored as a basis for building a theological understanding of mental health and mental disorder that is true both to tradition and to the insights of the contemporary social and human sciences, and that incorporates both immanent and transcendent accounts of Christian spirituality. We might have considered, for example, the narratives of Jesus in Gethsemane (Matt. 26.36–46; Mark 14.32–42; Luke 22.39–46), or experiencing temptation in the wilderness (Matt. 4.1–11; Mark 1.12–13; Luke 4.1–13). We might have explored the healings effected by Jesus within which there is no reference to the demonic, but within which we are made deeply aware of the psychological and social dimensions of the suffering of the person concerned (such as, for example, the woman with a haemorrhage in Mark 5/Luke 8). However, I would like to close with a reference to one passage, unique to Matthew's Gospel, within which reference is made by Jesus to a series of human conditions that, at least metaphorically (and sometimes literally), seem to be highly descriptive of the plight of those who struggle with mental ill health – hunger, thirst, exclusion, nakedness, sickness and captivity.

> Then the king will say to those at his right hand, 'Come, you that are blessed by my Father, inherit the kingdom prepared for you from the foundation of the world; for I was hungry and you gave me food, I was thirsty and you gave me something to drink, I was a stranger and you welcomed me, I was naked and you gave me clothing, I was sick and you took care of me, I was in prison and you visited me.' Then the righteous will answer him, 'Lord, when was it that we saw you hungry and gave you food, or thirsty and gave you something to drink? And when was it that we saw you a stranger and welcomed you, or naked and gave you clothing? And when was it that we saw you sick or in prison and visited you?' And the king will answer them, 'Truly I tell you, just as you did it to one of the least of these who are members of my family, you did it to me.' (Matt. 25.34–41, NRSV)

This is an eschatological story – a narrative – related by Jesus, which has both immanent and transcendent reference. It is set in the context of Jesus' teaching about the importance of praxis in relation to those in need. Perhaps it also implies some boundaries with which we are not always comfortable – those between well-being and want, or between inclusion and exclusion, for example. Thus it draws together many of the themes of our book. It is a narrative that attributes value to the work of caring for and helping those who suffer from mental disorder. It encourages us to think of Christ as one who associates himself with those who are vulnerable, and it encourages us to do likewise.

References

Cook, C. C. H. (2011), The Philokalia *and the Inner Life: On Passions and Prayer*, Cambridge: James Clarke.

Greenhalgh, T. and Hurwitz, B. (1999), *Narrative-based Medicine*, London: BMJ Publications.

Roberts, G. and Holmes, J. (1998), *Healing Stories: Narrative in Psychiatry and Psychotherapy*, Oxford: Oxford University Press.

Williams, R. (2000), *On Christian Theology*, Oxford: Blackwell.

Index

CPSIA information can be obtained at www.ICGtesting.com
Printed in the USA
LVOW01s1435031113

359638LV00006BB/92/P